Understanding and Addressing
Suicide Attacks

Understanding and Addressing Suicide Attacks

The Faith and Politics of Martyrdom Operations

David Cook and Olivia Allison

*Foreword by
Ambassador Edward P. Djerejian*

PRAEGER SECURITY INTERNATIONAL
Westport, Connecticut · London

Library of Congress Cataloging-in-Publication Data

Cook, David, 1966–
    Understanding and addressing suicide attacks : the faith and
politics of martyrdom operations / David Cook and Olivia Allison;
foreword by Edward P. Djerejian.
      p. cm.
    Includes bibliographical references and index.
    ISBN 978–0–275–99260–6 (alk. paper)
    1. Suicide—Religious aspects—Islam. 2. Suicide bombers.
3. Martyrdom—Islam. 4. Violence—Religious aspects—Islam.
5. Islam and politics. 6. Islamic fundamentalism. I. Allison,
Olivia, 1981– II. Title.
    BP190.5.S94C66   2007
    363.325'11—dc22   2007003037

British Library Cataloguing in Publication Data is available.

Library of Congress Catalog Card Number: 2007003037
ISBN-10: 0–275–99260–8
ISBN-13: 978–0–275–99260–6

First published in 2007

Praeger Security International, 88 Post Road West, Westport, CT 06881
An imprint of Greenwood Publishing Group, Inc.
www.praeger.com

Printed in the United States of America

The paper used in this book complies with the
Permanent Paper Standard issued by the National
Information Standards Organization (Z39.48–1984).

10 9 8 7 6 5 4 3 2 1

Every reasonable effort has been made to trace the owners of copyright materials in this book,
but in some instances this has proven impossible. The author and publisher will be glad to
receive information leading to more complete acknowledgments in subsequent printings of the
book and in the meantime extend their apologies for any omissions

Dedicated to our parents:
Dr. W. Robert and Elaine Cook, and Dr. Fred and Martha Allison
Thank you for your constant support through the years

Contents

Foreword

The seminal struggle for ideas between the forces of extremism and moderation in the Islamic world is the major challenge facing not only the Muslim countries but the world at large. Its outcome will have a major impact on regional and global peace and security. Its framework includes the political agenda of the Islamic radical jihadists and "the manipulation of religious norms," the Arab-Israeli conflict, Iraq, and the basic issues of political and economic and social governance in most of the Muslim countries. The lethal subset of this struggle is terrorism spawned by the Islamic radical jihadists. In this respect, the most prominent aspect of their methodology is suicide bombing and martyrdom operations—the subject of this important book by David Cook and Olivia Allison.

In order for decision makers and political leaders to formulate the necessary strategies and policies that can address effectively this fundamental challenge, it is essential to understand the forces at play objectively and analytically. Here there is much room for improvement. Good policy flows from realistic analysis and understanding. To combat terrorism effectively there has to be a comprehensive and strategic policy that deals with the major factors underlying the resort to terrorism as an instrument of the Islamic radicals to obtain their political ends: Namely, to destroy and overthrow the "near enemy," the impious regimes in the Muslim countries, weaken if not undermine the "far enemy," the states supporting the impious regimes and Israel, with an ultimate goal of reestablishing their extreme version of an Islamic Caliphate under the rule of *shari`a* law.

While the strategic goals of the Islamic radical jihadists are vast, their specific resort to terrorism with a focus on martyrdom operations and to suicide bombing as their preferred methodology poses a particularly difficult task to policymakers. Suicide bombings have demonstrated their ability to try to sabotage governments, undermine efforts to resolve the Arab-Israeli conflict, terrorize populations, achieve short-term political ends, and to recruit and radicalize new generations of martyrs. Indeed, they convey the impression that because they are willing to kill themselves for their cause, they cannot be stopped. Therefore, an objective understanding of the true nature of these martyrdom operations and suicide bombings is essential.

In a key conclusion the authors argue that

> the defeatism expressed in policy papers and news reports on suicide bombing is completely misplaced. Most previous policy papers have focused on financial or security measures, but these do not address the most unique aspect of suicide bombing. Suicide attacks inherently require a great deal of justification, primarily religious justification, because they involve killing oneself; thus far, no major policy study has highlighted this issue or identified it as a weakness in the West's discourse on the topic. We believe, however, that because this, the most sensitive aspect of these attacks, would not stand up to serious ideological confrontation if religiously based opposition to these attacks existed. We encourage policymakers and international political figures to spend more time in the future when discussing suicide attacks.

David Cook and Olivia Allison have made a significant contribution to our understanding of this pressing subject. They assert that suicide attacks are a politicomilitary weapon and, therefore, can be countered by "creative measures" that they put forward for policymakers to consider. They delve into the history of warfare and jihad in Islam, the political, economic, social, cultural, psychological, and religious underpinnings of these terrorists' acts. In this latter respect they make a compelling case that the religious aspects of suicide bombing and martyrdom operations are a key factor and must be addressed by active measures. This is an area that I would encourage U.S. policymakers to look at closely. The underestimated role of religion and culture in public policy is a real problem, especially since the demise of the cold war and the rise of religious, ethnic, and racial strife in the world.

The authors recommend holding Muslim clerics who incite suicide operations responsible for their words and making them accountable for this incitement. The authors explain that a Muslim cleric issuing a fatwa to promote a suicide act is a deliberate incitement to action. Equally important, they argue that within Islam there are critiques of suicide bombing based on the Qur'an that maintain that such martyrdom operations are in fact suicide, an act that is prohibited by the Qur'an. Here there is much scope for informational programs and activism by moderate clerics to counter the Islamic radical jihadists. One nuance in the current discourse in the Muslim community, that, however, does not give solace to non-Muslims, is Muslims questioning such operations that incur the loss of Muslim life, such as the mass killings in Iraq and Sunni-Shi`ite strife. The authors point out that what is missing from these critiques is that suicide attacks are immoral under Islam and that indiscriminate killing, especially of civilians, is wrong and should be condemned.

In a key conclusion, the authors state,

> All too often reading Muslim opponents of suicide attacks, one has the strong feeling that they either do not know that much about Islamic tradition or they are obscuring theses truths from their non-Muslim readership. Instead of end-lessly emphasizing the humane aspects of Islam, they should be confronting the problematic aspects. Until this problem is confronted squarely and honestly, radical Muslims will continue to control the discourse, intimidate their more moderate opponents and feel free to inflict suicide attacks wherever they wish, justifying these attacks using basic Islamic texts.

The authors propose, inter alia, that what is needed is not just for a single high-ranking Muslim cleric to issue a fatwa against suicide bombing (because this might even serve to taint that cleric with accusations of treasonous collaboration with the West). Instead what they suggest is to promote the ability of many Muslims to point out these religious problems with suicide attacks, such that it appears there is an antisuicide attack consensus.

Another major factor that the authors edify the reader on is the deep, historical sense of humiliation and victimhood on the part of Muslims that plays into the hands of the Islamic radical jihadists. They point out that, despite real grievances, many of the texts and myths advanced by Muslim radicals are based on irrational facts and conspiracy theories that should be addressed by "counterpropaganda, especially if spread by rival groups."

Closely related to this aspect of the issue is the major role of the media in the struggle with the Islamic radical jihadists. The authors correctly point out that the Internet and chat rooms have become a "global *madrasa*" that is a potent instrument for propaganda and recruitment of young peo-ple to the radical cause. They propose a number of sensible public diplo-macy approaches that can counter more effectively the messages of Muslim radicals. However, they also put into perspective "the concern that unfil-tered propaganda has been released (by al-Qa`ida and others) through Western media."

One of the most useful contributions this book makes is the model that the authors have designed to understand suicide bombings and to dispel the misperceptions about suicide bombers, for example, that suicide bombers are mostly poor, not religious, and driven more by political struggle. Their "Motivation Model" contrasts the goals of the organizers of suicide attacks and the individuals who carry out these attacks. The organizers are more driven by their ideological, territorial, and strategic motivations and goals, while the individual bombers are mostly driven by personal considerations of redemption, desperation, and eternal reward. This distinction is an important one to analyze the phenomenon of suicide bombing accurately and to craft successful policies to counter them.

Another important insight in this book is the stated goal to isolate potential suicide bombing recruits by focusing on converts and on newly radicalized Muslims' communications. The authors point out that suicide bombing has proven to appeal increasingly to Western converts to Islam. Here the militancy of Muslims who live and have been educated in Western democracies is especially troubling. They recommend that, instead of immediately shutting down Islamic radical jihadists Internet sites, monitoring these sites may be much more likely to produce relevant information concerning jihadist agendas and personnel.

In sum, this book is a valuable contribution to an understanding of the forces that underlie the current phenomenon of suicide bombing and martyrdom operations. Indeed, the authors describe the semantic relevance in Arabic of the phrase "suicide bombing" (*al-'amaliyyat al-intihariyya*), which is problematic in terms of the strictures of the Qu'ran, and the phrase "martyrdom operations" (*al-'amaliyyat al-istishhadiyya*) that tries to connote some religious legitimacy and justification to these acts. Our understanding of these factors and forces can do much to help policymakers craft more intelligent and effective policies to combat this form of terrorism.

Ambassador Edward P. Djerejian,
Founding Director of the James A. Baker III
Institute for Public Policy, Rice University

Preface

The martyrdom operations that some of the Muslims undertake against a usurper—occupier are one of the legal methods of fighting. Sacrificing one's soul so that "the Word of God is the highest" is one of the most meritorious sacrifices that gains the one who does it the favor of Allah.

—Taj al-Din Hamid `Abdallah al-Hilali,
Grand Mufti of Australia and New Zealand[1]

How is one to stop a determined attacker from killing himself in order to terrorize a population for political or religious ends? The goal of this book is to propose just such a policy to deal with the major group most likely to organize suicide attacks against the United States, its interests and its allies: radical Muslims. Probably no single action performed by contemporary violent groups evokes such passionate feelings as the specter of someone who seeks, by his/her own death, to inflict pain, destruction, and death on others for political or religious goals.

The terminology describing such actions reflects the polarity of the opposing worldviews. In general, the most widely used terms are "suicide attacks," with pejorative connotations, and "martyrdom operations," with laudatory undertones. For victims of a "suicide attack," such an attack begins with the suicide of the attacker and has the sole purpose of murdering innocents. For ideological supporters of such attacks, the term "martyrdom operations" conveys, first and foremost, the idea that the perpetrator is a martyr—a witness to the veracity of his/her cause—and second, perceived heroism (at least among Sunni Muslims since the mid-1990s).

One term occasionally found in recent literature on the subject is "homicide attack." This term frequently appears in American official and governmental reports, as well as in other publications and some media outlets. We consider this term to be vague and useless. Many suicide attacks do not actually kill anyone other than the perpetrator and yet still engender significant terror because of the (apparently) random nature of the attack. In addition, many other forms of attack are homicidal. The term "suicide attacks" best expresses that the attacker must die to initiate the action. Because this characteristic separates suicide attacks from all other attacks, the terminology used to describe them should reflect this.

In this book, we will use the term "suicide attacks" to express the actions we are analyzing, but in certain cases, we will also use the term "martyrdom operations." The use of the latter term, however, does not convey justification or support for any form of violent actions or for the political stance of the perpetrators or their ideological supporters. When we use this term, the purpose will be to express the meaning of the actions as they are perceived by those perpetrators or supporters. Avoiding the term "martyrdom operations" entirely would obfuscate the intensity of these groups' feelings. In addition, when we use the term "militant organizations" throughout the book, we are referring specifically to those militant organizations that use suicide bombings.

One seemingly pervasive attitude we have encountered in the course of our research is the idea that the suicide attacker, because of his/her choice of tactics, is undefeatable. Suicide attacks, however, are just another form of politicomilitary weaponry and, like any weapon, can be countered by creative measures. Throughout history, the appearance of major tactical weapons has always caused the development of new strategies and weapons to counter them.

Rather than yield to defeatism, we have identified the following guiding policy principles that would serve to stem the tide of suicide attacks.

1. Focus upon the religious aspects of the problem of suicide attacks. Many scholars and policymakers shy away from considering the role of religion as a key determining factor in creating suicide attackers, a factor that yet may be a cardinal, if not *the* cardinal, factor in the contemporary creation of radical Muslim suicide attackers.
2. Confront the problem of perceived humiliation among Muslims that has such a prominent role in the continual recruitment of suicide attackers.
3. Make political and religious leaders accountable for their continued support of suicide attacks. While many Muslim leaders insist that certain suicide attacks (mainly those that target Muslims) are illegitimate, they refuse to systematically condemn the genre as a whole. Doublespeak needs to cease, or the tactic will continue to be used and supported.
4. Engage the Muslim world in a discussion about suicide attacks, using its own communication means (such as existing and popular satellite television channels, Web sites, and other media).

We believe that preparations against suicide attacks and attackers are possible, and that with an adequate understanding of the issues causing suicide attacks, they can be aggressively confronted and contained. We have addressed our policy suggestions specifically to U.S. policymakers, but because of common interests, these policy suggestions are applicable elsewhere too—not just in Europe but in all countries facing the possibility of suicide bombings.

In order to accomplish the goal of containing suicide tactics, the initial roots and support for suicide attacks within the Muslim world must be examined and the messages communicated by the suicide attackers—both in the larger sense of leading by example and in the smaller sense of actual media-oriented messages—must be understood and neutralized. This book will first examine the roots of warfare and jihad within Sunni and Shi`ite Islam, the use of suicide attacks by Shi`ites, then by religious-nationalistic groups (such as Palestinians and Chechens), then by al-Qa`ida and its ideological affiliates. The book will then examine how militant groups employing suicide bombings conduct media operations and how the groups rely less on mainstream global media than on public and private grassroots forums ranging from chat rooms and discussion sites to video-trading sites such as YouTube and Google Video. From this analysis of militant organizations' media relations, we then address the perception that militant groups "use" Western media such as CNN and BBC to get their message out to the world. In a final section, we identify in the policy discussion of suicide attacks misperceptions that hamper the formulation of coherent and effective policy suggestions, and we propose new approaches to policy confronting the spread of this type of attack.

Acknowledgments

We would like to thank the numerous people and foundations that have assisted us in this research. An especially warm thanks goes to our readers, who were, first of all, our parents, Dr. W. Robert and Elaine Cook, and Dr. Fred and Martha Allison, for their criticism and support throughout the past two years. Our other readers were Daniel Allison, Dr. Akil Awan, Liora Danan, Ben Horne, Saira Karim, Elena Pavlova, and Abby Spencer. Many other people have answered our questions, made time to meet with us, supplied us with books and materials, or were of assistance in other ways. We would like to thank Ibrahim Ado-Kurawa, Mumtaz Ahmad, Bakhtiyar Babajanov, Suliman Baldo, Rick Barton, Muhammad Iysa Bello, Stephen Bongardt, Meghan Miller Brawley, Robert Brym, Jaime Burnell, Sabrina Chua, Charles Dahan, Kevin Farell, Rohan Gunaratna, Rosalind Hackett, Richard Haeder, Mohammed Hafez, Andrea Jackson, Bahar Jalali, Kris Kelley, Noorain Khan, Mas`ud Khalili, Sylvia Louie, Jason Lyons, Allen Matusow, Mike McGovern, Junaid Misbah, Hamid Munasser, Paul Murphy, Cindy Ness, Martha Olcott, Muzafar Olimov, Abdul Hakim Oripov, Reuven Paz, Jerrold Post, Khalid Rahman, Kumar Ramakrishna, Aaron Reese, Michael Roberts, Jean Rosenfeld, Yosof Safi, Basel Saleh, Badrus Sholeh, Izzat Soubra, Suzanne Staszak-Silva, Bob Tinsley, Kajsa Törnroth, Ambreen Tour, Melanie Walker, Quintan Wiktorowicz, Stacey Philbrick Yadav, and Barbara Young. All errors are, of course, our own responsibility. The index was prepared by Olivia Allison.

We were supported in our research by the Smith-Richardson Foundation and the Baker Institute for Public Policy at Rice University. We would like to thank the Center for Strategic and International Studies in Washington, DC and the Baker Institute for Public Policy at Rice University for allowing us to use their facilities to present our findings.

Some of the spellings in this book such as al-Qa`ida for the more common al-Qaeda or Usama bin Laden for Osama bin Laden, etc. conform more closely to the Arabic standards laid down by the *International Journal of Middle Eastern Studies*.

Chapter 1

Historical and Islamic Roots of Suicide Attacks–Martyrdom Operations

And some people sell themselves for the sake of Allah's favor.
Allah is kind to His servants (Qur'an 2:208)

The Marines stationed in Beirut, Lebanon were certainly not prepared for the explosive-laden truck detonated by a suicide attacker in their midst on October 23, 1983. Since September 29, 1982, the Marines had been stationed in various areas of Beirut, on a peace mission in the civil-war torn country (a civil war that was to continue until 1990). They were there ostensibly to protect the Palestinians from massacres, but more importantly to reinforce, together with detachments from France and Italy, a new political order that would leave the Christian Maronites in the ascendancy, as well as to enforce a peace agreement between the Christian-dominated Lebanese government and Israel then occupying the southern third of the country. This new order was unacceptable to many groups in Lebanon, among them the newly powerful Shi`ite majority. The Shi`ites were the dominant population in the southern part of the country, and most importantly also in the southern part of Beirut (the so-called belt of misery). On October 23, the Marines were stationed on the road leading to the Beirut airport right in the middle of the Shi`ite dominated area.

The barracks of the Marines were located next to the major road going to the airport, just a short distance from a Lebanese Army check-point. Although the barracks were protected by a number of sentry-posts, it had a weak spot: an empty field located just past the barracks on the way leading to the airport. There were two fences between that field and the compound protecting the building in which the Marines were sleeping that Sunday morning (at 6:22 a.m.), one of them a six-foot iron fence. It was no match for a yellow Mercedes-Benz truck carrying approximately 12,000 lbs of TNT. The driver made as though to turn around in the field, but instead swung back at the first fence, penetrated it, then hit the iron fence and went through it, jumped a sewer ditch and drove right into the back entrance of the building.

Even though the sentries had realized that they were under attack they did not have time to shoot at the driver before the awesome explosion knocked them down. While the Americans were trying to rescue any who had survived in the building, they came under sniper and mortar fire and had to restrain looters. The total number of American dead was 241, the largest number of Marines killed on a single day since Iwo Jima (1945). At almost the same time (three minutes later) that the Americans were targeted, French troops located at al-Ramla al-Bayda' were also attacked by a suicide bomber driving a truck; 58 were killed and 16 were wounded.[1] Although the group that supposedly carried out the two bombings identified itself as The Free Islamic Revolution (al-Thawra al-Islamiyya al-Hurra), most outsiders suspected the Shi`ite group Hizbullah. However, the identities of the attackers were never verified and are still unknown.

With this major attack, preceded on April 18, 1983 by the suicide attack on the American Embassy in Beirut (killing 63 people), the idea of radical Islamic suicide attacks upon Americans became well-known for the first time. The effect was fairly immediate: the Marines were withdrawn from Beirut on February 26, 1984. Although the terrorists had won this massive victory over the United States (as well as France and Italy, who withdrew as well), the West did not learn any major lessons concerning the tactics of suicide attacks. On September 20, 1984 the U.S. embassy in Beirut was suicide-attacked again, this time killing 24.

During the intervening years, Americans have seen a large number of suicide attacks, mostly on targets abroad, but occasionally up close such as the 9/11 attacks in New York and Washington, DC. Although the phenomenon of suicide attacks is far from being confined to radical Muslims, over the past ten years most other groups using suicide terrorism have either removed it as a tactic, established a moratorium on its use, or downplayed it considerably (with the exception of the Liberation Tigers of Tamil-Eelam [LTTE], fighting for self-determination in northern Sri Lanka). Only radical Muslims and some semisecular nationalist groups (the PLO and its off-shoots and the Kurdish PKK) in the Middle East still use suicide attacks on a broad scale. Ultimately, the bigger question for the U.S. government is how it should react to this type of terrorism. To answer that question requires an inquiry into this phenomenon and a study of the connections between the use of suicide as a weapon and some elements of Islam as they are understood by radical Muslims and their supporters throughout the Muslim world.

Radical Islam

Radical Muslims do not refer to themselves by this name; they call themselves simply "Muslims." They reject all labels and names conferred upon them by outsiders: fundamentalists, extremists, terrorists, radicals, and the like. From their point of view, they are attempting to reestablish the original Islam of the time of the Prophet Muhammad (d. 632), to create a unified Muslim state, and to revive the rule of the *shari`a* (the Divine Law of Islam). However, there is good reason for the outsider to label them as radical Muslims and to interpret the type of Islam they practice as something considerably different from Islam as it has been historically known.

Islam developed out of the Arabian Peninsula as a result of the uncompromising form of monotheism preached by the Prophet Muhammad against his pagan kinsmen. During the early years of his ministry in his home town of Mecca, Muhammad was quite unsuccessful, but after he migrated to the oasis town of Medina in 622, he and his followers, together with converts from the local tribes, founded a polity called an *umma* (a faith-based community) that spread across tribal boundaries and revolutionized Arabian society. After Muhammad's death the Muslim Arabs began a series of conquests that transformed the Middle East into its present identity. Older religions such as Christianity and Zoroastrianism died out (largely) as their adherents converted to Islam, and from Spain in the west to Central Asia in the east Arabic became the language of culture. Although because of European Christian advances, Spain was detached from the Muslim world in the fifteenth century, the rest of the region has remained Muslim until the present day.

In general, the history of Islam has been one of success. Prophet Muhammad managed to achieve success during his lifetime—something that Moses, Buddha, or Jesus were unable to do—and, in general, Islam has gained converts because of its worldly success rather than lost them because of its failures. Although it is certainly common among many religions and cultures to see followers of other religions as inferior, for most this attitude has been tempered by a collective memory of failure or persecution. Christianity was persecuted during its first three centuries and frequently lost battles and wars to the Muslims over a period of 1,000 years; Buddhists, Jews, Hindus, and others can say the same. Islam on the other hand has had few collective failures, and for the most part these did not leave much of an imprint upon the collective memory of the community. Wars against infidels have usually been won by Muslims, and from the time of the Prophet Muhammad there has been a close relationship between victory and Islam (even though Muhammad himself did not win all of his battles). Looking at Muslim history, it is easy to see the reasons why a Muslim might think that this long string of victories was God's way of demonstrating to the world that Islam is His final revelation and that all other religions are void.

Although the record of Muslim victory against European Christians is generally consistent between 634 and 1683, Europe and most especially Christianity have always been Islam's most fierce opponent. During the eleventh through the thirteenth centuries Europeans launched a series of counterattacks against Muslims, first in Spain (ultimately reconquered in 1492), then in Italy (reconquered by the end of the eleventh century) and also in Syria-Palestine. This last group of invasions, known as the Crusades, was launched by Pope Urban II (d. 1099) with the ostensible goal of aiding the Orthodox Christian Byzantine Empire (today Turkey), but with the secondary goal of liberating Jerusalem from the Muslims. This was accomplished in 1099, and the Crusader kingdoms managed to establish themselves in Syria-Palestine for about 200 years (more in Cyprus and other islands). This represented the only time during the premodern period that significant Muslim territory from what Muslims considered to be the core lands of Islam was detached and ruled by Christians. (Although the Mongol pagans invaded Iran and Iraq at the same time, they converted to Islam within a generation of their conquests.)

For Muslims, then, although Christian Europe for centuries presented no cultural or economic challenge, to Muslims it did present a military one. This challenge was renewed strongly at the beginning of the modern colonial period when Europeans began to take over large sections of the Muslim world. This colonial period was lengthy for peripheral areas controlled by Muslims—in India, Central Asia, and Indonesia for some 200 years—but for the core Middle Eastern region it was quite short—on average about 80 to 100 years. Lengthy or short, the colonial period and its aftermath have remained traumatic for many Muslims—above and beyond the sense that one has from non-Muslim colonized areas—and there is a collective sense of humiliation that pervades the writings and public statements of many in the Arabic-speaking Muslim world, as well as in other places.

The word "humiliation" (*dhill, hawan,* and many other cognates) is found with astonishing regularity throughout the corpus of radical Muslim writings (also beyond them, but that issue is not within the scope of this work),[2] and one cannot escape the fact that this feeling represents a selling point that radical Muslims use toward the larger Muslim community in order to preach their message.[3] This humiliation stems from the fact that today Islam (or the Muslim community) is not obviously in a dominant position, either politically, militarily, economically, or culturally. Nowhere in the world is Islamic law fully applied in the idealized version that radical Muslims propose. And Muslims are not masters of their own destiny; instead they are very much part of the process of globalization and Westernization. The fact that so many Muslims throughout the world, both in Muslim majority countries as well as in Muslim minorities in Europe and the United States, have embraced globalization and Westernization and have assimilated (at least partially) to these non-Islamic cultures is a source of horror and humiliation for the radicals (and others as well). For radical Muslims the solution to this problem is to recreate the boundaries between belief and infidelity.

It is at this point that radical Islam begins to diverge from normative Sunni Islam. Sunnism embraces a wide range of attitudes and interpretations of Islam. Although much of the discourse in parts of the Arabic-speaking Muslim world seems to favor the radicals, they are in fact very much in the minority everywhere. This minority status is because their interpretation and delineation of Islam rejects the Sufi mystical tradition of Islam to which the vast majority of Muslims worldwide belong. According to many radicals, Sufism involves association of others with God (*shirk*) because of Sufism's frequent invocation of holy men for the purpose of intercession. *Shirk* is the primary sin in Islam, and therefore from a doctrinal point of view, many radical Muslims place Sufis outside the boundaries by means of *takfir* (naming apparent Muslims "infidels"). This doctrinal aspect of radical Islam is one of the major ways it changes Islam as a whole, in addition to its radical rereading of Muslim history by cutting Sufism out.

However, several points must be made clear in a discussion on suicide attacks. Not all radical Muslims are violent; as a matter of fact, the majority are not. Most are quietistic, unlike the violent activists. These quietists involve themselves in various kinds of social work, missionary activities, and education. Although they share goals with violent radical Muslims— such as the creation of a Muslim state—and often have sympathy with their struggle (if not with their methods), and can join them unexpectedly, there is need to make distinctions between those who are dangerous and those who are not (discussed in chapter 8). Another point that must be clarified is that although today the vast majority of suicide attacks carried out by Muslims are in fact accomplished by radical Muslims, there are a number of other groups, usually of a socialist or nationalist bent, who have and continue to use such methods. Both the Lebanese resistance to the United States and Israel (during the period 1982 to 1986) and the Kurdish PKK (1994–2001) were of this bent, and some of the suicide attacks in Iraq may be more nationalist than religious in nature, as well.

Because the vast majority of suicide attacks associated with Muslims is the work of radical Muslims, and because these attacks represent a strong future trend for the most fervent ideological opponents to the United States, it is legitimate to dedicate this book to analyzing their strategy and tactics. But in doing so it is important that the reader does not forget that these are still only one type of violent group opposed to the United States in the Middle East and elsewhere.

Jihad

No discussion of martyrdom operations in Islam can proceed without a discussion of the concept of jihad. Linguistically, jihad indicates "struggle" or "exertion" that from the classical period has become a euphemism for fighting. When Muhammad first came to the oasis of Medina, according to the Muslim version of events, he came without any goods and his followers were equally penurious. Because the Muslims had been unjustly expelled from their homes in Mecca, to come to Medina they had the right to wage war against their pagan relatives in order to even out the economic imbalance. Verses encouraging jihad fill the chapters (*suras*) of the Qur'an that are dated to the Medinan period of Muhammad's life. Eventually a number of battles between the Muslim community and the pagan Meccans were fought, some of which were victories for the Muslims and some were not. In the end, Mecca was conquered by the Muslims in 630, and that could have completed the jihad. But by that time the mission of conquest and conversion had spread to the entire Arabian Peninsula, and pagans were given the choice between conversion and death.

Already during Muhammad's lifetime he had sent Muslim troops to fight the Christians in the Byzantine Empire (in the area of Syria-Palestine), where they were defeated. But verses indicating that the Muslims were to continue fighting Christians appear in the latest chapters of the Qur'an, including this decisive one (9:29):

> Fight those among the People of the Book [Jews and Christians] who do not believe in Allah and the Last Day, do not forbid what Allah and His Apostle have forbidden and do not profess the true religion, till they pay the poll-tax out of hand and submissively.

This verse was seen from classical times until the present day to mandate warfare against Christians, and most of the doctrine of jihad developed as a response to fighting Christians or at least Europeans, who are identified broadly in Arab and Muslim sources as Christians.

Jihad warfare in classical times had a contractual air about it. Qur'an 9:111 says:

> Allah has bought from the believers their lives and their wealth in return for paradise; they fight in the way of Allah, kill and get killed. That is a true promise from Him in the Torah, the Gospel and the Qur'an; and who fulfills His promise better than Allah? Rejoice then at the bargain you have made with Him for that is the great triumph. (see for a similar idea 61:10 also)

God offers the believers, the fighters especially, paradise in return for fighting and dying during the course of jihad.

However, although jihad developed out of this idea, it has a somewhat different connotation in Arabic than its contemporary understanding in the English-speaking world ("holy war," "unrestrained fanaticism," etc.). According to the legal sources, jihad was not merely any war in which Muslims were fighting against unbelievers, but one that was sanctioned by God (in the time of Muhammad) or by a divinely empowered representative. Today, since the office of caliph (successor to Muhammad) no longer exists, this sanctioning authority is usually held to be the religious leadership of Sunni Islam, the *`ulama'*. According to related religious theory, only this body of scholars and jurisprudents has the authority to declare an offensive jihad.[4] However, the situation is different when Muslims are attacked. When jihad is held to be defensive, then it is obligatory upon all Muslims, regardless of age or gender, to aid in fighting the enemy.

In addition to this stipulation, jihad is held to be a regulated form of warfare. There are rules concerning against whom jihad can be declared (unbelievers), the process that has to take place prior to its declaration (invitation to Islam), the type of combatants forbidden from fighting (women, children, aged, and monks), and the tactics that they are allowed to use. Discussions concerning all of these topics fill medieval and modern law books on the subject.

After reading this material, however, one questions its relevance to the present day. It is true that contemporary radical Muslims in their many struggles regularly publish discussions of the strategy and tactics of jihad, and questions are frequently directed to them concerning their authority to proclaim a jihad when they have no legitimate religious authority to do so. As we will see, radical Muslims have answers for all of these critiques and questions, some of which are relevant for policy concerning martyrdom operations. But in the end, to the outside observer, it seems that there are two different strains of authority at odds here: the first is the classical authority of the *`ulama'* who laid down the laws of jihad, and the second is the fighter who carries them out. Today the prestige of the *`ulama'* is low; with the exception of a few charismatic (and usually fiery) preachers who grab the headlines,[5] most are seen as the tools of various Muslim governments and not as independent religious figures.

The spiritual prestige of the fighters, the *mujahidin*, however, is high. From classical times they have often challenged governmental and religious elites, and today they do so once again in the guise of radical Islam. Their exploits capture the imagination of wide sections of the Muslim world that feel humiliated by the West and by Israel. Because of this prestige, the *mujahidin* have more and more arrogated to themselves the right to interpret jihad law and to even make (or break) rules as they go along. The classic example of this tendency is Usama bin Laden, who has no religious sanction to make the pronouncements that he is known to have made. But because he has spiritual prestige as a fighter in the field, his words are heeded by many.

Classical jihad doctrine divided the world into three basic divisions: the *dar al-Islam* (the abode of Islam), where Islamic law and norms reigned, the *dar al-harb* (the abode of war), where Muslims had the right to wage jihad, to pillage, and to take captives, and the *dar al-sulh* (the abode of truce), where Muslims had some treaty obligations. This tripartite division has little meaning in the contemporary world; some radical Muslims have even said that because there is no *dar al-Islam* anymore (because the *shari`a* according to their understanding and interpretation is not implemented anywhere), every country in the world is *dar al-harb* and thus subject to attack. Labels like this, or the general accusation of infidelity that radical Muslims make against other Muslims, especially Sufis, gives them the authority (in their own eyes) to open the field of battle broadly and to wage jihad wherever they feel it is necessary.

After the initial phase of aggressive Muslim conquests (seventh to eighth centuries), most Muslim interpreters of jihad emphasized that it should be used mostly when lands belonging to Muslims were attacked or Muslims were threatened by infidels. This theory of defensive jihad is still common today; however, whether it is still relevant at all is open to questioning. Since the rhetoric of dispossession, entitlement, and humiliation is so often to be found in the Arab Muslim world, as well as the larger non-Arab Muslim world, it is not difficult to justify an attack as "defensive." Today, writers on jihad often blur the distinction between "offensive" and "defensive" to the point that there is little meaning to these terms. Some radicals call for the reconquest of all lands that were ever ruled by Muslims.

Radical Muslims for the most part confine themselves to those areas, regions, or countries that are deemed by most Muslims to be under occupation or where there is a significant oppressed Muslim minority. The examples that are usually cited are Palestine (Israel), Iraq (United States), Kashmir (India), Chechnya (Russia), Southern Philippines (Philippines), Xinjiang (China), Southern Thailand (Thailand), and perhaps Burma.[6] But because the logic of radical Islam demands that jihad be waged against those who are preventing the creation of a Muslim state, warfare can and is expanded secondarily to countries with majority-Muslim populations in which there is no obvious persecution of the Muslim population. In these cases the government or the ruling elite is identified as apostate (through *takfir*) and thus the *mujahidin* are given free rein to fight them (such as in Egypt, Algeria, or Uzbekistan).

A third case are those Muslim-majority countries such as Pakistan and Iraq where sectarian conflict between Sunnis and Shi`ites results in counter-charges of *takfir*. Martyrdom operations frequently take place in situations of the first type (occupation) and in the third type (sectarian warfare), but rarely in the second type (antigovernmental jihad). For the most part those martyrdom operations that have occurred in situations of the second type have been against interests perceived as oppressive (police or governmental targets), foreign (tourism or the oil industry), or culturally invasive.

History of Islamic Martyrdom and Suicide Attacks

Within the context of Islam, martyrdom in general has a very respected position.[7] The word for martyr in Arabic, *shahid*, indicates someone who bears witness or testimony to the truth. It is a word that has passed into most Muslim languages beyond Arabic, and while it can be used in purely political, even secular, circumstances, it usually has strong religious connotations. The standard Qur'anic verses describing the martyr are 3:169–70:

> And do not think of those who have been killed in the way of Allah as dead; they are rather living with their Lord, well-provided for. Rejoicing in what their Lord has given them of His bounty, and they rejoice for those who stayed behind and did not join them; knowing that they have nothing to fear and that they shall not grieve.

Although there is no set definition given to the word *shahid* by classical legal authorities, in following the Jewish and Christian tradition, the title was conferred upon those who died for the sake of Islam. However, this group was (and is) comparatively small. Muslims were persecuted during Islam's very earliest period and some individuals and groups since that time have suffered for actually being Muslim or have died rather than convert to other faiths, but in general the title of *shahid* was given to those who died in battle for Islam or other circumstances listed below. This is a category of martyr that is rejected by both Judaism and Christianity, although both faiths allow for the possibility of a "just war."

Beyond the group of martyrs who die on the battlefield there are a whole range of other less widely accepted categories of *shahid*. One prominent tradition states:

> The Messenger of Allah [Muhammad] said: God Most High has established [the martyr's] reward according to his intention. What do you count as the circumstances of martyrdom? They said: Dying in the path of Allah [jihad]. The Messenger of Allah said: There are seven categories of martyr other than being killed in the path of Allah. The one who dies of a stomach complaint is a martyr, the one who drowns is a martyr, the one who dies of plague is a martyr, the one who dies in a structural collapse is a martyr, the one who dies in a fire is a martyr, the one who dies of pleurisy is a martyr, and the woman who dies in childbirth is a martyr.[8]

Many other circumstances of martyrdom are listed in various sources. Most of these are not relevant to the topic of martyrdom operations; a striking number, however, emphasize the issue of "intention." In other words, if a Muslim has the intention of doing a certain deed and is unable to carry it out before he dies, then it can be credited to him as if he had done it. This issue of intentionality will become important when we discuss justifications for contemporary suicide attacks.

Traditionally in Islam the body of the martyr is not washed, unlike all other Muslim burials. The rationale behind this is that the body of the martyr, because of its wounds, is actually pure and does not need to be purified or cleansed in any way prior to burial. Additionally, the martyr's wounds will continue to be present on his body until the Day of Resurrection when they will appear before God, and He will grant them access to heaven because of them. Unlike other dead, martyrs are not to be mourned at all, but there should be rejoicing at their deaths.

The rewards of the martyr are delineated in great detail in the classical sources. Already we have seen Qur'an 3:169–70, in which the martyr is promised heaven. Other promises are made as well in the tradition literature:

> In the sight of God the martyr has six [unique] qualities: He [God] forgives him at the first opportunity, and shows him his place in paradise, he is saved from the torment of the grave, he is safe from the great fright [of the Resurrection], a crown of honor is placed upon his head—one ruby of which is better than the world and all that is in it—he is married to 72 of the *houri*s, and he gains the right to intercede for 70 of his relatives.[9]

The last two qualities—of marriage to the *houri*s or eternally virgin women of paradise, and the right of intercession for relatives[10]—are the ones that have gained the most attention. From classical until contemporary times, most Muslims who cite Islamic literature or ideas in order to give their reasons for martyrdom usually cite one or the other of those reasons.[11] (This does not mean that there are not other reasons that Muslims give for martyrdom, such as vengeance, or that there are no other possible motivations that are covered up by citation of these two reasons.)

Although the *shahid* who dies on the battlefield or expires as a result of his wound has sought out (in a way) the circumstances of his or her death, his/her death is not at his/her own hands, and very often those who are known to have sought martyrdom in battle were in fact not granted it. This leaves open the question of seeking martyrdom in a more proactive manner. In classical Muslim literature, discussion of this type of martyrdom seeker came under the legal category of "the single fighter who charged a large number." Since it was understood that one who did this was either suicidal or suicidally brave there was some opposition to allowing such operations (which will be discussed below).

Suicidally brave (or stupid) charges of an enemy are known from military history around the world, and many military enterprises have put soldiers into dangerous situations, sometimes with little reason, but there is little global historical precedent for contemporary suicide attacks. Many fanatical organizations or individuals have assassinated prominent personalities throughout history, and it is tempting to see them as precursors of individual suicide attacks. The Ismaili sect of medieval Islam is the most obvious one (during the eleventh through the thirteenth centuries), but there are examples in other cultures, such as the Amida Tong of medieval Japan. These groups assassinated first for ideological reasons and then later for mercenary gains. But it is a stretch to see them as suicide attackers. There is no evidence that the Ismailis actually committed suicide either as part of their assassination plans, or in order to evade capture. Most of them seem to have at least attempted to flee after the assassinations and were killed by pursuers.[12]

Suicide attacks were discussed by Ibn al-Nahhas (d. 1411), a veteran of Muslim wars against the Crusaders, in his widely circulated book on jihad.[13] Although many legal scholars had discussed the issue of the "single fighter," their conclusions were not discussed in any of the classical jihad books other than that of Ibn al-Nahhas. Indeed, Ibn al-Nahhas, even though he permits the possibility of suicide attacks if there is some benefit in them for the Muslim side, is rather ambivalent concerning them and does not encourage them at all or give any positive examples of what benefits they have achieved for Muslims.[14] It is unclear what precisely a suicide attack during the premodern period could gain that could not be gained from a standard military attack,[15] and Ibn al-Nahhas saw much more benefit in single-combat situations.

This conclusion seems to be one that is proven from the historical circumstances. If one understands that suicide attacks are those attacks in that the death of the person is *necessary* for the operation to succeed—as opposed to those attacks that are suicidal or stupid in nature—then prior to the invention of dynamite or high-explosives, there would be little benefit in carrying them out. Although there are some documented cases of suicidal charges in colonial Muslim Asia from the nineteenth century, the evidence that we have for them is from the point of view of the European colonizer, and it is unclear what the purpose of the attacks were or what their religious justification was (if any).[16]

For this reason we date the beginning of suicide warfare to the Japanese *kamikaze*s of World War II (especially 1944–45), who in their final desperation turned their airplanes into bombs to attack American ships and soldiers. Although the *kamikaze*s succeeded in killing numbers of U.S. servicemen and terrorizing others, one cannot say that they had anything like a decisive effect upon the war. As will be seen during the discussion on contemporary Shi`ite jihad as waged by Iran and Hizbullah (chapter 2), the role of suicide attacks as a military (as opposed to a political or a religious) factor in conflicts is minimal. Suicide attacks can achieve mass casualties but as yet they have not won any wars. Nor did they significantly prolong World War II, although they might have contributed to President Harry Truman's decision to drop two atomic bombs on Japan at the close of the war, as he feared the mass casualties that an actual invasion of Japan would entail.

It was not until the 1980s and especially the 1990s that one finds the rise of terrorist organizations using suicide on a regular basis. However, this increase in the use of suicide attacks is not necessarily associated with radical Islam; as a matter of fact, radical Muslims were among the last to use this tactic. Hizbullah—the Shi`ite group fighting to expel the U.S., French, and Italian forces from Beirut and then the Israeli Army from southern Lebanon—and other Lebanese groups pioneered the broad use of suicide terror in the Middle East (discussed in chapter 2) in the 1980s. By 1990, the LTTE fighting in Sri Lanka for a Tamil homeland began to use suicide attacks on a regular basis and, despite several periods of truce, by 2001, had carried out at least 75 attacks. Others followed in their wake: the Kurdish PKK against Turkey in order to establish a Kurdish state during 1996–97, and Sikh separatists in Punjab (India) used a suicide attack to kill a chief minister.[17]

But all of these attacks are rendered somewhat quaint and simple when one considers the hundreds of suicide attacks that occurred in Israel launched by the Palestinians during 2000–05 (the al-Aqsa Intifada) and the hundreds of additional attacks that were occurring on an almost daily basis in Iraq against Shi'ite civilians and U.S.-led coalition forces in Iraq at the time of writing. Statistically, with the single exception of the LTTE, the overwhelming majority of suicide attacks at the time of writing are associated with Muslims, usually radical Muslims. Although there is no lack of non-Muslim insurgencies or disgruntled individuals or groups in the world, it is extremely difficult (as Mia Bloom demonstrated) to find among them any who carry out suicide attacks.[18] This raises the question of whether it has been easy to justify suicide bombing within Islam, and if so, why.

Contemporary Justifications for Suicide Attacks or Martyrdom Operations

When one begins to look at the literature on suicide attacks, it comes as somewhat of a shock to realize how broad the support for suicide attacks is among the Muslim religious leadership. The means by which this support is communicated is the fatwa (a legal opinion) that is usually solicited ostensibly by a (dis)interested member of the community on a given subject. Because of Islam's (especially Sunni Islam's) nonhierarchical structure, there is no binding effect of a given fatwa upon anyone other than the person who solicited it; nonetheless, it is striking how many fatwas there are supporting suicide attacks and how few there are opposing them, most coming from Western or Turkish Muslim apologists. This support for suicide attacks is not even—it is strongest for the Palestinians attacking Israel (especially during the al-Aqsa Intifada since 2000) and grows progressively weaker as one goes to other conflicts on the periphery of the Muslim world. And there are no mainstream `ulama who support the numerous suicide attacks that Muslim radicals carry out against Muslim civilians.

Of the 61 fatwas that we collected during our research,[19] 32 mention the Israeli-Palestinian conflict specifically; the remaining fatwas are divided up in the following manner: two mentioned Palestine and the entire world; two mention Chechnya, two mention the entire world, and one mentions India.

The other fatwas merely endorse suicide attacks in a general way without specifying a location. The fatwas from a geographical point of view are taken (in alphabetical order) from Bosnia (1), Egypt (6), Iran (5), Iraq (5), Jordan (3), Kuwayt (3), Lebanon (3), Pakistan (2), Palestine (3), Qatar (2), Saudi Arabia (10), Sudan (2), Syria (8), the United Arab Emirates (1), Yemen (1), in addition to those from non-Muslim countries (Australia, Great Britain, Russia, Chechnya, and South Africa) and one from al-Qa`ida.[20] The most interesting element about the fatwas, in addition to their geographic spread, is the breadth of the religious leadership's support for suicide warfare. Since one of the bases of Sunni Islam is consensus (*ijma`*) it is important to emphasize that this tactic has in fact achieved an approximation of consensus. It is possible to find only a very few opponents to suicide attacks that buck this consensus.

From a stylistic point of view, a standard fatwa is that of al-Shaykh Sulayman b. Nasir al-`Ulwan (Saudi Arabia):

> The sacrificial operations that are taking place in Palestine against the Jewish usurpers and in Chechnya against the Christian aggressors are martyrdom operations and legitimate (*shar`i*) forms of fighting. They have stunned the aggressors, proven their effectiveness and caused the usurpers to taste the bitterness of their crime, and the evil of what they have done such that the infidels have become afraid of everything and expect death from every direction. Some of the papers have mentioned that the criminal Sharon has demanded the stopping of these operations. Thus these operations have become a woe and destruction upon the Israelis, who have usurped the lands, violated honor, spilled blood and killed the innocent. The Most High said: "And make ready for them whatever you can of fighting men and horses, to terrify thereby the enemies of Allah and your enemy..."(Qur'an 8:60), and also: "Fight the polytheists with your wealth, yourselves and your tongues." (Abu Da'ud).[21]

Although al-`Ulwan cites both a Qur'anic verse and a tradition from the Prophet Muhammad, they are both quite general and could be applied to any form of jihad. All of his other arguments are political in nature. In the end, this fatwa relies upon the religious status of al-`Ulwan and not upon its actual logic. In general, this type of methodological carelessness is characteristic of fatwas supporting the Palestinians in their campaign of suicide attacks. A broad segment of Arab and Muslim opinion supports these attacks, and their legitimacy is not seriously debated, hence there is no need to supply detailed evidence to support them.

Such carelessness is not characteristic, however, of the radical Muslims who seek to justify suicide attacks beyond Palestine, in Chechnya, Afghanistan, and ultimately the entire world. Their arguments employ several verses from the Qur'an. These include Qur'an 2:208: "And some people sell themselves for the sake of Allah's favor. Allah is kind to [His] servants" (epigraph to this chapter), which seems to indicate that one who is willing to "sell themselves" for God's sake will earn God's favor (although in classical times this verse was never interpreted in that manner). From the Qur'anic story of David and Goliath, 2:249 states: "But those of them who believed that they would meet Allah said: 'How many a small band has defeated a large one by Allah's leave. Allah is with the steadfast'." "Meeting" God here, of course, is a euphemism for death. Other verses that are regularly cited are Qur'an 9:111 (cited above) and 2:96 that accuses the Jews of wanting to have a long life, implying that this is not something that the believers would want.[22] Traditions that are quoted by these fatwas are usually examples of people who sought martyrdom during the time of Muhammad by charging into the numerous ranks of an enemy, and not surprisingly most of the legal material from classical sources also follows the "single fighter who charges a large number." Most of the fatwas emphasize intentionality, the historical importance of which was discussed above. These fatwas claim that if the intention of the suicide bomber is pure, then his action will be received and rewarded by God as if it were jihad. It is uncertain, however, that these arguments would stand up to serious discussion in the Muslim world, were they to be examined in a context divorced from the political realities of today. Not one of them actually uses an example of someone who commits suicide during the course of killing large numbers of people (usually civilians).

Opposition to Suicide Attacks

Muslim opposition to suicide attacks has been quite muted, especially outside the West, probably because of political circumstances (passive support for the Palestinians against Israel, opposition to the goals and methods of U.S. foreign policy in the Muslim world), but possibly also due to the level of consensus that has developed around the issue of martyrdom operations, especially the perceived high spiritual authority of the *mujahidin* and their *`ulama* that has served to silence their would-be critics.

Different types of critiques of suicide attacks have, however, been leveled by Muslims. They fall into several categories:

1. *Critiques emphasizing tactics*: Since martyrdom operations frequently kill civilian innocents (as defined even by the loose standards of radical Muslims) and/or Muslims and violate other laws of jihad, Muslim scholars have critiqued or questioned the tactics involved.[23] Usually these critiques do not actually prohibit suicide attacks per se, but they would place such limitations upon the use of them (making certain that civilians or Muslims are not part of the target population) that effectively the advantages gained by their use would be nullified.

2. *Critiques emphasizing strategy and propaganda*: Martyrdom operations are occasionally critiqued by Muslims for bringing the reputation of

Islam into disrepute, destroying the moral basis for an otherwise legitimate cause (such as the cause of the Palestinians, the Kashmiris, or the Chechens)[24] or because they do not accomplish the military or propaganda goals claimed for them by their proponents.[25] Many Arab journalists criticize suicide attacks on these bases, enraging those attack organizers concerned with their public image (see chapter 6).

3. *Religiously based critiques*: Examples of these critiques are those of Nasir al-Din al-Albani, the famous Syrian traditionalist (also an intellectual mainstay of radical Islam), who maintained that martyrdom operations were suicide (prohibited by Qur'an 4:29) and that no amount of semantics can hide that fact.[26] Another critique appears in the radical Muslim jihad primer, *al-`Umda li-Jihad fi sabil Allah*. This treatise critiques suicide attacks on the basis of the fact that they are sought by those who desire fame, and that the true *mujahid* would not seek out such flamboyant operations.[27] This type of critique makes use of classical reservations stemming from the verse 61:4: "Allah loves those who fight in His cause arrayed in battle, as though they were a compact structure." Because martyrdom operations are operations of a single person, they violate the idea that jihad as a spiritual action should be a group activity. The feats of each individual should be known only to God in order to discourage those who seek personal fame.[28]

Most of those who have attacked the idea of suicide attacks have been `ulama independent of both the governmental authority and the influence of radical Muslims. These are rare, and most of those with stature have died during the 1990s or early 2000s.

Typical of them was Ibn `Uthaymin (d. 2001), whose fatwa concerning suicide attacks reads: "The person who places explosives on his body in order to put himself in one of the gathering areas of the enemy kills himself and will be punished in accordance with anyone who kills themselves, in Hell eternally, just as the Prophet [Muhammad] said: 'Whoever kills himself will be punished for it in the fire of Hell.' "[29] Unfortunately most of the other fatwas condemning suicide attacks are also laconic.

What is missing from these types of critiques is the idea that suicide attacks are immoral because indiscriminant killing of non-Muslim civilians without any warning is actually wrong (and not just tactically inexpedient or something that harms the image of Islam). The materials that come closest to this type of moral condemnation of suicide attacks are those of Turkish writers—usually followers of Fethullah Gulen or Bediazaman Nursi (d. 1960)—who at least work with the Muslim material and cite counterarguments that approximate the moral condemnation that is lacking in contemporary Muslim discussions. But even in the Turkish case, as with so many other Muslim antiradicals, a nationalistic tendency to apologetically defend their own history mars the result and makes it less than persuasive.[30]

In general, those Muslims who have criticized suicide attacks are unwilling to deal with the amount of support that the tactic has within the Muslim community, to confront head-on the Qur'anic verses and *hadiths* that radical Muslims and their supporters cite, and to bring out counter-arguments that demonstrate that they actually know the depth of the suicide literature in contemporary Islam.[31] All too often, reading Muslim opponents of suicide attacks, one has the strong feeling that they either do not know that much about the Islamic tradition or they are obscuring these truths from their non-Muslim readership. Instead of endlessly emphasizing the humane aspects of Islam, they should be confronting the problematic aspects. Until this problem is confronted honestly, radical Muslims will continue to control the discourse, intimidate their more moderate opponents, and feel free to inflict suicide attacks wherever they wish, justifying them using basic Islamic texts.

Models for Understanding Suicide Warfare

For the most part, European and American scholars, political scientists and strategists have dealt with the phenomenon of suicide attacks as part of a global phenomenon, without singling out radical Islamic variants. Israel has been the exception to this rule, which as it faces Palestinian suicide attackers has naturally focused almost exclusively upon Palestinian—not pan-Muslim—suicide bombings. Even though the majority of suicide attacks during the past 25 years (1980–2005) came from Muslim countries and was at least nominally Muslim, a considerable percentage has not. As noted above, the LTTE of Sri Lanka has provided by far the most consistently high numbers of suicide attacks during the period 1990–2000, although this steady supply vanished, beginning with the 2001 truce, through spring 2006.[32] But there is some reluctance on the part of scholars to identify Muslims, let alone Islam as a religion, with suicide bombing.[33] Even the Israeli scholars who could have understandably labeled suicide terror as "Islamic," as they might hope to derive political benefit from demonization of Islam, have preferred to describe their opponents as nationalistic.

The general constructs for dealing with suicide terror can be grouped into several categories:

1. *Top-down organizational theory*: Robert Pape's book *Dying to Win* provides the most coherent, statistically based discussion of suicide attacks and the rationale behind them and must remain the standard in the field. Pape portrays suicide terror as top-down, as a strategic choice by terrorist groups who are attracted to it by its success rate. According to Pape, suicide attacks happen only as a result of insurgencies against democracies, where occupations (or the perception of occupation such as Saudi Arabia) have religious differences from the occupied. The problems with his thesis are that he

dismisses or ignores the huge religious backing for suicide attacks in Islam, downplays the issue of individual initiative, and does not explain Muslim-on-Muslim attacks where there are no obvious Western interests (Pakistan, Bangladesh, Uzbekistan, Iraq to a large extent). In short, Pape's thesis goes a long way toward analyzing suicide attacks rationally, but his theory fails to explain occupations where there have been no suicide attacks or those suicide attacks that were carried out where there was no occupation.

2. *Intergroup competition theory*: Mia Bloom, in her book *Dying to Kill* and in other published articles, proposes a theory of competition, in which terrorists try to outdo one another. According to this idea, each group must go further and make more and more spectacular attacks of a suicidal nature in order to gain the attention that the terrorists need. Again, there is much substance to her argument, but it tends to ignore the fact that suicide attacks do not actually need to be spectacular in order to be terrifying. What they require is a state of continuity and regularity in order to drive a population into a state of hopelessness or perhaps frenzy.

3. *Economic theory (poverty explanation)*: This theory argues that suicide attacks are the weapons of the weak or the impoverished. First, this theory is based on (faulty and now discredited) research on suicide bombers' backgrounds as being "poor," compared to the majority in their respective societies.[34] As explained in chapter 8, this theory has been discredited by simple statistics. On an organizational level, this explanation claims that when there is a dramatic asymmetry in armaments between conflicting groups (Israel versus the Palestinians, for example), the disadvantaged group will naturally turn to terrorism and, lacking alternatives, will use suicide attacks. This theory is too simplistic, ignoring the fact that most radical Muslims are not impoverished and are in fact quite well educated and at least middle class. Furthermore, many radical Muslim insurgencies are relatively well funded (although, of course, not on the same levels as their Western military opponents), when compared to insurgents in other assymetrical struggles. The economic theory of suicide attacks ignores the numerous successful and failed insurgencies and even terrorist groups (some of whom have gained legitimacy in power) that have been in such dramatically disadvantaged situations and yet avoided the use of suicide terror.

Implications for the United States

Despite the best efforts of Muslim apologists to say differently, aggressive jihad is well-attested inside Muslim society, with strong examples from the life of the Prophet Muhammad and the Qur'an. This is a reality throughout the Muslim world and if apologists are unwilling to admit it, then their credibility is questionable. Also, basic ideas that are used by radical Muslims in order to promote suicide attacks are very well attested inside core Islamic teachings. No amount of denial will make that go away.

On the other hand, even a casual knowledge of equally core Islamic teachings reveals certain promising lines of counterargument that could be used to decrease sympathy for radical or nationalist Muslims who use suicide attacks. (It is unlikely that the true believers among militant radical Muslims will be persuaded, and, while it is probably useless to try to persuade them, it is still important to make these counterarguments to persuade potential sympathizers.) Accurate information—not apologetics—is necessary in order to combat the phenomenon of suicide terrorism; ignoring the role of Islamic justification in promoting this tactic will only perpetuate the problem.

The reality for the United States is that an astonishing number of Muslims believe that the United States is actively destroying or attempting to destroy Islam and/or commit genocide against Muslims. Theories of global anti-Islamic conspiracy are not new and have their roots in materials that have circulated since the mid-1970s.[35] But certainly under the Clinton and Bush administrations such conspiratorial paranoid thinking has been fleshed out considerably, to a large extent with judicious use of quotations from high officials of both these administrations.[36] Because this material has been so widely circulated and is so widely believed, there exists a narrative of global politics in the Muslim world that completely counters the one most in the West would give. This counternarrative is especially prevalent not only in Arabic-speaking areas but also beyond and is difficult for Americans to fathom.

The Muslim world's sense of persecution, humiliation, and offense perpetrated by the United States and its close allies (usually the United Kingdom, Australia, Canada, and Israel, with a few others occasionally appearing in publications) cannot be overemphasized. Understanding the prevalence of suicide attacks against the United States and its allies should start with an understanding of the significance of perceived humiliation; countering these attacks will have to take into account the reality of this perception and the existence of numerous oppression narratives. Some of these narratives are indeed based on real events and Western policies (e.g., Guantanamo Bay prison conditions, Abu Ghraib prisoner abuse, lack of intervention in response to Israeli strikes on its neighbors, among many others) that nurture the culture of conspiracy theories and humiliation narratives. As we state in the policy-recommendation chapter (chapter 9), the real and perceived roots of this humiliation should be addressed in any policy attempting to deal with these attacks.

Chapter 2

Shi`ites Pioneer the Military Use of Suicide Attacks

> *This martyrdom paradigm is the result of the initialization*
> *program of the Islamic Movement . . . and by it the material*
> *advantage of the enemy will be crippled and its power nullified.*
>
> —Muhammad Fanish[1]

The Hizbullah and the other radical groups in Lebanon could not have known that their victory over the United States on October 23, 1983 in Beirut would be the high water mark of the effectiveness of suicide attacks' military use. Although many groups since 1983 have used suicide attacks for military reasons—as well as for political and religious reasons—and others have managed to kill far more people than the 241 Marines and 58 French troops killed in Beirut on that day, no one has ever managed to complete a major attack against a military target, inflict mass casualties, *and* reap tangible military benefits from doing so. Almost all future mass-casualty suicide attacks would be attacks against civilians, some of which would also reap political rewards for the groups that carried them out.[2] The experience of the Hizbullah in southern Lebanon would also exemplify the law of diminishing returns.

Shi`ite attitudes toward jihad and martyrdom are slightly different from those Sunni ones described above.[3] The historical experience of Shi`ites has been one of persecution at the hands of Sunnis. Shi`ites believe that the Prophet Muhammad's family has the legitimate right to rule the Muslim community and that this right is accompanied by hidden or gnostic knowledge passed down the family. Historically, the most important experience for Shi`ites was the murder of the Prophet Muhammad's grandson, al-Husayn, at Karbala (today in southern Iraq), at the hands of a government militia in 680. This murder is the defining moment in Shi`ite martyrology and indeed, in the development of Shi`ism as an independent movement within Islam. For Shi`ites the blood of al-Husayn was shed unjustly, and those who murdered him—the spiritual ancestors of Sunnis—are irredeemably guilty of his murder. Moreover, since many Shi`ite sympathizers abandoned al-Husayn to his fate, Shi`ites are also guilty of his blood for not rendering him aid at the critical moment.

Guilt feelings stand at the heart of a great many Shi`ite teachings. Al-Husayn was not the only descendent of the Prophet Muhammad to attempt to gain power; many others did as well, almost all of them unsuccessfully. For the first three centuries of Islam, hundreds of Prophet Muhammad's descendents and immediate family were either murdered or imprisoned and tortured by the ruling Umayyad or `Abbasid dynasties. These people form the heart of Shi`ite martyrdom stories that are told and retold throughout the Shi`ite yearly calendar (which focuses upon the deaths of prominent figures). All of this bloodshed and guilt means that Shi`ites have a different view of martyrdom than do Sunnis. For Sunnis the martyrdom process is closely connected with jihad and victory; even in death one does not lose the ultimate victory of attaining paradise. However, for Shi`ites the martyrdom process is a mournful one and whatever victory can be gained from it will have to be deferred until Judgment Day when God will ultimately set everything right.[4] While Sunnis have been the majority (in most places) and closely connected with the government and the process of ruling as well as with the expansion of Islam (either through conquest or through missionization), Shi`ites have always been the underdogs. With the exception of Iran and a few other states in North Africa and India, Shi`ites have always been divorced from the government.

All of this background is helpful in understanding why martyrdom and martyrdom operations have been a fit in Shi`ism, while among Sunnis the literature concerning the legality of martyrdom operations is vast and essentially highlights the problematic position of this tactic within the religion. (Although there is little active opposition to suicide attacks in the Muslim world from an intellectual or religious point of view, the legal-religious case for them within Islam is still quite weak.)[5] Shi`ites have never been concerned with this issue. One illustration of different approaches to the problem of legitimization is the very term used for suicide attacks. Among Sunnis, very early writers such as `Abdallah `Azzam (founder of al-Qa`ida and mentor of Usama b. Laden) did use the term "suicide attacks" (*al-`amaliyyat al-intihariyya*) in the mid-1980s,[6] but later Sunnis began to use the term "martyrdom operations" (*al-`amaliyyat al-istishhadiyya*) in order to give the operations some glory and religious legitimacy.[7] Shi`ites also used the term "suicide attacks" early[8] and have gradually moved to using "martyrdom operations" but have never completely avoided the term "suicide attacks." Only those who have very cautiously come out against suicide attacks, however, use the former term now.[9] Nonetheless, to date, Shi`ites have never produced the huge legitimizing literature for suicide attacks that one finds among Sunnis. The issue of using these attacks was simply nowhere near as jarring for Shi'ites as it was for Sunnis.

Iran

Until the mid-1970s, few outside observers thought that Shi'ites would be a potent political force. Shi'ites existed in large numbers in Iran (where they were the majority population), in Iraq (where they were probably already the majority population), southern Lebanon, Pakistan, Afghanistan, India, and eastern Africa. In none of these locations were the Shi'ites politically active. But the appearance of the Ayatullah Khumayni in Iran in 1978, bringing about the fall of the Shah of Iran, heralded a vast change in worldwide Shi'ism. Khumayni preached an activist version of Shi'ism that harkened back to the activities of al-Husayn, who, according to Khumayni, aggressively confronted injustice and was willing to die for his beliefs. Khumayni tried to formulate an Islamic state along these activist principles—and in opposition to the more conservative quietist `ulama—that would export revolution around the Muslim world. Although Khumayni's revolutionary call was limited in its appeal, since Shi'ites are very much the minority in Islam, this call had an effect even among Sunnis.[10]

The revolutionary call was most feared among the Arab states that bordered Iran and had large Shi'ite populations or minorities, such as Iraq, Bahrain, and Saudi Arabia (about 15 percent of which is Shi'ite). The Iraqi regime of Saddam Husayn, who had taken power in 1980 (although he had been a dominant force in Iraq for the previous ten years), either feared the effects of the Iranian revolution upon the Shi'ite population of Iraq or desired the oil-rich ethnically Arab province of Khuzistan and decided to attack Iran in September of that year. Most likely, Saddam Husayn was also impressed by the chaos then reigning in Iran and thought he could take advantage of it.

Whatever the reason, the Iraqi invasion of Iran was a desperate moment for the revolutionary Islamic government. Because of its foreign policy, Iran could count upon no major or even minor power in the world to support it. Most of its weaponry was American-made and inherited from the time of the Shah, but because of the 1979–81 hostage crisis (in which American diplomats were held in Tehran), the United States was a mortal foe. Additionally, because most of the upper ranks of the armed forces had supported the Shah, Iran had effectively no military. Iraq's early success in conquering significant parts of Khuzistan led to a mass popular mobilization of suicide attackers by the Iranians.

Wave after wave of these suicide attackers would sweep across the battlefields, effectively demining the Iraqi positions and overrunning them. Hundreds of thousands died, all with special keys fastened around their necks symbolizing their entry into heaven once dead. The sacrifice of these children or youths was essential for the Iranian forces behind them to then secure their positions and eradicate the Iraqis. But, given the secretive nature of both the Iranian and the Iraqi regimes, the true number of those who died during the 1980–81 campaign to repulse the Iraqis will probably never be known.[11]

Today the Iranian regime continues to preach the rhetoric of suicide attacks or martyrdom operations. On a regular basis, there are sign-up sheets where prospective suicide attackers or battalions can register, and there are repetitive threats to employ armies of suicide attackers against the United States, Israel, or any of the other enemies of the Iranian regime.[12] For all these threats, however, it is the Shi`ites of southern Lebanon who have actually been able to fight and defeat the United States.

Lebanon: Expel the United States

At the same time the Iranian regime was preaching Islamic revolution, the Shi`ite population of southern Lebanon was being awakened for the first time. Although Shi`ites were probably already a significant minority in the 1960s and 1970s, they were little noticed by the Maronite Christian and Sunni Muslim elites of Lebanon. Many of the Shi`ites were villagers or existed in poverty in the vast slums of south Beirut. Throughout the 1970s, much of southern Lebanon was effectively under the control of the Palestinian Liberation Organization (PLO), which used this location to carry out periodic attacks against Israel. Israel invaded southern Lebanon in June 1982 and occupied about a third of Lebanon in an effort to expel the PLO and to deny the Syrians influence in the area. This invasion was coupled with an attempt by the Maronite Christians to reassert their old dominance over the country as a whole in tandem with the Israelis.

Unfortunately for both the Maronites and the Israelis, neither of them had taken the Shi`ite population into consideration. While the Shi`ites initially seemed to have welcomed the Israelis who rid them of the PLO domination, this welcome quickly turned to hatred when the Israelis showed no signs of leaving. Through 1983 and 1984, western powers such as the United States, France, and Italy tried to impose some type of order upon Beirut, at first to facilitate the exit of the PLO in 1982 and then (from the point of view of the Sunni and Shi`ite populations) to enforce the Maronite-Israeli ascendancy. By 1983, the first suicide attacks against western interests began to happen, culminating in repeated suicide attacks against the U.S. Embassy in Beirut, the Marines, and the French forces (already detailed). All of these attacks had their effect and eventually the foreign forces withdrew in early 1984, leaving Beirut and part of southern Lebanon in the hands of the Shi`ites.

Southern Lebanon: Hizbullah, Israel, and the Southern Lebanese Army

The defeat of the Western powers did not, however, necessarily have much effect upon Israel. Already during 1983 and 1984, while suicide attacks were happening in Beirut, Israeli forces were targeted with some highly successful suicide attacks. The first of these was the suicide car bomb against the Israeli military headquarters in Tyre (southern Lebanon), which killed 74 on November 11, 1982.[13] Although this attack took place almost a year prior to the attack on the Marines (detailed in chapter 1), no one seemed to have understood that this type of car bomb would be highly effective in killing large numbers of people inside a building, were it to be detonated under the right circumstances. Indeed, the Israelis themselves were again targeted in Tyre on November 4, 1983, just 10 days after the Marines and the French had been hit, and lost 60 people.

Starting from these initially spectacular attacks, Hizbullah and its offshoots in Lebanon began to launch a number of suicide operations against the Israeli forces, especially after the United States, French, and Italian troops left Beirut and there were no significant foreign targets left in the city. Although some of these Hizbullah attacks against the Israeli military were successful, usually against convoys, an equal number killed none but the perpetrator. But these attacks convinced Israel to withdraw from most of southern Lebanon into a self-proclaimed "security zone" by June 1985. Pape's conclusion that suicide attacks are effective is demonstrated by the experience of Hizbullah against its two major foes: the Western powers in Beirut and the Israelis in southern Lebanon (1982–89).[14]

Limitations to the effectiveness of suicide bombings existed, however, from a purely military point of view. According to Pape's account, Hizbullah carried out a total of 20 suicide attacks between 1985 and 1986 and a further group of five random attacks between 1985 and 1999. Most of these attacks were directed against the South Lebanese Army (SLA), a group supported by Israel and made up mostly of Christians. Seven of the first group of attacks killed a total of 108 people, but the other 13 attacks caused minimal deaths—in many cases only the perpetrator.[15] Of the five random attacks in the later grouping, one managed to kill eight Israelis traveling in a convoy, but all of the others killed only the perpetrator. Significant numbers of fatalities were overwhelmingly achieved in earlier attacks; the later attacks were insignificant.

Although it is unclear whether there was indeed an operational Hizbullah decision to avoid suicide attacks from the end of 1986, examination of the group's tactical operations leads us to this conclusion. Suicide operations can deliver a lethal blow to a military opponent, but military personnel over a period of time (and given enough losses) will take the security precautions that render such operations ineffective. Indeed, although Hizbullah continued to fight against the SLA and the Israeli Army between 1986 and 2000, when Israel withdrew from southern Lebanon and the SLA collapsed, it rarely used suicide operations. Moreover, when celebrating its victory over Israel in the summer of 2000, Hizbullah did not make the mistake of attributing this victory to suicide attacks,[16] but correctly pointed out the higher significance of rocket attacks. This same strategy was apparent in the July–August 2006 war between Israel and Hizbullah. Hizbullah personnel did not carry out any suicide attacks against Israel.

The increasing irrelevance of suicide attacks against the Israeli military during the 1990s, however, did not limit their use against civilians, especially those in areas of the world completely unprepared for this type of warfare. On July 18, 1994, the Ansar Allah (apparently an offshoot of the Hizbullah) carried out a deadly suicide attack against the Asociación Mutual Israelita Argentina (or the Israeli-Argentine Mutual Association) building in Buenos Aires, Argentina, killing approximately 86 and wounding at least 236. As so often had been the case, this attack was carried out by a truck bomb filled with ammonium nitrate that was driven into the front of the building. This attack had followed a bombing attack against the Israeli Embassy in Argentina on March 17, 1992 (which killed 29). The 1994 attack was a truck bombing, and the fact that it was a suicide attack was not publicly known for a lengthy period following the blast (most probably the investigation of this attack has been held up for political reasons; Argentina has apparently been reluctant to highlight the role of Iran in the attack).[17]

Although there has never been final proof indicating the role of Hizbullah, the attack followed the kidnapping of Mustafa al-Dirani (a leader of Hizbullah) on May 21, 1994, and was followed by a number of other attacks associated with Hizbullah. Additionally, the suspected bomber, Ibrahim Berro, was commemorated by Hizbullah as a martyr for an operation on the same day. Hizbullah likes to present itself as an organization that focuses its violence upon Israel and does not attack any other country (although apparently Jewish or Israeli organizations worldwide are legitimate targets), however, and the organization promotes itself as a political and economic power in Lebanon. Whether this policy will remain in place in the future is difficult to know. However, it seems likely that Hizbullah will continue to remain heavily influenced by Iranian policy and be a proxy for Iranian policy goals vis-à-vis Israel and, to some extent, the United States.

Shi`ites in Southern Iraq

As in Lebanon, the Shi`ite population in southern Iraq has been largely ignored until the recent past. Although most probably a majority since the middle of the nineteenth century, Shi`ites were not well represented in the government in Baghdad. This lack of representation was especially pronounced during the reign of Saddam Husayn (1980–2003), who based his regime to a large extent upon the minority Sunni population. With the overthrow of Husayn by the American invasion in 2003, it seemed that a pro-American Shi`ite domination of Iraq had begun.

The differing currents within the Shi`ite Iraqi population and the intense resistance put up by Sunnis (see chapter 5), however, have made that conclusion more questionable as the years have passed. The Shi`ites can generally be divided into the majority conservative faction headed by Ayatullah `Ali al-Sistani who succeeded the more pro-American Ayatullah Muhammad al-Baqir al-Hakim (killed by a massive suicide attack in August 2003), and the more militant Muqtada al-Sadr faction that is anti-American. During the 2004 uprising against the U.S. occupation (jointly between Sunnis and Shi`ites), Muqtada al-Sadr did make some statements in favor of suicide attacks. While he and his followers, the Mahdi Army, were besieged in the holy city of Najaf, he is reported to have said, "We will resort to suicide operations, and we will become human bombs."[18] However, nothing ever came of these threats. Hundreds of suicide attacks have taken place in Iraq since the summer of 2003, most of them targeting Shi`ites and a number of them targeting their most holy places (Karbala, Najaf, Samarra, and other prominent mosques in Baghdad), but interestingly not once have Iraqi Shi`ites attacked Sunnis with a suicide bombing in return. (The subject of Sunni suicide attacks in Iraq will be covered in chapter 5.)

Implications for the United States

Shi`ites are extremely important for the United States. The negative relationship with Iran over the past decades has colored most Americans' perception of Shi`ism and perhaps given some people the impression that Shi`ites are irredeemably anti-American, but there is little evidence to support that conclusion. All major Shi`ite factions voice to some degree anti-American rhetoric (with the exception of some top leaders in southern Iraq, who can be called pro-American), but with the exception of the 1983–84 interval in Lebanon, this rhetoric has not been backed up by any serious force.

Recently, Shi`ites have been remarkably quiescent in the use of suicide attacks even in the face of extreme provocation. With the exception of Hizbullah during the period 1982–96, there is no example of contemporary Shi`ites participating in the current campaign of suicide attacks by radical Muslims against the United States, its allies and its interests. Even in southern Iraq, where since mid-2003 Shi`ites have been continually targeted with suicide attacks, Shi`ites have not responded in kind. Increasingly since the middle of 2004, however, Sunnis and especially Sunni radicals have been targeted by Shi`ite murder squads that have taken vengeance upon the Sunnis for various attacks.

Pakistani Shi`ites have also seen their leaders attacked and their worship sites desecrated repeatedly since 2001 by Sunni suicide attackers. Like their Iraqi counterparts, Pakistani Shi`ites have not once responded with a suicide attack. This conclusion should not be taken to mean that Shi`ites in either southern Iraq or Pakistan have been passive; on the contrary, they have responded violently to attacks upon them. But not once have they used suicide attacks. Given the huge provocation that Shi`ites have had to endure in both Pakistan and Iraq for being targets of hundreds of suicide attacks, one can safely conclude that they are not likely to react with these types of attacks in the future.

There are also no cases of Iranian Shi`ites who have utilized suicide attacks, although certainly Iran produces more official propaganda in favor of such attacks than does any other single country in the Middle East. Today Iran stands at the forefront of those countries that the United States opposes because of the former's nuclear ambitions. Iranians fear the possibility that the United States might invade it in the same way as it did Iraq and have probably prepared martyrdom units to oppose such an invasion.[19] From an American point of view, however, it is unlikely that such an invasion would be carried out, so it is uncertain whether there will be a situation in which Iranians will be massed for suicide attacks against the United States.

Chapter 3

Are Suicide Operations the Weapon of the Disadvantaged?

Every day the earth absorbs the blood of the righteous, and
[it] kneels in front of the graves and bows before the martyrs of grace.
This is part of the price of pride and honor, liberation and salvation.
This is the dowry of those with "lovely eyes," a substitute for paradise.
"Lo! Allah has bought from the believers their lives and their
wealth in return for Paradise."[1]

There is no conflict situation on earth that is more polarizing than that of the Israeli-Palestinian conflict. Since the creation of the state of Israel in 1948 (and even before), resolving this conflict has been the bane of many statesmen. The roots of the conflict go back to the irreconcilable claims of political Zionism to found a state within the region of geographical Palestine (the territory given to the British for a mandate by the League of Nations in 1918) and the wishes of the local Arab population, both Muslim and Christian (later called Palestinians), to have a state in that same area. Zionist aspirations were driven by the historical claims of the Jewish people to the region of Palestine, as well as the desperation created by the genocidal drive of European anti-Semitism culminating in the Holocaust. Arab claims were driven by equally historical roots, and the fact that in 1947–48, when the United Nations agreed to partition Palestine, they were the majority population.

The Arabs of Palestine did not develop their society during the period of the British mandate (1918–48) but instead wasted their energies on internecine warfare. Consequently, when partition was announced in 1947, although the Arab population opposed it, they were ineffectual in confronting the Jews militarily and had to rely upon the aid of surrounding Arab states. These states, namely Egypt, Jordan and Syria, all had claims of varying degrees of legitimacy to the region of Palestine, and thus when they invaded Palestine in May 1948 (at the moment of Israel's independence), they did so with the aim of aggrandizing their own territories.

On the Israeli side, the remaining Arab population was viewed as a problem, and there was either a policy of encouraging the Arabs to leave (sometimes through the application of terror) or a calculated policy of expulsion. A number of Israeli politicians and military figures believed that Israel as a state would not be viable with a large hostile Arab minority within its borders. From the Arab states' perspective, the foundation of Israel was fundamentally unjust, and thus they refused to resettle the Arabs of Palestine within their own countries. These refugees were kept in large refugee camps both in geographical Palestine as well as in the surrounding states. The result of the 1948 war was unfavorable to the Arabs of Palestine, but far less unfavorable to the Arab states surrounding it, most especially Jordan, which annexed the central territory of Palestine (henceforward called the West Bank).

For the Arabs of Palestine the defining moment came in 1967 when the important Arab states surrounding Israel—Egypt, Jordan, and Syria—were all decisively defeated and a portion of their lands occupied. This event, while disastrous to the prestige of the elites of these countries, enabled the Palestinians (now referred to by this name) to develop their own nationalism, and eventually to found the Palestinian Liberation Organization (PLO).[2] Initially, the PLO pursued a policy of armed attack against Israel, using the neighboring countries as bases (especially Jordan and then Lebanon), coupled with flamboyant terror operations throughout Europe (usually in alliance with local leftist groups) and the Middle East to publicize their cause. However, both of these tactics proved to be counterproductive as the neighboring Arab states turned against the PLO during the 1970s and 1980s, and its terror operations caused opposition to Palestinians to harden. By the late 1980s, the PLO was forced gradually to accept Israel's existence and by 1993 had signed a peace agreement with it.

The principal factor causing this relative moderation was the outbreak of the first Intifada in December 1987. The Intifada was a local outburst of violence against the Israeli occupation that focused upon building sympathy for the Palestinian cause by portraying the Israelis as brutal aggressors. For the most part, the organizers of the first Intifada emphasized a low level of violence, playing to the world media for sympathy, and noncompliance with the Israeli authorities. Even before the beginning of the first Intifada, radical Muslims, influenced by the Egyptian Muslim Brotherhood, had begun to make headway among Palestinians. By 1988, they had founded Hamas, which henceforward would be their militant expression. Although the first Intifada gained the Palestinians some propagandistic points, by 1991—when the first negotiations between the PLO and Israel began—they were no closer to achieving a state.

Initially the Oslo peace accords that were signed by 1993 seemed to promise the Palestinians a state and led to a decrease in terror operations. However, Hamas never saw itself as being bound by the Oslo accords and continued to use violence. After the massacre perpetrated by the Jewish radical Dr. Baruch Goldstein in the Tomb of the Patriarchs-Khalili Mosque in February 1994, Hamas decided to take revenge by using suicide attacks, a first for the Palestinians. It is difficult to know where they got the idea from, since suicide attacks had not been used by Hizbullah for some years prior to 1994. No justification for the change was given at the time, but since 1997 a prodigious number of justifications have been written (below).

During the initial phase of suicide terror from 1994 to 1998, 26 operations were carried out by Hamas and the smaller radical Islamic group, Islamic Jihad. The individual tactics will be examined below. During this period, while the PLO was transforming itself into the Palestinian National Authority (PNA) and conducting intermittent negotiations with Israel concerning withdrawals from the West Bank and Gaza and the establishment of the Palestinian state, the support for suicide attacks was low, except in cases of revenge for certain Israeli actions.

This changed after the failure of the Camp David negotiations, hosted by President Bill Clinton in July 2000. These negotiations were supposed to be the final status negotiations between the Israelis and the Palestinians. No agreement was reached and the talks collapsed. A few months later, after Israel's then-opposition leader Ariel Sharon's visit to the Temple Mount/Haram al-Sharif (the site of the Dome of the Rock, the Al-Aqsa Mosque and the ancient location of the Jewish Temple), the al-Aqsa Intifada began (September 28, 2000). There does not seem to be much doubt that this intifada was sparked by the Palestinian leadership at first as a negotiating tool but later became a popular struggle. Suicide attacks were not present during the first month of the Intifada, beginning only on October 26. Even then the suicide attacks (approximately 12) until June 1, 2001 were quite ineffective and killed mostly just the bomber and a maximum of two or three others or merely wounded people.

From the summer of 2001 until the beginnings of the truce initiated by Palestinian President Mahmud `Abbas (Abu Mazin) in 2005, the suicide attacks went through a number of phases. In general, there was a pattern of quiet after every major operation, with suicide attacks then gradually building up to another major operation that generated a strong Israeli response. The major exception to this rule was the suicide attack campaign that lasted from December 1, 2001 to the end of May 2002. While until the end of 2001, the suicide attacks had been almost exclusively the property of Hamas and Islamic Jihad, from that point onward all of the Palestinian factions, including groups associated with the PLO (al-Aqsa Martyrs Brigades) and the secular-Marxist Popular Front for the Liberation of Palestine (PFLP), joined in. Although this unity of action was to some extent broken by the Israeli response of reoccupation of the cities of the West Bank during the end of that period, some coordination remained until the end of the Intifada in 2005. Only the PFLP, the smallest of the Palestinian factions, did not participate in the suicide attacks after the end of 2003.

Strategy

One of the problems with the Palestinians is the lack of unity when dealing with strategy. Nominally, the goal of the PNA during the 1993–2000 period, and continuing until the present, had been to establish a Palestinian state on the territories of the West Bank and the Gaza Strip, with its capital in East Jerusalem. (Many Israelis suspect that this goal is merely preparatory to further territorial goals.) In order to achieve this goal, the strategy has been to apply international and especially American pressure on Israel to gain concessions. When these concessions failed to materialize in 2000, the response of the PLO and its supporters was violence, but usually not directed at Israel proper (behind the 1967 lines). Hamas and the Islamic Jihad have different goals stemming from radical Islamic beliefs, and precluding any option other than the establishment of an Islamic state over all of geographical Palestine. With this goal in mind, it is to the advantage of both of these groups to prolong the fighting and to maximize the number of dead in order to make any return to negotiations difficult.

Although the Palestinians pursued a coherent strategy until the middle of 2003,[3] it was not until the period between December 2001 and late May 2002 that this strategy involved suicide attacks in any major way. The basic problem of the al-Aqsa Intifada was how to get the message of the Palestinians out to the world, and at the same time make the conflict real enough to Israelis that they would want to withdraw from the territories that the Palestinians wanted. Although there was disagreement about this between the PLO and the Hamas, those differences were played down in the short term. This strategy had to be accomplished while the Israeli Defense Forces vastly outnumbered the Palestinians and were much better equipped. Additionally, to some extent the Palestinians had been spoiled by the memory of the positive news-media coverage that the first Intifada had given them; they expected a similar treatment during the second Intifada and were often resentful when that was not accorded them.

In public discussion of suicide attacks, militant groups presented these attacks in terms of a disadvantaged and poor state of oppressed people fighting a world-class power supported by the United States. Palestinians frequently said that they would only rely upon suicide attacks to even out this imbalance, and that no one had the right to judge them for using the tactics of desperation. However, this argument is not necessarily persuasive when the number of popular insurrections that employed nonviolent means or low-level guerilla warfare without recourse to attacking civilians indiscriminantly is considered.[4] An alternative argument emphasized that suicide attacks were the only way to balance out the severe Palestinian casualties with similar casualties on the Israeli side. It is true that most of the Israeli casualties during the al-Aqsa Intifada were caused by suicide attacks. But the fact that virtually all of these casualties were civilians and located inside the 1967 boundaries of Israel tended to bring most Israelis to the conclusion that the Palestinians wanted to kill them all—leading them to support harsher policies against the Palestinians. These attacks failed to endear them to the international public as well: Scenes of Israeli civilian casualties, viewed on TV screens throughout the world, tended to make international audiences much less sympathetic to Palestinian suffering, to the point where by the end of 2002 the whole conflict was deemed "hopeless" and unimportant, compared to mass-casualty terrorist attacks threatening Western countries at home.

During the suicide campaign of 2001–02, one can see the effects of a protracted series of suicide attacks, sometimes day after day, or with several on the same day, upon a civilian population. Because of the close proximity of the Palestinians to Israel (and Palestinians' knowledge of Israeli society gained from working inside Israeli territory), the Palestinian factions were able to keep this suicide campaign up for almost six months. Israel's breaking point was reached on March 27, 2002, when `Abd al-Basit Muhammad `Awdah wheeled a cart filled with explosives into a hotel Passover celebration in Netanya, killing 29 and wounding about 150. This operation had been preceded by 16 suicide operations since the beginning of December 2001 and was followed by five more operations within a week. It led directly to Israel reoccupying the major cities of the West Bank during the following months, against which there was surprisingly little international protest.[5] Effectively, the suicide campaign had significantly decreased international support for the Palestinians. By the summer of 2002, major Palestinian intellectual and social figures signed a petition calling for an end to suicide attacks.[6]

However, because of the disintegration of the PNA (as a result of the Israeli reoccupation during this time), the Palestinian groups themselves increasingly fragmented, with each group vying to outdo the others in taking vengeance upon the Israelis without any apparent strategy. As the Israelis became aware that there was no authority among the Palestinians that could or would call off the suicide attacks, they took the route of building a barrier between them and the Palestinians. This barrier has had the effect of removing the easy access of Palestinians to Israel and has significantly decreased the number of successful suicide attackers (although the number of *attempted* suicide attacks still remains extremely high). Once again, the building of the barrier—to which there has been surprisingly little international protest—highlighted the fact that Israel still dominates the situation and can, in the end, impose its will without provoking international reaction.

It is interesting to note the close connection between the prevalence of suicide attacks and Islam among the Palestinians. Christians have not supplied any of the Palestinian suicide attacks, despite the fact that they are approximately 2 to 5 percent of the population and are an integral part of the semisecular PLO and the leftist PFLP that have made numerous suicide attacks.[7] Although the stated goals of most of these suicide attackers are nonreligious, usually nationalistic, the fact that Christians are entirely unrepresented (as opposed to the situation in Lebanon during the 1980s when Christians supplied a high percentage of suicide attackers against Israeli targets) demonstrates the increasing Islamization of this conflict.[8] At every point suicide attacks have failed to bring positive benefits to the Palestinian side, but for years after this became apparent, most Palestinian factions continued to use them. The reasons for this are complex and need to be examined for their implications for future use of suicide attacks. They can be summarized into three reasons: parity of violence, believing the justifications for suicide attacks, and the creation of a heroic image.

Justifications

More justifications for Palestinian suicide attacks have been published than have been for any of the other conflicts discussed in this book.[9] This fact means that there is a comparative embarrassment of riches with regard to the Palestinian use of suicide terrorism that compares unfavorably with the lack in other areas. Palestinian strategy and tactics are widely discussed in Arabic by both Palestinians and non-Palestinians, and there is a substantial body of religious literature designed to demonstrate that these attacks are not only in accord with Islamic law on the waging of jihad but actually represent the pinnacle of jihad. This last, exaggerated claim most probably is designed to cover up the actual weaknesses of the other arguments. On the other hand, the materials produced for the Palestinians have spilled over into other conflicts, despite the best attempts of many establishment `ulama to prevent this. Indeed, most of the arguments justifying suicide attacks against Israelis are used by al-Qa`ida and other radical Muslim groups with only slight changes, and often with a contemptuous dismissal of the idea that the use of suicide attacks should be limited to Israel. Later in this volume, we will note the insidious effect of the broad acceptance of Palestinian arguments supporting suicide attacks upon the larger Muslim world.

There is no doubt that Nawaf Takruri synthesized most of the best arguments, and his collection, al-`Amaliyyat al-istishhadiyya fi al-mizan al-fiqhi (*Martyrdom Operations in the Legal Balance*), which has gone through numerous editions since it was first published in 1997, is the premier book on the subject. Takruri starts off by giving the reader 18 paradigmatic operations taken from all over the Muslim world (he even includes one from the Sudan), but focusing upon the Palestinians. He then attempts to present the primary objection against the use of suicide attacks by Muslims, which is that they are actually no different from suicide. This idea was refuted by promoting the idea that true suicide was only the result of depression and loss of hope in the future whereas martyrdom operations (now referred to as *al-`amaliyyat al-istishhadiyya*, in contrast to the earlier Hizbullah formulation of "suicide attacks," *al-`amaliyyat al-intihariyya*, in chapter 2)[10] constitute the epitome of hope and self-sacrifice. This formulation has been embraced by all subsequent radical Muslim promoters of suicide attacks.

Takruri laid down seven benefits of suicide attacks that are also foundational:

1. They cause the most terror to the Jews.
2. They are the least costly to those opposing the Jews, since the one who carries them out is himself the weapon.
3. These types of weapons even out the imbalance between the Muslims and the Jews. Previously the Muslims were being killed and killed; now they are "killing and being killed" (Qur'an 9:111).
4. These operations make the Jews think a thousand times before carrying out a massacre or an exterminating operation on the Palestinian civilians, since these types of operations are what the Jews can expect in return.
5. The one who carries out these attacks, if his action is one devoted to God, intends to terrorize enemies and to uplift the Word of God (Qur'an 9:41) as a method of causing fear to aggressors and to weaken them, and to bring happiness and a return of resolve to the hearts of the Muslims...he has attained the rank of the martyrs.
6. These operations spread the spirit of the love of jihad and martyrdom throughout the [Muslim] community—which its enemies fear and make every attempt to abort from the community.
7. They cause many non-Muslims throughout the world to know the true creed of Islam.[11]

He also lists two negative aspects to the suicide attacks:

1. The one who carries out such an operation is killed by his own hand and not by that of his enemy—a fact that makes these operations similar to suicide.
2. Some of the people who are killed in these operations are civilians, such as women and children, who are forbidden to kill, and that makes aspects of the operations contrary to the laws of fighting.[12]

This summary of the benefits and problems of suicide attacks more or less details the problems that all Muslims dealing with the subject have had to either confront or avoid. Takruri over the course of his book is at pains to demonstrate that the two problems he lists are refuted. But he is able to do this only by rationalization; he is not able to bring any examples from the time of Muhammad that would truly serve as a precedent for martyrdom operations. As we will note, the issue of the killing of civilians is a continuous problem for the Muslim apologists of suicide attacks. While specifically with regard to the Israeli-Palestinian situation most authors rationalize the problem by either saying that they are doing to the Israelis what the Israelis are doing to the Palestinians or that there are no true civilians among Israelis (because most people serve in the army), when radical Muslims started using suicide attacks against other Muslims these arguments sounded quite hollow.

Tactics

It is impossible to deal with all or even a reasonable number of the approximately 120 successful suicide attacks that the various Palestinian factions unleashed upon Israel during the 1994–2005 period. Many of these attacks were extremely minor and either only wounded people or killed a small number. Even these "unsuccessful" attacks, however, are significant for the overall creation of an insecure environment. But the most important paradigmatic attacks are the ones in which the suicide attackers attempted new or unusual tactics.

Although suicide attacks started earlier, the four coordinated attacks in 1996 (two on February 25, and one each on March 3 and 4) truly established the standard tactic for driving the Israeli population into a state of terror. These bombings had been preceded by the assassination of Yehye `Ayyash, the Hamas operative who had developed the tactic of suicide bombing among the Palestinians several years before, at the end of 1995. Simultaneous bombings of Bus 18 in Jerusalem (killing 26 people) and an attack on a bus stop in coastal Israel started the first round. During the interval, there was considerable anger among Israelis, but not the terror that can happen after random suicide attacks. Then there was a second round, during which the bus line was hit again (killing 19 people), and then a day later a major mall in Tel Aviv was attacked (killing 20 people). With the exception of the last attack (by Islamic Jihad) all of the attacks were carried out by Hamas.

The hysteria that was created after the final pair of attacks was incredible and demonstrates that suicide attacks, when they are sustained and prolonged, can actually drive a society into panic. Security measures that the Israelis took during the week interval between the first bombing of Bus 18 and the second one were ineffectual, and these attacks disproved the "urban myth" that suicide attackers would not attack the same targets more than once in such a short time period. However, because there was no significant popular (let alone governmental) support for continued suicide attacks among the Palestinians, this style of suicide attack had to wait for the second Intifada to come into fruition.

The negative Palestinian reaction to the sustained attacks of early 1996 (which contributed significantly to the election of Benjamin Netanyahu, the Likud candidate in the Israeli elections in May 1996) led to a hiatus in suicide terror. But by the middle of 1997, as Netanyahu was perceived by many Palestinians as being an obstacle to negotiations, there were a number of other attacks. The most innovative of these attacks was the triple suicide bombing of Ben Yehuda St. in Jerusalem on July 3, 1997. This attack involved three suicide attackers who positioned themselves throughout this popular pedestrian thoroughfare and detonated themselves killing 16 and wounding 178. Although these suicide operations were among the first to try and achieve mass casualties in a public place, they achieved limited success. The lesson that Hamas learned was clear: in order to maximize casualties, suicide attacks had to take place in confined locations. Buses were ideal, open spaces were not (unless there was already a crowd gathered and there was some way to confine the blast).

The initial suicide attacks of the al-Aqsa Intifada were comparatively low in casualties. This trend ended on June 1, 2001 when Hasan Husayn al-Hotari detonated himself in a crowd of revelers waiting to enter a popular nightclub in Tel Aviv (the Dolphinarium). This attack signaled the beginning of spectacular terror attacks that had the effect of emptying out many popular gathering places and establishments in Israel during the next two years and significantly changing local social patterns. It was followed up by another spectacular attack on the Sbarro restaurant in the middle of Jerusalem (killing 15 people) on August 9, 2001. Both of these attacks took place in areas previously considered to be "safe" by Israelis and were probably chosen for that reason.

Although the high-profile al-Qa'ida suicide attacks of Septetember 11, 2001 led to a short-term decrease in the use of suicide terror by the Palestinians, since the Palestinian leadership did not want to be identified with al-Qa'ida, such attacks resumed at a massive level toward the end of 2001. This suicide campaign reached its peak with the attack of `Abd al-Basit `Awdah on the Park Hotel in Netanya (along the coast of Israel) on March 27, 2002 (during the Passover seder). This massive attack, carried out quite brazenly by `Awdah, who wheeled a bomb disguised as a food cart into the midst of a large group of diners, led directly to Israel's reoccupation of the cities of the West Bank. However, the political price that the Palestinians were paying for such attacks was also clear when virtually no international bodies protested this reoccupation.

For the most part, foreigners have been absent from the Israeli-Palestinian conflict. Although there was a great deal of sympathy for the Palestinian cause on the part of the neighboring Arab countries (and the Muslim world beyond), none of the governments would allow any of their citizens to join the Palestinians in attacting Israel. Unlike the later situation of Iraq, the borders between Israel and its neighbors are not porous and three of its neighbors (Egypt, Jordan, and Syria) have strong, stable regimes with no desire to provoke a war with Israel—regardless of how much sympathy they might have for the Palestinian cause. However, since European tourists are very common in Israel, the possibility of recruiting either a European Muslim or a European convert to Islam to carry out a suicide attack in Israel was much more feasible and more attractive.

Steven Smyrek, a German convert to Islam, was the first outsider to try a suicide attack. In 1997 he was arrested after flying to Israel for a suicide attack on behalf of Hizbullah. Although he was exchanged in 2004 as part of a prisoner exchange with the Hizbullah, he remains, according to his own statements, determined to carry out a suicide attack.[13] Asif Muhammad Hanif and Omar Khan Sharif, two British Muslims of Pakistani descent, remain the major examples of foreign Muslims helping out in the Palestinian suicide campaign. On April 30, 2003, after having been recruited by Hamas in Gaza (and after having been given a ride into Israel by aid workers), both of them went to Mike's Place, a popular club in Tel Aviv. Hanif's bomb detonated and killed three people, but apparently Sharif's did not detonate, and he fled the scene. Several weeks later his body, having drowned, washed up on the seashore. The use of two British Muslims heralded the radicalization of the British Muslim community and the future suicide bombings of July 7, 2005 in London, and the desperation or strength of the Palestinian factions.

In general, the tactical sophistication of the suicide attacks against Israelis decreased significantly after the summer of 2002. In part, this was due to the broadening of the phenomenon of suicide attacks. Suicide belts had become widely available to individuals, and the power of the Palestinian factions had become diffuse and somewhat disorganized. The targets, which initially had been groups of people in enclosed areas (buses, nightclubs, and restaurants), now became widely varied. However, the cumulative effect of suicide attacks was maintained with remarkable consistency until it began to peter off at the end of 2004 and the beginning of 2005. As the barrier that the Israelis constructed became more and more real, there were serious logistical difficulties in placing a suicide terrorist within Israel itself. This fact had two ramifications: first, it spelled the end of personal suicide attacks, since successful suicide attacks had to be planned and organized by the Palestinian factions as some type of tactical innovation (usually closed off immediately afterward as the Israelis became aware of it), and second, it directed more of the attacks against Israeli settlements, which had been attacked rarely but were located beyond the barrier. However, as the attack of April 17, 2006 at a Tel Aviv restaurant (killing nine people) proves, the tactic is still capable of causing terror, now that Israelis have been lulled into some security.

Creation of a Culture of Martyrdom and the Projection of the Heroic Image

One of the most important by-products of the suicide attack campaign of the Palestinians during the al-Aqsa Intifada has been the development of a full-scale martyrology.[14] Classical Islam had developed some martyrologies, especially among Shi`ites, and to some extent this heritage was utilized by nationalists against European colonialism. But in general, these martyrologies had not encompassed an entire people. Because of the violent nature of the al-Aqsa Intifada (as opposed to the first Intifada), there are an abundance of martyrs—at least 4,000 to 5,000 according to Palestinian counts. The first and best-known of them is Muhammad al-Durra, killed under somewhat mysterious circumstances on September 30, 2000 during a confrontation between the Israeli army and Palestinian forces at the Netzarim junction in the Gaza Strip. Although the entire scene, with its touching pictures of al-Durra's father attempting to shield his son from the bullets flying around them, was photographed by Talal Abu Rahma (a photographer for *France 2* television station), there remain questions as to whether the footage was doctored. For the Arab and Muslim world, however, Muhammad al-Durra remains the paradigmatic martyr of the al-Aqsa Intifada. As an innocent child, supposedly killed in cold blood by the Israelis, he is symbolic of the suffering of the Palestinian people overall. Not surprisingly, stories about him are the first ones featured in most martyrologies about the conflict.[15]

Suicide attackers appear in great numbers inside these martyrologies. One of the important legacies that the suicide attackers leave behind is the martyrdom video, which is usually filmed several days before their mission and includes some type of explanation as to why they intend to carry out a martyrdom operation. The imagery used in these martyrdom videos is impressive: the attackers are often wrapped in green Islamic flags, with heroic slogans embroidered upon them. Usually they will appear with weapons in hand or sometimes with the suicide belt wrapped around their waists.

Another important legacy is the after-martyrdom celebration in which the oral history of the martyr and whatever operation he has carried out will be established. Most very religious martyrs encourage their loved ones not to mourn them (unlike other dead), and consequently this event has the form of a "wedding celebration," in which the martyr is "married" to the *houris* of paradise. Even the female suicide attackers have these "wedding celebrations," although it is not clear to whom they are married.[16] Inside the martyrologies, the suicide attackers are almost always given the motive of vengeance.[17] Although Islamic motivations of redemption and personal salvation appear, they are comparatively muted; more often the salvation seems to be national and collective.[18] Suicide attacks in general are presented as the last resort of a people pushed beyond their limits and who need to restore parity with the enemy. It is difficult to gauge the responses of the families as presented in the martyrologies, sometimes they appear to be proud of what their children have done, other times sad and worried (since mid-2002, Israeli soldiers almost always came to destroy the houses of the families of suicide attackers, so the families often had to move out quickly). But there was some additional ambiguity as female suicide attackers began to appear among the Palestinians.

Female Suicide Attackers

Proportionally the subject of female suicide attackers has attracted more attention than any other category of suicide attacker.[19] Traditionally women did not fight in jihad, other than a very few examples to the contrary. The stringent rules of sexual modesty that Islam places upon the woman—rules that hamper her maneuverability—together with the problem that a woman could be raped by an enemy make it difficult for the idea of women fighters to be accepted within Muslim countries. The vast majority of the extant jihad materials were written with men in mind. However, the changing norms of (even) Muslim societies have caused certain scholars to raise the question of women fighting in jihad, at least theoretically. The general consensus of this discussion is that women can fight in jihad if the battle is against an invading enemy and their help is needed. However, women fighting in jihad is clearly a matter of last resort.

From the first Intifada (1987–93) the participation of women was integral. Women were seen as being the better representatives of the Palestinians in nonviolent protests. Soldiers were less willing to attack women and sometimes sensitive to searching them thoroughly. And Palestinian women participated en masse in the first Intifada, deeming their participation to be a sign of equality. The al-Aqsa Intifada, however, has been a military uprising and while there have been nonviolent protests, the overwhelming arena of action has been military. This fact presents a quandary for Palestinian women who want to be involved.

This quandary was resolved by Wafa Idris on January 27, 2002 during the course of the 2001–02 Palestinian suicide campaign. Idris delivered a bomb to the center of Jerusalem, killing one person and wounding around 150 (it is still uncertain whether this was a suicide attack, however, or whether her bomb was detonated by another figure). Although one cannot say that this was a spectacular attack, it had the effect of skewing the profile of the likely suicide attacker—now women were as suspect as men—and it galvanized the support of the Arab world. To have women carrying out suicide attacks together with men proved to be a very powerful propagandistic tool in such an honor-shame society. Women's martyrdom videos were often played with the express purpose of shaming men into fighting or at least supporting the Palestinian cause financially.[20] Traditionally the only acceptable role in Arab society for women in battle was to encourage the fighters. But occasionally a young woman would be placed in the center of the battle on a camel in order to ensure that the tribe did not give ground lest they lose her (she was never harmed if captured by the other side, but the humiliation for her tribe was immense). Female suicide attackers then fulfilled this role, but they also had a redemptive aspect, since the vast majority of Palestinian female suicide attackers have been compromised in some way (illicit sexual relationships or pregnancies, barrenness, or other family dishonor). The importance of varied motivations will be explored in chapter 8.

Not surprisingly, although in general suicide attacks had until the middle of 2001 been associated with the more religious Hamas or the Islamic Jihad, with the semisecular al-Aqsa Martyrs Brigades (part of the PLO) or the Marxist PFLP lagging behind, it was the secular nationalists who pioneered female suicide attackers. Two full years of suicide attacks occurred before Hamas was willing to use women attackers, and even then only once (Reem al-Riyashi on January 14, 2004 in Gaza, killing four). Islamic Jihad proved to be much more willing to adopt female suicide attackers, sending in several before Hamas. It seems that Hamas took the religious problems of women suicide attackers very seriously and really used them only as a last resort.[21]

One cannot say that the performance of female suicide attackers in their attacks was nearly as impressive as the response to their mere appearance on the scene. In general, their attacks have been very minor, with the exception of that of Hanadi Jaradat on a restaurant in Haifa on October 3, 2003, killing 19 and wounding 60. Her motive was certainly vengeance, although she was apparently also sexually compromised and left a detailed will listing her motivations:

> I know that I shall not bring back Palestine. I fully know this. However, I know that this is my duty for Allah. Believing in the principles of my faith, I respond to the call. I now inform you that, Allah willing, I shall find what Allah has promised to me and to all of those who take this path—gardens which Allah has promised us, in which we will live forever...it is my duty to the religion of Allah—and my obligation to Him—to defend it [Palestine]. I have nothing before me other than this body, which I am going to turn into slivers that will tear out the heart of everyone who has tried to uproot us from our country.[22]

Despite her compromised position, Jarradat obviously hopes to find salvation in paradise as a result of her actions. Her motivations are a mix of nationalism, despair, and belief in the salvational effectiveness of the suicide attack. Although it has been difficult to assimilate female suicide attackers into the overall Islamic mythology of martyrdom, words such as these are similar to those voiced by male suicide attackers in their videos.[23]

Nationalist-Islamic Resistance Movements: Chechnya

Like the Palestinians, the Chechen movement in southern Russia began as a secular nationalist one. The history of Chechnya had been a rocky one—after the initial Russian conquest during the 1830s and 1940s, their heroic leader Imam Shamyl had led a revolt from 1834 to 1858. Although this revolt was ground down by Russian strength, the Chechens remained rebellious. During World War II, the Communist dictator Josef Stalin exiled the entire Chechen population from its ancestral homeland on the northern side of the Caucasus Mountains. The Chechens returned only in the middle 1980s. When the USSR collapsed in 1991, the Chechens began to agitate for independence. Although the Russian answer to this request was no, effectively Chechnya slipped away from Russian control such that by 1994–95 the Russian Army had to invade it. This turned out to be a fiasco, and when the Russians withdrew in 1996, they left thousands of dead soldiers behind.

In 1999, however, they came back. Using a bombing campaign that had transpired in Moscow during that year—which was never tied to the Chechens—as an excuse, the Russian Army invaded again and leveled everything in its path. By 2001, the country was nominally pacified, but there are still substantial guerilla groups that operate throughout the region. Initially Chechen independence was tied to local nationalism, and as the north Caucasus had always been a stronghold for Sufism, there was no radical Muslim presence. But this changed throughout the 1990s as more and more radical Muslims from the Middle East or Afghanistan came to fight in Chechnya. Gradually they gained local followers such as Shamyl Basayev, the charismatic leader of some of the Chechen militias. It is difficult to tell, however, whether the appearance of the first suicide bombings in Chechnya was a manifestation of the power of radical Muslims. In almost none of the cases do the motivations of the Chechens—apart from vengeance against the Russians—seem to be using traditional Islamic terminology of jihad or martyrdom.

One of the earliest suicide attacks in Chechnya was carried out on June 9, 2000 by Hawa Barayev, a young woman who according to the hagiographical accounts killed 27 members of the Russian Special Forces when she drove a truck filled with explosives into their building. Barayev has become famous because not only was she apparently the first Chechen suicide attacker, but she was also the occasion for radical Muslims to write a legal opinion on whether her action was legitimate or not. This fatwa, "The Islamic Ruling on the Permissibility of Martyrdom Operations," penned by the Saudi al-Qa`ida leader Yusuf al-`Ayyiri, was the first major legal opinion to move the focus of martyrdom operations away from the Palestinians.[24]

Immediately following Barayev's suicide attack, there were a series of at least eight other attacks during the following two months, clearly demonstrating the desperation felt by the Chechens. None of these, however, was a spectacular attack and all were directed at military targets. Once again, after an initial lapse of security exploited by Barayev, the Chechen experience proved that suicide attacks have little military value and did not hamper the Russian army at all. But while the initial suicide attack campaign wound down in 2000, there were several spectacular suicide attacks against military targets during 2001 and 2002. These were spaced out so that the Russian guard was down.

By 2002, a new organization the Riyad al-Salihin Martyrdom Brigades had appeared in Chechnya and changed the tactics of suicide attacks to focus upon civilians. The first attack of this group, on December 27, 2002, involved an attack on the government complex in the capital of Grozny, killing 83 and wounding 210. From May 12, 2003 until the middle of 2004 this group claimed at least 11 major suicide attacks. The targets ranged from hospitals to trains, several airplanes, and an attack on a rock concert in Moscow. All of these operations, in addition to others such as the attack upon a school in Beslan (September 2004) were apparently attempts to publicize the Chechen conflict and to inflict casualties among the Russian population similar to those already suffered by the Chechens. Although it seems that since the summer of 2004 the Chechens made an operational decision away from suicide attacks, it is unclear whether this is a short-term tactic or a long-term strategy.

The ideology of the Chechens is much less Islamic than even the semisecular elements of the Palestinian factions. Although some of the Islamic slogans are used, and radical Islam has made some inroads into Chechen society, it seems that in every case known thus far, vengeance against the Russians has been the primary motivation for suicide attacks. In the video "No Surrender," Hawa Barayev and her sister Luisa appear in a dialogue and use a large number of standard Muslim tropes for justification of suicide attacks. But in the end, Hawa Barayev appeals to the manliness of her viewers:

> Our forefathers would have killed anyone who tried to get tough with their women but today Muslim women are getting attacked and raped in front of those who claim to be men—they have no sense of jealousy for their Muslim sisters' honor to the extent that they sit and drink tea while listening to this appalling news!! Do you consider yourselves men?[25]

A much larger number (proportionally) of Chechen suicide attackers have been women, many of them purportedly war widows or women who were raped by the Russian soldiers.[26] Thus, there may be an element of redemption in the motivations for female suicide attackers like those of the Palestinians.

Implications for the United States

The United States does not border upon either the Palestinians or the Chechens, and thus there is a limit to how much one can learn from the experiences of Israel or Russia. Although Palestinian suicide attackers have killed American citizens in Israel, both the Palestinian and Chechen groups remain focused upon their primary foes, Israel and Russia. For the United States, the principal issue is its support for Israel that is seen throughout the Muslim world as a justification for suicide attacks perpetrated by globalist radical Muslims such as al-Qa'ida, and for this reason both the Palestinian experience and to some extent even the Chechen experience has ramifications for policy.

We reject the idea that poverty or being ill-equipped against a superior foe creates the necessity for using suicide attacks, as Palestinian spokesmen and apologists have stated repeatedly.[27] But there is a connection between the continuation of suicide attacks and the compensation that is paid to the families of the bombers. For the first three years of the second Intifada (2000–03), Saddam Husayn of Iraq paid a sum to the families of bombers in order to make up for the loss in economic support. This sum of money that sometimes reached $25,000 or more raises the question of whether some of the bombers actually commited suicide in order to better their families' economic situation. While there is no real evidence that this was in fact the case—and after 2002 the Palestinian suicide attacker had to take into consideration the fact that the Israeli military authorities usually demolished their families' home as a deterrent—there may have been a downturn in the number of suicide attacks after the support from Saddam Husayn was cut off. In other words, we find it doubtful that Palestinian suicide attackers actually killed themselves for the sake of money for their families, but it is likely that this financial support artificially propped up the numbers of suicide attackers for a considerable period. Rather than assume that this drop was related only to the lack of money going to suicide bombers' families, it is important to note other concurrent developments in the conflict such as the death of Palestinian leader Yasir Arafat, Israel's building of the security fence, and organizations' own changing tactics. Regardless, we find it difficult to see how this compensation, however, will have any relevance to conflicts outside the Israel-Palestinian arena. None of the suicide attackers associated with al-Qa'ida, with the Chechens, or with Iraq are known to have received compensation to their families after their deaths.

Although it is unlikely that the United States would ever have to face a local population bent on suicide attacks, both Israel and Russia have demonstrated the methods that can be successful in defeating these attacks. The barrier that Israel has built on its borders has effectively removed the threat of a sustained Palestinian campaign like that of 2001–02. Russia has taken a different method: effectively it has given rule of Chechnya into the hands of a small group of very ruthless Chechens, headed by Ramzan Kadyrov, who have suppressed the radical Muslims in the region. Morally, however, these methods present problems for the United States. In dealing with suicide attackers, the question that frequently recurs is whether one must descend to barbaric or cruel methods to combat them. This is nowhere more evident than with al-Qa'ida.

Chapter 4

Self-Sacrifice Against the "Great Satan": Al-Qa`ida and Martyrdom Operations

If I had ten arrows I would fire them all at [America],
and I would not fire even one at anybody else.
I swear by God, that if it were possible for me to carry out
a martyrdom operation against them I would
not even wait an hour to do it.

—Nasir al-Fahd[1]

For the United States the most visible aspect of contemporary radical Muslim use of suicide attacks is that of al-Qa`ida. The al-Qa`ida organization was founded in 1988 by the Palestinian `Abdallah Azzam (assassinated in 1989) and the Saudi `Usama bin Laden, and it is still headed by the latter. Al-Qa`ida's goals include (but are not necessarily confined to) insuring the withdrawal of Western armed forces and cultural interests from the Middle East specifically and from the Muslim world in general, and the eventual establishment of a pan-Muslim state that will be led by a caliph. Other goals include fighting and winning a number of conflicts of a religious-nationalist bent, most especially Israel (geographical Palestine), but also in Chechnya, Kashmir, Afghanistan, Iraq, the Philippines, southern Thailand, and Burma where Muslims are being oppressed (as al-Qa`ida and in some cases a substantial part of the Muslim world sees it), as well as attempting to change the character of Islam as a whole, which will be discussed below. Thus, al-Qa`ida's goals are grand and diverse, and most importantly for the United States, these cannot be achieved without either the defeat of the United States or a radical change in its foreign policy.

Al-Qa`ida was born in the border region between Pakistan and Afghanistan as a result of the guerilla warfare initiated by both the United States and

Pakistan against the Soviet occupation of Afghanistan (1979–89).[2] This initiative from the point of view of the United States was supposed to drain the resources of the USSR and to bog it down in an unwinnable war that could possibly spill over into the Muslim republics of Central Asia. From the point of view of Pakistan, support of the Afghani *mujahidin* was supposed to obtain the valuable support and favor of the United States and the Western world, and additionally to counteract the influence of its traditional opponent India (who had also enjoyed good relations with the USSR) and to obtain economic resources from both the West and the rich Arab Gulf states. For the short-term, all of these goals were realized by all parties.

However, fostered by Pakistan, especially by its powerful intelligence service, the ISI, and almost unnoticed by the United States, another influential movement was being born at that time. Frustrated by the lack of progress in fighting Israel during the 1970s (especially among radical Muslims), the Palestinian `Abdallah `Azzam came from Saudi Arabia, where he had been teaching, to establish training camps for volunteers to fight the Soviets. These volunteers came from all over the Muslim world, although the majority (at first) came from the Gulf states of Saudi Arabia and the U.A.E. Eventually large numbers were to come from North Africa, and from Southeast Asia (Malaysia, Indonesia, and the Philippines) as well. Although it cannot be said that the eventual victory of the Afghan *mujahidin* in 1992 was due to these volunteers, they contributed substantially to several key campaigns.

To these volunteers `Azzam preached a salvational form of jihad that, although based upon the classical sources described in chapter 1, demonstrated some differences. Prior to the time of `Azzam, among Sunnis, jihad had been an ideal, but one that was controlled to a large degree by either a Muslim government or by the religious leadership (the `ulama'). In general, both of these groups were quite reluctant to call for jihad. Although the word was occasionally used in the antiimperialist struggles of the early and mid-twentieth century, and especially in the conflict with Israel, its religious content was played down. Only after the Arab defeat of 1967, does the religious emphasis upon jihad increase somewhat. But even then the concept was controlled to a large degree by governments or religious elites.

Although `Azzam was not the only one to call for change—other ideologues in Egypt, Saudi Arabia, and Pakistan also had a hand in this process—because he lived in a military zone (Peshawar, in the Northwest Frontier Province of Pakistan), he was able to focus upon jihad as a lifestyle. For other ideologues this jihadi lifestyle was hypothetical; they never held a gun or lived in military quarters, let alone participated in actual combat. `Azzam emphasized that jihad defined the nature of true Islam, and that Muslims who did not participate in military jihad did not hold the same spiritual rank as those who did. This was a considerable change from classical Islam. Moreover, he preached that because of the occupation of Muslim lands (at that time Afghanistan and Palestine), jihad was a personal obligation upon every Muslim. The implication of this idea was that each Muslim who did not come to fight was a lesser Muslim or perhaps not a "true" Muslim at all.

Many Muslims responded to this message, and it was from this doctrine of salvational jihad or lifestyle that jihad the ideal of al-Qa`ida was born. The unity that the various ethnic groups of Muslims felt in the jihad camps of Pakistan was something that had not been felt among Muslims for some centuries, and for many it was a transformative experience. This experience gave the fighters a sense of Islam as a global phenomenon, a unifying feeling that is similar to that of the annual *hajj* in Mecca. For the first time in centuries Muslims from all over the world fought for the ideal of Islam as a whole. And they won, according to their own perception, without outside aid. This problematic conclusion (because of the role of the United States in supporting the *mujahidin*) was eventually to imbue al-Qa`ida and its ideological offshoots with a powerful sense of confidence, destiny and support from God.

In the immediate wake of the end of the Afghan experience (1989–92), most of the jihad fighters drifted: either back to their homes, where many were instrumental in setting up local antigovernmental jihad movements (such as the GIA in Algeria and the Jama`a Islamiyya in Southeast Asia) or to new fields of jihad such as Bosnia-Herzegovina (1992–95) or Chechnya (1999–2001). The formative phase of al-Qa`ida, however, was after Usama bin Laden returned to Afghanistan in May 1996. Between 1990 and 1996, Bin Laden drifted: first to Saudi Arabia, and then—with his increasing opposition to the Saudi government and religious elite—to Sudan, where he lived between 1992 and 1996. In 1994 he was deprived of his Saudi citizenship, and by 1996 the Sudanese government, itself an alliance between the military and the radical Islamic movement of Hasan al-Turabi, was under pressure to expel Bin Laden. The only place where Bin Laden could go was Afghanistan.

By September 1996, the radical Islamic movement of the Taliban, which was a group of graduates of Pakistani *madrasa*s who had banded together to found an Islamic state in Afghanistan, had taken Kabul (the capital). Already by July 1996, Bin Laden had proclaimed a jihad against what he characterized as the American occupation of the Muslim holy land of Saudi Arabia. He hailed two bombing operations against the Americans in the kingdom—one on November 13, 1995 in Riyadh and the other a suicide attack in June 25, 1996 in Dhahran—as representative of the desire of the Muslim Saudis to expel the non-Muslim foreigners. (Most likely neither of these two operations can be actually ascribed to al-Qa`ida or its influence.)[3] This proclamation was framed in terms of the classical *hadith* attributed to Prophet Muhammad that commands Muslims to "Expel the polytheists (*mushrikin*) from the Arabian Peninsula"[4] and has some considerable popularity among Muslims worldwide.

Bin Laden throughout his career has been a uniter, and this is one quality that makes him a powerful, albeit symbolic, leader. Unlike so many of the other factious radical groups that are forever splitting apart and squabbling about doctrine, Bin Laden tries to speak in broad generalities, without delineating his exact platform and to focus the violence of his followers on the outside world instead of on each other. His spiritual prestige stems not from any deep Islamic learning, although he is capable of citing classical materials, but from his battlefield experience in Afghanistan, from his personally ascetic lifestyle, and from his clear black-and-white vision of the world. In general, Bin Laden has promoted a very clear message: Americans and Westerners must leave Saudi Arabia.

It is to Bin Laden's fortune that a great many of his side messages flow naturally from this one central message. Because Saudi Arabia is (arguably) the center of the Muslim world and because it promotes itself as a country in which Islamic norms are maintained in a very vocal manner, Bin Laden and al-Qa`ida are able to critique a very visible standard and measure themselves up to it (or it to them). The fact that Saudi Arabia is dependent politically and in many ways culturally upon the United States is easily translatable from a propagandistic point of view to the overall dependence of the Muslim world upon the west. If al-Qa`ida can succeed in establishing the boundaries it demands between Islam and infidelity in Saudi Arabia, then that achievement would be so powerful and symbolic that it might very well signal the beginning of a pan-Islamic state.

It is also to al-Qa`ida's advantage that the fight to rid Saudi Arabia of Western influences will be a protracted one. Just as it was in the interests of Hamas and radical Muslims over all to prolong the struggle with Israel, so prolonging a struggle with Saudi Arabia and by extension the United States continually provides a lodestone for new recruits and material for propaganda. It is doubtful whether even if the United States were to fully withdraw from the Arabian Peninsula, that al-Qa`ida would give up such a valuable selling-issue for new recruits. The perception that its followers are defending the holy places against desecration by the infidels is simply too powerful to throw away.

By 1998 Bin Laden had gained powerful supporters, not only from the Taliban (who, while aiding his movement overall, never became his followers and remained at odds with al-Qa`ida on several key issues), but also from radical Muslims all over the Muslim world. Al-Qa`ida despite its claims, however, never became a truly globalist radical Muslim movement. While it accepted recruits from every ethnicity as long as they were Muslim, the higher leadership was always Arab. Only Hambali of the Southeast Asian Jama`a Islamiyya (JI) ever sat on their higher councils. Of the various Arab countries the dominant influences in al-Qa`ida during the Afghanistan period were first of all Egyptian and then Saudi (and Gulf Arab). Curiously, very few Syrians, Palestinians, or North Africans were represented in the upper ranks of al-Qa`ida. Although there were many South Asians close by from Pakistan, Kashmir, India proper, and Bangladesh (some of whom signed the 1998 declaration), none were represented in the higher ranks of al-Qa`ida.

Al-Qa`ida's support came overwhelmingly from the Gulf (especially Saudi Arabia). This is nowhere better illustrated than in the issue of finances. Bin Laden, although possessed of a substantial fortune (although not impressive in Saudi terms), had lost most of his money during his interlude in Sudan and the rest was frozen by the Saudi government. In order to finance operations, he and al-Qa`ida relied heavily upon donations especially from Gulf Arabs.

After this initial period of establishment, al-Qa`ida went through three major phases: early operations; September 11, 2001 and its immediate aftermath; and finally transformation into a loosely linked terror organization. The early operations are all major suicide attacks against the United States or its interests (the specifics of which will be covered under "Tactics"). These operations served to highlight the importance of the group, and to signify to the Muslim world that it meant to carry out serious operations. While some of these operations, such as the ones at the U.S. embassies in Nairobi, Kenya, and Dar es-Salaam, Tanzania on August 7, 1998, caused massive loss of life, in general these operations were highly symbolic rather than mass-casualty oriented.

September 11, 2001 was considerably different—while it too was symbolic, mass casualties were an integral part of the symbolism. This operation in which 19 highjackers took control of four separate American planes and used three of them to attack the two towers of the World Trade Center in New York, and the third to attack the Pentagon, was easily the most spectacular attack that al-Qa`ida has ever carried out. It could be said that al-Qa`ida as an organization, and its offshoots as well, has coalesced around this operation, since it symbolized the willingness to fight Americans within the United States, to not take into account what the reaction of the United States would be, and to demonstrate to the (Muslim) world at least that there was no reason to be afraid of the United States.[5] Much of al-Qa`ida's propaganda machine focused and to some extent still focuses upon the publicity it received as a result of this operation. The terrorist attacks of September 11 also raised the bar of expectations considerably, since future al-Qa`ida operations will inevitably be judged against it.

However, in the immediate aftermath of September 11, al-Qa`ida suffered a number of serious losses that even led certain factions within it to question whether such high-profile suicide attacks were to the benefit of the group.[6] Whereas between 1996 and 2001 al-Qa`ida had a secure base in Afghanistan under the protection of the Taliban regime, as a result of provoking the United States into directly confronting it (with American armed forces as well as through the Afghani Northern Alliance), it lost that base. This fact has had numerous ramifications that will be discussed below, in the strategy section of this chapter. Because al-Qa`ida has not been able to find a new country that can or will host it, it cannot conduct formal training of recruits or promote the sense of pan-Islamic unity (by bringing all recruits to the same camps) that was one of its greatest attractants. Its communications are severely hampered and although it has continually managed to carry out major operations, the spectacular operations al-Qa`ida craves are increasingly carried out by subsidiary groups who are not under close scrutiny (see chapter 5).

Although Usama bin Laden and his closest associate Ayman al-Zawahiri remain at large, and without a doubt their successful evasion of the American dragnet is a powerful propaganda tool in their favor, their immediate access to operations is limited, and their most talented subordinates are regularly arrested. They are potent symbols to their supporters and sympathizers but impotent threats (at least for the present).

A Culture of Martyrdom

Even more than for the Palestinians it is important for al-Qa`ida to cultivate a culture of martyrdom throughout the Muslim world. In some ways the symbolism that al-Qa`ida fosters is its prime contribution to the development of globalist radical Islam. By promoting the idea that Muslims should be a community of martyrdom (and not just individual groups among them, such as the Palestinians), al-Qa`ida seeks to make a radical transformation in Islam overall. As with so many of the other elements of jihad, `Abdallah `Azzam was the one who initiated this sea-change. Although radical Islam overall is hostile to Sufi mysticism, `Azzam essentially adopted its cult of holy men but changed it into a cult of martyrs. This is best exemplified in his *Ayat al-Rahman fi jihad al-Afghan* (*Signs of the Merciful One in the* jihad *of Afghanistan*), a comparatively short treatise in which he details the miracles associated with the fighters, and most especially with their bodies after their deaths, in Afghanistan. This martyrology is a clear attempt to focus attention upon the miraculous as a sign of God's favor in jihad, and to create a type of spectacle that will be watched and admired by Muslims.

Many of the jihad struggles since the time of `Azzam have followed in his footsteps. Martyrologies are now published about the first Afghan conflict (1979–89), the wars in Bosnia-Hezegovina and Chechnya, and about the struggle in Afghanistan (2001–present day) and Iraq (2003–present day).[7] In each one of these martyrologies an idealization of the figure of the martyr is made so that others will want to follow that person. Usually the martyr is said to have gone through a process of rejecting society. He will have to travel through difficult circumstances, sometimes against the wishes of his family (although not always), without succumbing to the many temptations that could distract him from the goal of martyrdom. These distractions sometimes include women who will try to seduce him, material pleasures that will lure him to want to stay in this world, and the desire for post-martyrdom fame that would taint its purity. Although not every single martyrology contains all of these elements, most will contain a selection.

As portrayed in the martyrology, as the martyr comes ever closer to his death, he is separated out from his fellow fighters. They remember him later as being pious, helpful, and superior in his fighting skills, but alone and always desirous of the next world. Often they will see him in dreams foretelling his impending death (these dreams also appear after his martyrdom to confirm that it was accepted by God). The martyr in his dying moments is described as a "lion" that pounces upon his prey, and it often takes a large number of infidels to actually kill him. According to the hagiographical materials, his body is preserved, uncorrupted, for long periods of time after his death, sometimes years. It will emit the pure smell of musk and sometimes the blood from the wounds will continue to flow.[8] On occasion the martyrologies tell us that the bodies of the *mujahidin* render other Muslim fighters aid at key moments.

All of these hagiographical elements of the image of the martyr are designed to recruit future fighters and to project to the outer world the image that the *mujahidin* are unstoppable. In the end, the success of a martyrdom operation lies not just in the terror it provokes among a given population, but in the fact that the fanaticism (or perceived fanaticism) that causes it cannot be stopped and can strike at any time. The video or testament that the martyr usually leaves and is aired after an operation is part of that process of terrorization (and will be discussed in chapter 6). Al-Qa`ida itself has pioneered a number of Internet propaganda methods such as the Internet magazine, although a number of its offshoots, such as those in Iraq, have developed these methods much further.

Strategy

The strategy of al-Qa`ida has gone through several phases, all of them based upon its understanding and interpretation of Prophet Muhammad's life and confrontations with his pagan opponents during the seventh century. The fact that these strategies are fairly confining gives al-Qa`ida's opponents a certain edge; however, in response the group has demonstrated considerable ingenuity in creating new variations on older themes.

Since the basic goals of al-Qa`ida are to rid the Muslim world of western influence, to establish a caliphal Muslim state, to foster a state of permanent salvational jihad, and to eventually convert (or at least conquer) the entire world to Islam, its strategy has to fulfill these goals. Al-Qa`ida's principal ideological opponents are not the western world but the Muslim religious elites and the governments that prop up these religious elites. In al-Qa`ida's view, these two groups working in tandem are themselves puppets of Western interests and would fall were Western governments to reduce or end their support. Al-Qa'ida sees itself as a vanguard (*tali'a*) of Muslims that is leading by example, and that will raise the consciousness of the Muslim community through carrying out spectacular attacks, so that they can rise up against the apostate non-Muslim regimes that hold them in a state of coerced quiescence. When the Muslim masses rise up against these elites, they will demand the establishment of a Muslim state under the *shari'a* that will embrace all Muslims worldwide. Eventually this state will be headed by a caliph.

In order to fulfill its goals al-Qa'ida can take several strategies:

1. Establish a Muslim state in part of the Muslim world and gradually add on to it (the example of Afghanistan).
2. Attempt a simultaneous or near-simultaneous series of uprisings all over the Muslim world that will establish the unified Muslim state.
3. Provoke the West, especially the United States, into attacking the Muslim world openly in the hope that Muslims worldwide will join al-Qa'ida and defend Islam or that the war will drag on for a long time and that gradually large numbers of Muslims will join.

This latter strategy is the one that was adopted in the wake of the September 11 attacks.

The reason why the first two strategies were rejected has to do with al-Qa'ida's desire to minimize Muslim casualties. One of the basic reasons why the radical Muslim groups that fought Muslim governments during the 1990s failed (in Egypt and Algeria especially) was the fact that they had permitted and even encouraged large-scale slaughter of Muslim civilians. Al-Qa'ida is clearly determined to avoid that mistake.

There are several paradigms with which al-Qa'ida has worked. The first, which was prevalent prior to the September 11 attacks, was that of the Ahzab. During 627, Prophet Muhammad and the Muslims were besieged in the oasis of Medina by a group they called the Ahzab (the Confederates, title of *sura* 33 of the Qur'an)—a large confederation of various tribes and mercenaries gathered by Muhammad's tribe and opponents the Quraysh, against him. The Muslim community was divided between those Muslims who followed Muhammad and those the Qur'an calls hypocrites (who were sympathetic to his opponents or at least resisted his leadership). One Jewish tribe of the three that had been originally in Medina when Muhammad arrived, the Banu Qurayza, either was negotiating with the Ahzab or was about to start negotiating. Since this tribe was located behind the Muslims' positions, this put Muhammad and his followers in the position of having to defend the oasis town against outward opponents (the Ahzab), as well as to battle off hypocritical followers and the Jews located behind their lines.

Al-Qa'ida did its best to follow Prophet Muhammad's strategy of manning the defensive lines, and presenting themselves as the guardians of Islam against foes outside and inside. According to the Qur'anic and traditional accounts, God defeated the Ahzab by sending a wind against them, and destroying their food supplies. Muhammad and the Muslims then were able to turn on the Jewish tribe, and slaughter it, and then eventually to isolate the hypocrites and either execute them or assimilate them into the community. Ideally, the attacks of September 11 should have worked in the same manner, and the Muslim world should have rallied to the defense of Afghanistan and the Taliban, since President Bush labeled the "War on Terror" a "crusade."[9] This comment was and is still easily translated in Arabic and other Muslim languages as a declared war against the entire religion of Islam.

However, things did not work out according to this strategy, although the world Muslim population is overwhelmingly hostile toward the "War on Terror" and suspicious of Bush's motives. Nonetheless, Muslims have not risen up against the "apostate" or "hypocritical" regimes that al-Qa`ida and its ideological offshoots detest. Thus, other strategies have been formulated, the most popular of which is a strategy patterned upon the figures of Abu Basir and Abu Jandal.[10] Again from the life of Muhammad, after the latter signed a treaty with his Meccan pagan opponents in 628, he was obliged to turn over to the Meccans any of their number who converted to Islam and sought refuge in Medina. Abu Basir and Abu Jandal were two Meccans who had converted to Islam and came to Medina but were turned over to the Meccans under the terms of the treaty. But the two of them managed to kill the Meccans who had come to take them away, and instead of going back to Medina they founded a small guerilla group dedicated to attacking the Meccans. Eventually the Meccans were willing to give up the stipulation that converts to Islam be handed over to them, and the fugitives were able to rejoin the Muslim community in Medina.

It is not entirely clear how this paradigm can be useful to al-Qa`ida and its followers. The original story seems to imply that even though Prophet Muhammad, who defined Islam, approved of turning over Muslim converts to the pagan Meccans, Abu Basir and Abu Jandal were obedient to a higher law, perhaps to what they saw as the spirit of Islam (in opposition to unbelievers). Today al-Qa`ida members are regularly handed over to the United States and other Western powers by Muslim governments in somewhat the same manner as Muhammad handed over Abu Basir and Abu Jandal. However, as will be seen in the next chapter, unlike Abu Basir and Abu Jandal, many contemporary radical Muslims have been unwilling to restrain their anger at Muslim governments and even at the Muslim masses for betraying them. While the earlier al-Qa`ida, like Abu Basir and Abu Jandal, refrained from attacking Muslims and focused its violence against non-Muslims alone, since 2003, that record has become much more ambiguous. At the present time, al-Qa`ida is seeking to adopt or modify another paradigm under which to operate. One can be certain that whenever they do, it will be modeled upon the operations of Muhammad or his early Companions.

In order to convey its strategic message, al-Qa'ida and its ideological offshoots have discovered that martyrdom operations are close to perfect. Martyrdom operations demonstrate the self-sacrificial nature of the movement carrying them out and show both the Muslim community and the world that Muslims are willing to die for what they believe in. They maximize the casualties and terror of the victims while minimizing that of the Muslims (ideally). Used progressively and methodically, suicide attacks can drive an enemy into a state of hysterical panic. This panic can cause the government or the population of the targeted country to act in an indiscriminantly brutal manner or to make statements that will alienate any Muslims likely to be sympathetic. In the end, al-Qa'ida wants to create boundaries between Islam and infidelity, boundaries that it feels have been destroyed by the process of globalization and the dominance of the United States and other Western powers. Its overall strategy will proceed from these basic imperatives.

Tactics and Justifications

From a tactical point of view, al-Qa'ida during the first two phases (early operations and September 11) demonstrated a considerable versatility and ingenuity. In general, operations proceeded according to the classical rules of jihad: usually Bin Laden made a major proclamation or threat prior to an operation (so that the infidels had a chance to repent), and the operation was carried out immediately. Al-Qa'ida needed to establish its credibility during this period and to differentiate itself from other Arab and Muslim organizations that regularly made empty threats. In that way, it attracted effective people to its cause.

The operation against the two American embassies in Nairobi, Kenya, and Dar es-Salaam, Tanzania, on August 7, 1998, established al-Qa'ida's typical modus operandi. Both of these bomb attacks were suicide attacks, they were timed close together in order to maximize the terror, and they were both highly lethal. The fact that in both cases very few Americans were killed[11] seemed irrelevant because of the high-profile nature of the attacks, and in fact, unlike later operations, no justification was made of the mass casualties (including many Muslims).

While the tactic of attacking civilians remain problematic, even for al-Qa'ida (at least in terms of its image), the attack against the U.S. destroyer *Cole* while it was in Aden, Yemen, on October 12, 2000, was against an entirely military target. The boat piloted by the two suicide bombers took the *Cole* by surprise (killing 17 sailors and wounding 39 others), thus demonstrating the potential weakness of military targets. But overwhelmingly, as with Hizbullah, the Palestinians, and the Chechens, and will be noted in chapter 5 with regard to Iraq, suicide attacks have no military value. Indeed, al-Qa'ida has only targeted a relatively low number of actual military targets. Suicide attacks against a military target do not usually kill more than two to four people, except in cases when there is an abnormal grouping of military personnel together in a relaxed or unprepared state. For this reason they lack the element of a spectacular assault that al-Qa`ida craves. However, in the case of the *Cole*, al-Qa`ida did manage to pull off a successful attack against a target that from its point of view was an affront to the Muslim world: a representative of the American military docking freely in Muslim waters. Although from al-Qa`ida's point of view the attack on the *Cole* was a success, it was not one that gained them much publicity outside of Yemen. From a tactical point of view, the bombing of the *Cole* was probably a one-time success; other attempts such as that against the *Sullivans* in 2000 (prior to the attack on the *Cole*) and against the Fifth Mediterranean Fleet in 2003 were failures because of logistical problems. But since al-Qa`ida is prone to target the same type of targets time and again, this type of attack will probably happen again as well.

The major and paradigmatic attack of al-Qa`ida was the September 11, 2001 attacks upon New York and Washington, DC. This series of attacks, which maintained the 1998 embassy attacks standard for synchronicity and boldness of execution and which topped all previous terror attacks for the number of people killed, was the perfection of a set of failed attacks that had preceded it since 1995. In December 1994, members of the Groupe Islamique Armeé (GIA), the dominant radical Muslim group in Algeria at the time, had highjacked an Air France plane with the intention of taking it to Paris and crashing it into the Eiffel Tower or at least exploding it over the city. This attempt was foiled by French commandos who stormed the plane in Marseilles and killed the highjackers, miraculously without killing any of the passengers. Other attempts by Ramzi Yusuf, the planner and coordinator of the first World Trade Center attack in 1993, to highjack planes in the Pacific were also failures.

However, Khalid Sheikh Muhammad (Ramzi Yusuf's uncle, and an al-Qa`ida planner) managed to formulate a workable plan during 1999–2000 involving four planes, with the possibility of additional planes as a follow-up.[12] This plan in itself had been pared down from an initial concept of 10 planes, with additional planes to be highjacked in the Pacific region. Rightly Bin Laden rejected this further element as too complicated with the possibility that it might endanger the more important American element of September 11. The pattern within al-Qa`ida planning appears to be to propose the grandiose and then to pare back to the realistic.

The choice of personnel was also well-thought out; Muhammad chose five for each of the successful missions, and four for the last unsuccessful mission. (United flight 93 was delayed slightly leaving Newark and was highjacked later than the others, with one fewer highjacker. After the passengers realized what was happening, they attacked the highjackers and almost overcame them, forcing the latter to down the airplane prematurely.)

The numbers were neither so many that they were wasteful nor so few that they were unable to complete their mission. What is remarkable about September 11 attacks is that it is one of those few conspiracies in history where all of the participants knew that they were going to die as a result of their actions[13] and yet kept silent and in no way (knowingly) betrayed the operation, even to say goodbye to their families. The only exception to this statement was the pilot of United flight 93, Ziad al-Jarrah, who mailed a goodbye letter to his girlfriend, Aysel Senguen, in Germany. But this did not compromise the operation at all, since the letter arrived after September 11, and in any case did not allude directly to what Jarrah was about to do. For this reason it is necessary to realize that even comparatively larger groups of suicide attackers associated with al-Qa`ida will be able to keep secrecy and perform their operations. Unlike with the Palestinians, there are no examples of al-Qa`ida suicide attackers giving up before their missions were complete or knowingly giving away a plot.

Symbolism is of crucial importance to al-Qa`ida, and this was best exemplified on September 11. Peripheral or easier targets were eschewed; there was no attempt to lead up to the truly significant targets by stages. Instead, perhaps realizing that such an attack could never be duplicated, al-Qa`ida chose the World Trade Center, the Pentagon, and perhaps the White House (or the Capitol), all symbolic of the economic, military, and political power of the United States. In attacking the World Trade Center, al-Qa`ida emphasized that its failure to destroy the Twin Towers in 1993 was merely a prelude and proved that it is relentless in its desire and ability to destroy key targets. Just because a target has proven resilient earlier does not mean that it will not be targeted again. From the point of view of the United States, this means that the targets chosen on September 11 will very likely be targeted again.

Another element of symbolism that is important to al-Qa`ida is the underdog, nontechnological, heroic image that it seeks to project. This image was also solidified on September 11. Deliberately al-Qa`ida sought to master the United States' implements of technology in order to use them to destroy it. On a regular basis al-Qa`ida makes statements indicating that it has contempt for the personal courage of the U.S. military forces and that the latter because of their cowardice avoid personal combat and hide behind their superior technology. On September 11 al-Qa`ida managed to take that vaunted technology away from the Americans and point it at their most sensitive institutions. The message in this tactic is clear: the United States thinks that its victory is inevitable because of its technology, but in fact God will prevail and aid the *mujahidin* in a supernatural manner in order to neutralize this technological advantage. *The Last Night*, the manual left by the highjackers instructing them how to act during the period leading up to the attacks, says: "All of their devices, their [security] gates and their technology will not save them nor harm [anyone] without God's permission."[14]

Despite al-Qa`ida's vast success in the September 11 attacks, it is worth remembering that this was only part of an overall plan to continue terror operations of an escalating nature inside the United States that has (as yet) failed. The security measures taken by the United States, while too late for the victims of September 11, have prevented any serious follow-up attacks. Although al-Qa`ida and its ideological affiliates have succeeded in carrying out a number of suicide operations in Europe, the Middle East, and other places since that time, al-Qa`ida itself has remained frustrated in that it has not been able to equal or better the terror of September 11 on American soil. One can count on there being further attempts (though not necessarily using suicide), since al-Qa`ida has demonstrated its relentlessness.

September 11 has an additional importance for al-Qa`ida and its ideological offshoots: it enabled them to develop justifications for mass-casualty suicide attacks that have no connection to the Palestinian cause. Most of the pro-suicide attack literature in the Muslim world has been written for the Palestinians; with the Chechens there was movement away from this focus upon the Palestinians. Ultimately, with the September 11 attacks, there was a complete break away from these two nationalist-Islamic causes. The major justification for September 11 was penned by Yusuf al-`Ayyiri (leader of al-Qa`ida in Saudi Arabia, killed in June 2003), called *Haqiqat al-harb al-salibiyya al-jadida* (*The Reality of the New Crusader War*).[15] Although a large number of religious justifications have been written since then—al-`Ayyiri managed to publish his within a week of September 11—the basic lines of thought that differentiate al-Qa`ida's operations from those of the Palestinians were established at that time.[16]

Whereas with regard to Israel, apologists such as Takruri did not have to defend the actual use of suicide attacks so much as make certain that they were not considered to be suicide, al-`Ayyiri has to defend the killing of mass numbers of apparent innocents. This he does by employing several arguments developed by radical Muslims during the 1990s:

1. Democracies elect their governments and pay taxes to them. Therefore, everyone in a democracy is criminally responsible for the deeds or misdeeds of the government. Hence there are no innocents.[17]
2. When the target of the *mujahidin* is surrounded by large numbers of innocent infidels it is permitted to kill them because they constitute "human shields." Without such an allowance their choice of targets would be severely limited or they would lose the element of surprise because they would have to warn the innocents prior to the attack.
3. *The "mangonel" argument*: Since the Prophet Muhammad is known to have used a mangonel—a spring-loaded catapult designed to lob payloads of rock (and later explosives) over the walls of a city—it is possible to use weapons on the principle of the mangonel that will kill civilians indiscriminately. This argument is stretched very thin, however, when used for suicide attackers because usually they can and do see their targets (the whole point of a human "smart bomb")

and therefore cannot be compared to a load of rock. Nonetheless, this argument is considered by radical Muslims to be a strong one and is usually the basis for their legitimization of mass-casualty attacks and even the use of weapons of mass destruction.

All of these arguments are backed up quite impressively by citations from the Qur'an (that are sometimes overly selective) and the tradition literature. Theoretically it would be possible for important Muslim scholars to refute them, but as yet none has done so.

The major problem that al-Qa'ida has faced in justifying suicide attacks since September 11, however, has not been merely the issue of the mass casualties, but the fact that *Muslims* are regularly killed by these attacks. This is the point where al-Qa'ida and its offshoots have been the most defensive, and where they have lost significant support. Since the attacks of September 11 killed Muslims, al-'Ayyiri had to answer why that was justified. He gave the following points:

1. The "human shield" argument is the same as the argument against innocent infidels. If Muslims are living among legitimate targets of the *mujahidin* then the former are effectively human shields for the infidels, and the *mujahidin* have the right to attack without warning.
2. Muslims who are helping the infidels, living in their countries and benefiting from their systems, are seen by jihadists as having apostasized from Islam because of that close association. This gives the *mujahidin* the right to attack them or at least not to take their presence into consideration.[18]

These arguments have fallen flat among Muslims, and although they have reappeared when there has been a controversial operation by one of al-Qa'ida's offshoots—the first Bali bombings of October 12, 2002, the Riyadh bombings of May 12, 2003, the London bombings of July 7, 2005, and the 'Amman bombings of November 9, 2005—in each of these cases there was a strong refutation published by scholars who otherwise were sympathetic to radical Islam.[19] Thus, while suicide attacks within Israel have not raised significant opposition among Muslims, widespread use of suicide terror in Muslim countries or against non-Muslim civilians has.

Implications for the United States

Al-Qa'ida is the enemy of the United States. This is a fact that is inherent in the nature of the organization and will not change unless al-Qa'ida changes in a way that is not presently discernable. And the United States will continue to be its major foe. As the logic of al-Qa'ida is that a Muslim state will not be achieved as long as the United States continues to prop up, from its point of view, illegitimate governments in the Muslim world and continues to support Israel, there can be no compromise with the United States. Moreover, its support to a large degree is dependent upon its continuing ability to launch large-scale attacks upon the United States; without that perception, al-Qa'ida would not be able to command financial and material support in the Arab and Muslim worlds.

However, it remains an open question how far al-Qa'ida will go in its attack upon the United States. So far, the favored method has been martyrdom operations either against the United States on its soil (September 11), against its military personnel (around the world), or against its expatriate population (especially tourists).[20] While Shaykh Nasir al-Fahd (cited at the beginning of the chapter) has indeed issued a notorious fatwa legitimizing the use of nuclear weapons against the United States—using the same religious justifications as were previously employed for mass-casualty suicide attacks—it is unrealistic for al-Qa'ida to aspire to actually carry out such attacks.

In general, al-Qa'ida, as Pape has analyzed it, is not an apocalyptic organization. It seeks religious-political goals, and the domination of Islam within the world, but it does not want to actually destroy the world or kill such large numbers of people as in a nuclear attack. Al-Qa'ida desires parity and an end to what it perceives as the humiliating circumstances of the current power structure. To that end it will probably *seek* nuclear weapons, but it is doubtful whether they would be used:

> God mandated this religion to spare the blood of humanity and to lift the head of mankind, to realize completely servitude towards God, Lord of creation, but in a time when the Muslims are constrained, and their enemies dominate them because of these weapons it is not possible for them to remain with their hands tied under the excuse that it is fate, but it is incumbent upon them to be serious in preparing power that will make their side feared and to repel their enemies from them.[21]

This is the general logic that one finds in countless documents coming from al-Qa'ida: the idea that casualties should be balanced. Sulayman Abu al-Ghayth, the spokesman for al-Qa'ida, spoke of the right of the Muslims to take 4 million American lives in return for the deaths that the United States has caused among Muslims worldwide. The tactics that al-Qa'ida is most likely to employ for this type of revenge will be high-profile operations, ideally one after the other, with an ever-increasing scale of destruction, but not one or more nuclear explosions.

It is also important to remember that since the September 11 attacks, al-Qa'ida has effectively become a minor player in the world of globalist radical Islam. Its leaders are confined and have little operational sway over the larger radical Muslim community. But al-Qa'ida accomplished its major goal: it proved that the United States can be attacked in a major way; it demonstrated to the Muslim world that fear of the United States was not warranted. Breaking this psychological barrier (as well as presenting the religious justifications that al-Qa`ida or its supporters have produced) was its most significant contribution. Today al-Qa`ida exists mostly as an exemplar to radical Muslims worldwide and does not maintain effective control over a large organization. The spectacular suicide operations occurring in the recent past have been farmed out by al-Qa`ida to other radical groups, some act with very different agendas than those of al-Qa`ida or perform on their own with al-Qa`ida as a model.

Chapter 5

Spreading Martyrdom Operations; Purifying the Muslim Community

Your democratically elected governments continuously
perpetuate atrocities against my people all over the world.
And your support of them makes you directly responsible,
just as I am directly responsible for protecting and avenging
my Muslim brothers and sisters...we are at war and
I am a soldier. Now you too will taste the reality of this situation.

—Muhammad Siddique Khan[1]

Global martyrdom operations have spread far beyond the control of al-Qaʿida. In the wake of the fall of the Taliban regime in December 2001, while al-Qaʿida continued to maintain operations, it increasingly spread its more spectacular operations, to subsidiary and/or loosely affiliated organizations. In addition to (or perhaps tied to) this phenomenon, the use of suicide attacks increased among radical Muslims, especially in Pakistan, in local sectarian conflicts. This trend, while unrelated to the overall globalist radical Muslim struggle against the United States, occasionally involves some of the same groups. However, it must be stressed that although al-Qaʿida maintains some relations with a great number of radical Muslim organizations throughout the world, there is by no means any sense of unity among these disparate groups. Some of them are willing to work together for a brief period of time or are infiltrated by people sympathetic to the goals or methods of al-Qaʿida, some organizations are "highjacked" (even briefly) by a leadership that is willing to subordinate itself to globalist radical Islam, but then that leadership can be deposed. (A good example of this phenomenon was the Moro Islamic Liberation Front (MILF) of the southern Philippines, which in the mid-1990s was highly sympathetic to al-Qa`ida but since that time has avoided associating itself with the organization because of a change in leadership that made the organization more conservative.)

All of these local variants mean that although al-Qa`ida is regularly "credited" with any spectacular mass-casualty suicide attack against Western interests or allies in the Muslim world or on its periphery,[2] this attribution cannot always be taken for granted. Nor does the willingness of al-Qa`ida to give itself "credit" for such attacks necessarily prove its influence; today al-Qa`ida competes with a large number of similar organizations for preeminence. Although the fact that al-Qa`ida was responsible for the September 11 operation always gives it a good deal of believability and prestige, its statements are not always accurate. It is also not unusual for smaller, shadowy organizations to give credit to al-Qa`ida for certain operations, either because they would like to promote the fiction of unity among radical Muslim organizations or because they would like to avoid the retributive attentions of Western governments. Once a prominent figure has taken responsibility for other actions, it may be convenient for numerous groups to assign "credit" or "blame" to that figure for actions that are deemed odious by world opinion, regardless of who carried out these deeds. The late Abu Mus`ab al-Zarqawi (killed June 9, 2006) of al-Qa`ida in the Land of the Two Rivers (Iraq) was one such figure.[3] Thus far it has been impossible to establish whether he is really responsible for the many suicide attacks for which he has taken responsibility.

However, in the end, the question of responsibility is an operational question to be dealt with by military authorities. The ideological responsibility of al-Qa`ida in helping to create an environment in which martyrdom operations are one of the primary tactics used by radical Muslims is clear. This chapter will explore how various different radical groups have continued with that legacy since September 11, 2001.

South Asia: Pakistan, India and Bangladesh

The people of Pakistan have suffered from the use of suicide attacks that were pioneered in the region by al-Qa`ida and have now turned sectarian. Because of Pakistan's history, geography, and sectarian divisions, the tactic of suicide terror has taken root more in this land than in any other country that is not in an obvious state of civil war. Pakistan was founded by the Muslim leadership of India who did not want to live permanently under Hindu majority rule. The British colonial rulers obligingly created two Muslim majority regions (eventually Pakistan and Bangladesh) to which many of the Muslims of the subcontinent immigrated, and from which many of the Hindu and Sikh inhabitants emigrated. This process of a population transfer in 1947–48 left hundreds of thousands dead and it divided what had been until that time a cultural unit.

The issue of Kashmir was and is the most problematic between Pakistan and India. Kashmir is located in the extreme north of India's geographic territory and shares a border with China. Although its ruler at the time of partition was a Hindu, the majority of its population was Muslim. In 1947 the ruler did not want to join either Pakistan or India, but when Kashmir was invaded by Muslim tribesmen from Pakistan, he called upon India for aid. Thus Kashmir came to be partitioned, with approximately one third of its territory in Pakistan ("Azad Kashmir") and the rest in India (with the exception of a segment occupied by China in 1962). Kashmir is the only Muslim-majority province of India (even though approximately 12 percent of India's population is Muslim), and in 1989 a separatist movement launched a campaign to liberate Kashmir from Indian rule. It is doubtful that the initial separatist movement wanted any form of union with Pakistan and probably could have been satisfied with some form of autonomy within the context of India. Over the course of the following years, however, this initially nationalist rebellion has taken on an increasingly Islamic tone.

Pakistan began supporting the separatist movement in Kashmir as the war against the USSR in Afghanistan was winding down in 1989–92. Large numbers of fighters were available from the Afghan conflict, and atrocious stories of persecutions of the Kashmiri Muslims were circulated throughout the Pakistani press to drum up support for their cause.[4] Together with the desire of successive Pakistani governments to promote an issue that could distract their citizens from other social issues inside Pakistan, these factors led to the creation of a number of movements to aid the Kashmiris in their struggle. Chief among these was the Harakat al-Mujahidin, first led by Fazl ur-Rahman Khalil (until 2000) then later by Faruqi Kashmiri; the Jaysh-i Muhammad (changing its name many times), led by Masood Azhar; the Lashkar-i Tayba, led by Hafiz Muhammad Saeed; and the Hizb al-Mujahidin, associated with the more mainstream Jama`at-i Islami. (Although all of these groups except the Hizb al-Mujahidin are now banned by the Pakistani government, some exist under other names.)[5]

Literature on the suicide attacks in Kashmir blurs the line between suicidal operations and actual suicide attacks.[6] There are a comparatively large number of *fedayin* (martyrdom-seeking) squads among the Pakistani-supported militant groups. Lashkar-i Tayba especially has been known for sending small groups of *fedayin* who typically attack units of the Indian Army, or all too often civilians, and fight until they are killed.[7] These groups strictly speaking are not suicide attackers; even though they do die, they are not the agents of their own deaths, and their deaths are not inevitable for the operation's success. In general, suicide attacks in Kashmir have taken the form of an explosives-filled car ramming an Indian Army unit or convoy.[8] Occasionally, as with the assassination attempts upon President Perviz Musharraf of Pakistan (below), also there are also selected attempts at assassinating Indian government officials such as the foiled attempt upon the life of Ghulam Nabi Azad on November 2, 2005 when he was due to be sworn in as chief minister of Kashmir. The suicide attacker was stopped by the police and detonated himself prematurely, killing 4 people and injuring 14.[9]

The balance of suicide attackers in Kashmir have been male and Pakistani (apparently), although at least one was female (October 13, 2005, from the Jaysh-i Muhammad).[10] For the most part, they have not carried out operations that stand out as mass-casualty attacks when compared to the other operations carried out by the same groups. In other words, the radical Islamic groups in Kashmir, unlike the Palestinians or the Iraqis, have been unable to come up with a formula that produces large numbers of casualties. It is unclear whether the use of suicide attacks helps these groups gain any particular notice: outside of Pakistan and India, few in the world are aware of or monitor this conflict.

On a different front, the social tensions in Pakistan between the Sunni majority and the Shi'ite minority have grown. Starting in the mid-1970s, the Sunni population has concentrated on enforcing doctrinal rules through Pakistani law (a process that continued massively between 1977 and 1989). This process led first to the banning of the Ahmadi sect in 1984, and the adoption of highly literal interpretations of Islamic law, and then to the appearance of militant anti-Shi'ite groups (Sipah-i Sahaba and Lashkar-i Jhanghvi). These latter groups began in 2000 with an attack on the *Nawa-e Waqt* newspaper in Karachi (interestingly, with a female suicide attacker) on November 6, 2000. Although there were attacks in 2001, they were not mass-casualty ones. Mass-casualty attacks came with the May 8 and June 16, 2002 attacks on foreigners (9 French killed in the first attack, 12 outside the U.S. Consulate in Karachi), both of which are associated with al-Qa'ida (perhaps), and both involved ramming car-bombs into either a convoy or a building.

These attacks opened up a major campaign of tit-for-tat attacks between Sunnis and Shi'ites, starting with the July 4, 2003 attack on Shi'ites in Quetta that killed 53 Shi'ites. All of these attacks are characterized by heavy death tolls, usually between 20 and 60, and increasingly since 2004 they have been focused upon the sanctuaries or sacred rites of the opposing sect.[11] Mosques are increasingly targeted during worship, a pattern that is either replicated by a similar campaign in Iraq or is replicating the Iraq campaign. Although Shi'ites have responded to Sunni suicide attacks with violence, they have not carried out any suicide attacks. The only major exception to these types of attacks have been the the assassination attempt upon President Musharraf on December 25, 2003, and the attacks once again upon the U.S. Consulate in Karachi on March 6, 2006. Because Musharraf has moved strongly against radical Muslims in Pakistan since September 11, 2001 and has turned over hundreds of suspected al-Qa'ida members to the United States, it is obvious that radical groups would want to assassinate him. They attempted to do so in a complicated pair of suicide attacks, with a pair of massive truck-bombs that were only a few seconds off when they rammed his motorcade in Rawalpindi (15 Pakistanis died during the attacks). The suicide attackers, one of whom was linked to the Jaysh-i Muhammad, while the other was from Afghanistan, clearly had inside information to know with such accuracy about Musharraf's schedule.[12]

In other areas of south Asia, only Bangladesh has seen the growth of suicide attacks spearheaded by the radical Muslim Jama`at ul-Mujahidin, led by Mawlana Abdur Rahman. Like the objective of other radical groups, the goal of this group is to impose a *shari`a* state, and it seems to have some links with al-Qa`ida. On November 29, 2005, 9 people were killed and about 40 wounded when a series of suicide attacks were carried out in various parts of the country. This campaign was seen as the culmination of a series of bombings during July 2005 that were attributed to the same group. However, suicide attacks do not seem to have much popular support in Bangladesh, and after Abdur Rahman and his fellow radical leader Bangla Bhai (leader of the Jagrata Muslim Janata Bangladesh) were arrested in March 2006, it seems that the trend, at least during the short term, will not continue.

Pakistan's sectarian violence generates little attention in the foreign media, but it does present a problem for Pape's thesis concerning suicide attacks. The sectarian suicide bombings are not directed against any Western targets, with the few exceptions mentioned above, and Pakistan itself is not a democracy. However, the sectarian hatreds in Pakistan are quite strong and have begun to spill over into neighboring countries. The presence of large numbers of Taliban supporters along the border with Afghanistan, together with some members of al-Qa`ida, is, no doubt, fueling this spillover.

Central Asia and Afghanistan

While Pakistan's radical groups seem to have embraced the use of suicide terror quite effectively, those in Central Asia and Afghanistan—while occasionally influenced by Pakistanis—have not done so. The history of radical Islam in Afghanistan dates to the time of the Soviet occupation (1979–89) when the *mujahidin* spearheaded the fighting against the communists. Despite the brutality of the Soviet occupation, in accordance with Pape's thesis that suicide attacks are primarily directed against democracies, there are no examples of such attacks during that period. Subsequent radical Islamic governments such as the Taliban (1996–2001), while inviting Bin Laden and al-Qa`ida to come to Afghanistan, where they essentially took over the state, had an ambivalent relationship with globalist radical Islam. However, al-Qa`ida performed various military support functions for the Taliban, including supplying fighting units, and therefore earned the gratitude of the Taliban. Two days before September 11, 2001, al-Qa`ida managed to send a pair of suicide attackers to kill Ahmad Shah Mas`ud, the leader of the Northern Alliance opposing the Taliban; he died several days later.

When the Taliban regime collapsed in December 2001, its leader Mullah `Umar and other top leadership began to lead a small guerilla campaign against the Afghan government under Hamid Karzai and its international forces (mainly American, but with significant European deployments as well). This conflict was exacerbated by the fact that the Taliban regime had been supported by the Pushtun tribal group that comprised a majority in the southern part of the country and historically had little influence in Kabul, the capital (where the northern Tajiks and Uzbeks tended to dominate). Today while Ahmad Shah Mas`ud tends to be viewed as a hero by the Tajik population in the north, his cult does not extend south of Kabul. Since the Pushtuns have wide connections across the border in Pakistan, it is strongly suspected by both Afghani and American officials that the Taliban and whatever is left of al-Qa`ida have taken refuge in this remote region and use it as a power base.

For the most part, until 2003 there was virtually no use of suicide terror in Afghanistan. It appears that, since at least 2004–05, a close relationship has developed between tactics used in Iraq and those in Afghanistan (including kidnappings and beheadings).[13] Therefore, it is not surprising that, after the suicide attack campaign began in Iraq in 2003, there have been several attacks upon coalition soldiers in Afghanistan. Even so, by November 2005 there had been only seven attacks, most of them detonated prematurely or against soldiers (foreign or Afghanistani). The targets were mostly in the north, many in Kabul, and in areas where foreigners congregated such as Internet cafes or shops that catered to tourists or aid workers. Since November 2005, there have been at least 91 such attacks, and the focus has shifted to the south (although spectacular attacks still frequently take place in the north), especially against the American and international troops in the area of Kandahar and Helmand provinces (both of which are known strongholds of the Taliban).[14]

A number of assassination or specific target attacks have taken place, such as that on June 1, 2005 at a mosque in Kandahar during the funeral of Mawlavi `Abdallah Fayyaz (a pro-government cleric assassinated by the Taliban). This attack killed a number of high-ranking government officials (killing a total of 19 people and wounding 52), and its strategy seems to be similar to attacks in Pakistan. The famous Blue Mosque in Mazar-i Sharif (traditional burial site of `Ali b. Abi Talib, Prophet Muhammad's son-in-law) was also attacked by a suicide bomber on December 14, 2005. The patterns behind these attacks seem familiar: For the most part these are not attacks that are mass-casualty in nature but focus upon a few soldiers or foreigners, or selected Afghani anti-Taliban figures. Only recently have the attacks begun to focus upon holy sites—such as those in Iraq and Pakistan—or killed large numbers of civilians (e.g., July 22, 2006, killing 8; August 28, killing 17; September 26, killing 18; September 30, killing 12). It seems very likely that this pattern is due to the influence of Iraqi tactics. With mass-casualty attacks increasing, it seems likely that the focus will shift away from soldiers to civilians, despite the Taliban's recent apologies for civilian casualties.[15] To curb casualties in populations more likely to be sympathetic (i.e., in the south), these attacks are more likely to concentrate upon Kabul and the other larger cities in the north and west.

Further to the north, after the collapse of the USSR in 1991, five largely Muslim Central Asian states were born. All today are still ruled by the remnants of the Soviet elite, but of those only Uzbekistan and Kyrgyzstan have had a significant radical Islamic opposition.[16] Uzbekistan is an authoritarian state ruled by President Islam Karimov. There are several Islamic opposition fronts, the most radical of which is the Islamic Movement of Uzbekistan (IMU). Since Uzbekistan, like all of the Central Asian republics except Kazakhstan, was gerrymandered into a patchwork of almost unconnected parts by the Soviets (in order to weaken it and to further their own control), it is a difficult place for a guerrilla group to operate. The most Islamic section of the country, the Ferghana Valley, is divided from the rest of Uzbekistan by a mountain range (closely patrolled by the military) and is also divided between two other countries, Tajikistan and Kyrgyzstan. Although the borders are permeable, and smuggling and drug-running are extremely common in the area, the valley is also difficult terrain for a guerrilla group to control because it is so flat. For this reason the IMU's operations have been mostly localized to the mountainous terrain of Tajikistan and Kyrgyzstan, with periodic operations down into the valley. Throughout the 1990s and until 2001, the IMU would train in Taliban-controlled Afghanistan and then return to Uzbekistan during the summers.[17] Since the fall of the Taliban, the IMU has lacked a secure base from which to operate.

While the IMU has had little success launching operations in the two-thirds of the country not located in the Ferghana Valley, there have been other sources of opposition to the Karimov regime. Already during the Soviet period there were a number of public suicides in Tashkent or in the Ferghana Valley to protest anti-Muslim policies.[18] This tradition was continued by a number of suicide attacks against the widely feared *militsia* (police) during March 28, 2004. At least 47 people were killed (according to the government accounts), both civilians and police. A number of the Uzbek suicide attackers, strikingly, were women.[19] Then on June 30 of that year, suicide attackers targeted the U.S. and Israeli embassies as well as the Uzbek Prosecutor-General's Office, killing three bombers and four police officials. This latter bombing is usually interpreted as a protest against the trial of 15 radical Muslims, supposedly tied to the earlier bombings that were happening at the same time. In both cases, the organizational affiliations of the bombers are unclear. Although the Karimov regime was quick to label various radical Muslim groups, such as the IMU and Hizb al-Tahrir* (a very improbable claim), no one claimed responsibility for these attacks.

---

* The organization's English-language spelling is usually "Hizb ut-Tahrir."

The IMU was never very strong in Tashkent, far from its home base in the Ferghana Valley, and it is difficult to see what it would have gained from these attacks in any case. Rather than lumping these suicide attacks into a broader pattern of violent uprisings directed by some outside or internationally connected Muslim group (such as the 1999 bombings or the 2006 Andijon protest/massacre), we believe it is more accurate to view these suicide bombings as somewhat of an aberration for the country and region. Therefore, while it is likely that Uzbekistan will continue to experience unrest in the future, the tactic of suicide bombing did not receive any respect or inordinate success, per se, and is somewhat unlikely to be used in the future.[20]

Southeast Asia

The region of Southeast Asia is the location of the largest concentration of world Muslims. Radical Islam here is an import from the Middle East and is fostered through networks of the Muslim educational system, the *pesantren* (similar to a *madrasa*). While the vast majority of *pesantren* are not open to radical Islam, there are about a hundred that are known to be fertile fields for recruitment into radical groups. After Indonesia's independence from Dutch rule in 1946, Muslims in central Java (the major and most populous island) set up a state called Dar ul-Islam (sometimes referred to as the Republic of Islam) that would be governed exclusively by the *shari`a*. Eventually this movement was suppressed in the 1960s, but many of its followers and support networks went underground during Suharto's rule (1966–98). Several of the members of Dar ul-Islam, most prominently Abdullah Sungkar and Abu Bakr Ba`asyir, founded a radical *pesantren* at Ngruki (near the conservative city of Solo, in eastern Java), which became the center for a movement they called *Jama`a Islamiyya* (or JI). JI was intended to promote the same sort of society within a society that Dar ul-Islam had originally intended, but with a pan-Islamic focus. To this end, Sungkar and Ba`asyir sought to unify all of the Muslims in Southeast Asia, not merely in Indonesia, but also in Malaysia, Singapore, Brunei, Thailand, and the Philippines, under a *shari`a* state. When both of them fled to Malaysia in the 1980s to escape the repression of Suharto, they were able to realize part of this vision in Malaysia.

But the real expansion of JI came after the fall of Suharto in 1998 when a series of weak governments ruled Indonesia. Militias sprang up all over the archipelago to enforce *shari`a*, to intimidate Christians and others, and to engage in petty lawlessness. In that atmosphere, Ba`asyir and JI were able to establish a number of cells all over Southeast Asia that were eventually to form the nuclei of a future Islamic state. In this they were aided immensely by the feeling that Muslims were being persecuted in the Philippines and in Thailand.

Both of these conflicts have older roots. While the population of the Philippines was mostly converted to Christianity during the Spanish colonial rule (1500–1898), a significant "Moro" (Muslim) population remained in the southern area of the country. This minority was gradually dispossessed during the twentieth century by internal migration, so that the originally "Moro" area today is actually majority Christian. The Moros established several different liberation fronts: the Moro National Liberation Front (MNLF), which has a left-wing orientation, and the Moro Islamic Liberation Front (MILF), a radical Islamic group. Throughout the 1990s while the MNLF engaged in periodic negotiations with the Philippine government, the MILF drifted closer to globalist radical Islam and established ties with al-Qa`ida. However, since 2002 the MILF has renounced these ties, and more radical members have drifted into Abu Sayyaf, a small group that has never concealed its support for al-Qa`ida.[21] Although non-Filipino radical Muslims have tried to encourage the development of suicide attacks within the Philippines, especially by groups of converts to Islam, apparently their success has been nil thus far.[22]

In southern Thailand, three provinces have close historical and religious ties with Malaysia (immediately to the south), and a low-level Muslim rebellion has been going on for the past several decades. But only recently has it acquired any of the rhetoric of radical Islam and there is no evidence for al-Qa`ida's involvement at all.[23]

All of these conflicts guarantee that JI has a number of operational fronts. Apparently, however, the move toward suicide terror in 2002 was premature. According to JI's charter, violence should only be employed after the group has successfully established its cadres within the entire region and thus has the support network needed to make the transition into a *shari`a* state. On October 12, 2002, there was a pair of massive explosions in Kuta, the tourist section of the (mostly) Hindu and heavily touristed island of Bali. One suicide attacker had entered Paddy's Bar and blown himself up, while another, taking advantage of the people streaming out of the establishments surrounding it, detonated a massive vehicle bomb. The result was 202 people killed, a large number of whom were Westerners (mostly Australian). Although the security arrangements of the JI cell that sent the suicide attackers were not enough for them to escape detection—most of them were arrested within a couple of weeks of the bombing—their tactics had the hallmark of globalist radical Muslim attacks. They chose Bali because of the presence of Hindus (who they despise), and their primary targets were tourists, whose provocative behavior (drinking, dancing, etc.) is an affront to a *shari`a* state.[24] Thus they were able to make the Hindu population suffer economically for catering to tourists: JI's strategy worked so well that they did it again on October 2, 2005.

The Bali terror attacks marked a considerable shift for JI and apparently have led to a split in the organization. One part of the group, led by

M. Nooruddin Top and Azahari Husin (both Malaysians recruited by Ba'asyir during his exile in Malaysia), has continued to use suicide terror, initiating attacks on the J.W. Marriott Hotel in Jakarta on August 5, 2003 (15 people killed) and on the Australian Embassy in Jakarta on September 9, 2004 (11 people killed), as well as the second Bali bombings, in which 30 were killed. Like the first Bali bombings, the Marriott and the Australian Embassy attacks focused upon foreign targets and involved car bombs. Both were (fortunately) timed incorrectly, so the fatality count, while significant, did not approach the number killed in the first Bali bombings. However, the second Bali bombings were different, employing not car bombs but three separate suicide attacks on different restaurants and night clubs around the island of Bali. While the bombings were thematic in the sense that the strategy was clearly to maximize the number of casualties by attacking multiple locations (and thereby also increasing the terror), these attacks were also not as deadly as the first Bali bombings (although they have devastated the economy of Bali). Nonetheless, the fact that JI has seemingly abundant suicide attackers makes the second Bali bombings just as chilling as the first.

While much of JI appears to have rejected the tactic of suicide terror against tourists—even Ba'asyir himself did so (after the second Bali bombings), a significant group centered around Imam Samudra, the spiritual leader of the earlier bombings, appears to have embraced it. Imam Samudra, while on death row, penned the powerful book *Aku Melawan Teroris* (*I Am Against Terrorism*) to justify the Bali bombings. In it he makes use of the vast literature in Arabic supporting suicide terror and points out that similar bombings in the Middle East against Israelis and others had been justified by various Muslim religious leaders. Imam Samudra attacks the arguments of figures such as Takruri and Yusuf al-Qaradawi, who have sought to confine suicide attacks to the Israeli-Palestinian conflict, by pointing out (as al-Qa'ida did previously) that the logic employed by these legal experts could be applied to other situations, such as Indonesia.[25] The influence of his book has been such that more mainstream religious leaders have been trying to counteract it by writing refutations.[26]

Although Nooruddin Top's associate Azahari Husin committed suicide rather than face capture by the Indonesian police on November 10, 2005, Top himself and a number of other JI leaders remain at large. Reflecting the split in JI, Top broke off from the group in January 2005 and formed his own group, which he called Tanzim Qa'idat al-Jihad. It seems clear that by forming this group Top wants to duplicate the success of al-Zarqawi in Iraq, who also has associated himself with al-Qa'ida. This should not, however, be taken to mean that JI is "al-Qa'ida's Southeast Asian branch" or that there is any operational control between the two groups.[27] Rather, it should be understood that inherent in JI's original foundation was the creation of a "society of Muslims" and that in fact the radicals in JI led the group prematurely into conflict mode with the Indonesian government. Top's breakaway group will need to resolve those internal conflicts to remain operational and will probably be responsible for additional suicide attacks in the future. But it remains an open question whether this small group can mature and grow, even though a surprising number of Indonesians support suicide attacks,[28] as do pockets of Muslims elsewhere, especially in the Middle East.

Middle East and North Africa

Despite all of its attempts, al-Qaʿida has largely failed in the Middle East (other than Iraq). Although the organization continues to be able to recruit malcontents and suicide attackers from many places in the Middle East, Usama b. Laden's call of February 11, 2003 to "liberate" Jordan, Morocco, Nigeria, Pakistan, Saudi Arabia, and Yemen has yet to bear any fruit.[29] In fact, the suicide attacks that al-Qaʿida was to carry out in Morocco and Saudi Arabia during that year set the progress of radical Muslims in both countries back significantly. Similarly, the suicide bombing in ʿAmman (Jordan) on November 9, 2005, for which al-Zarqawi claimed responsibility, caused support for al-Qaʿida to drop dramatically. Prior to mid-2003, hostility toward the United States as a result of the U.S. support for Israel and the perceived attack upon Islam (and other factors) meant that there was a good deal of passive support for al-Qaʿida in Saudi Arabia, Jordan, Morocco, and other states (it is impossible to judge its support in countries such as Syria that are not free). Additionally, few governments, despite the September 11 attacks, took the radical Islamic challenge to their societies seriously. And apparently quite a number of the religious leadership who supported the use of suicide terror against Israel really believed that it could or should be confined to the Israeli-Palestinian conflict.[30]

This confinement would not last. Starting with Riyadh, the capital of Saudi Arabia, on May 12, 2003, there were coordinated suicide attacks on three compounds housing Westerners (and non-Saudi Arabs as well) that killed 34.[31] These bombings were followed by further suicide attacks on November 8, 2003, which killed 17.[32] The first attacks were quite successful in targeting Western interests, but the second ones killed mostly foreign Arabs. Both of these attacks signaled the beginning of an al-Qaʿida mini-revolt within the kingdom. While there were a large number of suicidal operations in which the operatives did not expect to return (such as the Khobar operation of May 29, 2004), there were no further suicide attacks until February 16, 2006 when five suicide bombers tried to drive cars into the oil processing facility at Abiqaiq (the largest oil processing plant in the world) and were shot dead.[33] It seems that al-Qaʿida realized the close relationship between successful suicide attacks and reconnaissance after the November 2003 attacks, because, perhaps as a result of being on the run, the suicide attackers had made an incorrect assumption concerning the identity of the people living inside the compound they attacked. Killing numbers of Arabs led to a backlash against al-Qaʿida in Saudi Arabia. This backlash, together with the repressive tactics of the regime and the fact that a large number of previously radical `ulama were co-opted into opposing al-Qa`ida, has contributed to its lack of success.

The May 12 attacks were immediately followed by similar attacks in Casablanca on May 16, 2003, in which there were five separate attacks timed more or less together (within 30 minutes). The Casablanca attack was thematic in that, like the September 11 attacks and the second Bali attacks, it was a series of coordinated attacks: upon a Jewish community center, the Belgian consulate, a Spanish restaurant and club, and a hotel. Taken together they represented those institutions that radical Muslims despised— just as al-Qa`ida had sponsored a suicide attack on the Jewish synagogue in Jerba, Tunisia the previous year (April 11, 2002).

The most violent of all the North African radical Islamic groups, the Algerian GIA (Groupe Islamique Armeé or the Armed Islamic Group) and its successor the GSPC (Groupe Salafiste pour la Prédication et le Combat [the Salafist Group for Preaching and Combat]), however, have almost never—other than their attempt in Paris in 1995 and several isolated attacks—used suicide attacks at all.[34] These groups have been fighting against a dictatorial military regime that was willing to use extreme and even barbaric methods against them.

Nonetheless, the fact that there were some suicide attacks against these regimes calls into question Robert Pape's thesis that radical groups do not use suicide terror against dictatorships, which he outlined in *Dying to Win*. But despite these attempts, it seems that using suicide attacks against domestic targets has not gained a base within North African society: while many Moroccans have participated in suicide attacks, they have tended to go to Iraq.[35] The question of what will happen if and when these recruits return home from Iraq, still bent on suicide attacks, is an important one, however. Perhaps, if Iraq functions as a "school" for radical Islam in the way that analysts fear, suicide terror might reappear in North Africa.

Of all the countries in the Middle East, Egypt should have been the most expected site for suicide attacks. Radical Islam has a deep history in Egypt, and starting with `Abd al-Salam Farag's *al-Farida al-gha`iba* (*The Neglected Duty*), written in the early 1980s for the small group who assassinated Egyptian president Anwar al-Sadat in 1981, there are central texts detailing the rationale for suicide attacks.[36] Additionally, the Egyptian press has praised the Palestinian suicide attacks very highly, and a great many Egyptian clerics are on record supporting suicide attacks (albeit against Israel). All of this publicity concerning suicide attacks made it basically inevitable that eventually they would be used in Egypt. Radical Muslims from the two major groups of al-Gama`at al-Islamiyya and the Egyptian Islamic Jihad (EIJ) mounted a serious attack upon the Egyptian regime of Husni Mubarak during the 1990s focusing upon Egypt's tourist industry (the source of much of its income), but they never used suicide attacks in Egypt, even at the moments when the insurgency was failing in 1995–97.

This fact may have been due to the heightened security in Egypt, because the EIJ had carried out two suicide attacks in 1995: on October 22 in the Bosnian town of Rijika (killing only the attacker) and on November 19 at the Egyptian embassy in Islamabad, Pakistan (killing 16). This latter operation was closely associated with the future al-Qa`ida leader Ayman al-Zawahiri (soon after that time to become Usama bin Laden's right-hand man), and he wrote one of the earliest justifications of suicide attacks in Sunni Islam because of the opposition that the tactic aroused.[37]

But starting in October 2004, after a lull of eight years, the radicals—perhaps associated with EIJ since the Gama`at had by that time renounced violence—began to target tourists again, first in the Sinai Peninsula. This region, bordering on the Gulf of Aqaba and possessing some of the most beautiful diving locations in the world, has always been popular with tourists (both Israeli and European). Suicide attackers drove into the Taba Hilton lobby on October 4 and blew up a massive truck bomb, together with another attack on a camping site, killing 34 people.

While this attack could be categorized (perhaps) as an EIJ and al-Qa`ida joint operation possibly managed from Iraq, in retrospect it seems clear that Egyptian radicals were coming back into action again after a long hiatus. On April 7, 2005 a suicide attacker blew himself up in the midst of the Khan al-Khalili, the popular (tourist) market of Cairo. Several weeks later, members of the self-same cell (apparently) attacked in a double attack—one man in Ramses Square (another popular tourist location in Cairo, next to the train station), his sister, and his fiancée blew themselves up together near the Citadel near a tourist bus. Although the logistics of the last segment of the attack are problematic—it is possible that the two women were carrying out a conventional attack, and committed suicide during the process—the whole operation seemed to prelude the type of romantic suicides that one sees in Iraq (next section). Both of these Cairo incidents seem to have been rather ill-planned; although they were directed against tourists and accomplished their presumed goal of frightening foreigners away from Egypt, the perpetrators did not make the preparations necessary to maximize casualties. Both operations looked very much like individual militants on the run deciding to carry out suicide attacks on the spot.[38]

This was not the case with the Taba attack or with the Sharm al-Sheikh attack, also in the Sinai, at a popular tourist location, that followed on July 23, 2005. This latter attack was one of the most deadly attacks ever in Egypt, with 88 people killed, and over 150 wounded. Like at Taba, the suicide attackers targeted hotels and a market with very powerful truck bombs, and simultaneously exploded another device nearby (apparently to cause people to panic, but it was mistimed). The Sharm bombings killed mostly Egyptian workers in both the hotel and the market, since the tourist accommodations in the hotel were located too far away from the lobby (where the truck exploded) to be harmed. To date the affiliations of both the Taba and

Sharm attackers are unclear, as is their relationship with either al-Qa`ida or local Egyptian radical groups.[39] It is very likely that the next wave of Egyptian radicalism, when it begins again, will employ suicide terror because of the Egyptian economy's vulnerability to even the smallest attacks on tourists.

Jordan could also be said to have a similar tourism-related vulnerability, but perhaps this country will be inoculated by the experience of its first suicide attacks in the capital, Amman, on November 9, 2005. Like Egypt, Jordan has a history of radicalism, and discussion of Palestinian suicide attacks against Israel has very wide currency and sympathy in all walks of society. Most of the booklets on the subject of suicide attacks cited in this study were published in Jordan. Living across the Iraqi border and having close historical and familial ties with Iraq has led Jordanians to express a strong sympathy with the Sunni suicide campaign, usually defining it as "legitimate resistance." This support was epitomized by the leadership role that Abu Mus`ab al-Zarqawi (originally a Jordanian) has taken among the Iraqi Sunnis (below), and most especially by the suicide attack of Raed Albanna from the city of al-Salt in Jordan on February 28, 2005 in Hilla, Iraq, which was one of the most deadly attacks ever. After Albanna's death, his family carried out the traditional "marriage" ceremony to celebrate their son's marriage to the 72 *houris* in Paradise. This celebration led to Iraqi-Jordanian tension.[40]

Given this background, apparently most Jordanians thought themselves to be immune from suicide attacks until the November 9 attack. In an attack that parallels a number of romantic suicide attacks from Iraq, four attackers, including a husband-wife duo, attacked the Radisson Hotel,[41] the Hyatt, and the Days Inn virtually simultaneously, killing 57 and wounding at least 120. The Radisson attack was accomplished by the husband-wife team in the middle of a wedding celebration, killing a large percentage of the revelers. However, the wife's bomb failed to go off, and so she received permission from her husband to flee, which she did and was arrested a few days later. There are a number of problems with this operation. It is difficult to understand why Zarqawi, who took responsibility for it, thought that it would be popular to attack such an obviously civilian trio of targets, even though he characterized them as "dens of spies." And indeed, the Jordanian people strongly attacked the idea that they could be legitimate targets for suicide terror throughout November 2005, leading ultimately to Zarqawi's family disowning him and calling on November 21 for his blood to be shed. In retrospect, it seems clear that the callousness and detached quality of the Iraqis and their foreign allies, who had authorized hundreds of similar suicide attacks against civilians in Iraq, had led them to believe that they could act similarly in Jordan without repercussions. This assessment was wrong.

In the long run this attack may mark a downturn of domestic radical Muslim suicide attacks in the Middle East outside of the Palestinian and

Iraqi campaigns. The pattern for Middle Eastern operations has been that in Tunisia, Morocco, Jordan, and Saudi Arabia, after an initial suicide attack or a very few suicide attacks, their native popular support dried up—usually because of their choice of targets or because of the repercussions from the regimes in the wake of such attacks. Without the perception that there is occupation, the existence of a large permanently aggrieved population, or the acceptance of mass casualties among civilians, a radical Muslim campaign using suicide attacks cannot be sustained. Despite the fact that they do not have majority-level support, popular opinion does matter to radical Muslims. Even in the extreme case of Algeria, where the radical Muslim fighters have used the most brutal and callous tactics against civilians in their campaign since 1992 to establish an Islamic state, there has been virtually no appearance of suicide attacks, probably because the native population would not support them. If the local population does not support the attacks, they are more likely to report planned attacks to authorities, as is discussed in chapters 8 and 9, so this is an important element to understand. Despite this, however, the Middle East could still face a future of radicals, who have become calloused in Iraq and come back to fight in their home countries after the war is over.

Iraq

No conflict has engendered more suicide attacks than that in Iraq between the Sunni and the Shi'ite Arabs, with occasional attacks against United States and international forces,[42] the Kurds, and various international aid agencies. All of the suicide attacks have been initiated by the Sunnis, a fact that is not surprising given Iraq's history. The country of Iraq is an artificial creation of colonialism, in which the British stitched together three very disparate provinces from the Ottoman Empire: the province of Mosul (mostly Sunni and Kurdish but with some substantial minorities of Arabs and others), the province of Baghdad (mostly Sunni and Arab but with Shi'ite and Christian minorities), and the province of Basra (almost entirely Shi'ite and Arab). Historically, the Shi'ite population, which from the beginning of the twentieth century comprised a majority,[43] was ruled by a Sunni minority from Baghdad. This situation persisted and worsened, especially under the regime of Saddam Husayn (1979–2003), in which the Shi'ites were largely deprived of political representation. The reason for this deprivation was the fact that Husayn had provoked a war with the Islamic Republic of Iran in 1980 (chapter 2) and was afraid that the Shi'ite population of Iraq would have sympathy for their co-religionists in Iran. In fact this did not happen, as Husayn (eventually) managed to frame the war as a "Arab versus Persian" war, rather than a Sunni versus Shi'ite war and thus garnered support in Iraq and within the larger Arab World, and even from the West (which feared the influence of Iran).

After the conclusion of the Iran-Iraq war in 1988, Husayn needed to rebuild Iraq's shattered economy and so decided to invade the small neighboring country of Kuwait in August 1990, to which Iraq had some historical claim. Kuwait also possessed a high percentage of the world's oil and had taken measures that angered Husayn by lowering the price of oil that stymied Iraq's economic recovery since Iraqi oil was forced to follow the market price. By invading Kuwait, though, Husayn provoked the United States into the conflict, and the result of that was his military defeat in February–March 1991. Foolishly, the United States deliberately provoked the Shi'ite population of southern Iraq to rise up in revolt against Husayn, without, however, giving the revolt any support. Husayn crushed this revolt easily and from that time ruled as an absolute dictator, increasingly relying upon the Sunnis of Iraq to support him and giving them patronage in return. Throughout the mid-1990s, there were reports of Iraqi attempts to gain weapons of mass destruction (banned by the terms of the 1991 settlement), and by 2002 in the wake of the September 11 attacks, the U.S. administration of George W. Bush decided to use its political capital to attack Iraq and remove Saddam Husayn from power. The pretext for this attack was the possibility that Iraq either already had or was going to immediately gain weapons of mass destruction. Unfortunately for President Bush and for a number of his supporters in the United Kingdom and Europe, the *causus belli* of Iraq's weapons of mass destruction turned out to be entirely a fantasy.

Initially the invasion, which began on March 20, 2003, seemed to be a success. The United States managed to assemble an international coalition, albeit heavily dominated by the United States and United Kingdom, that quickly defeated Saddam Husayn's armies and occupied Baghdad. Although the invasion eventually (although not initially) found some support among the Shi'ite population of southern Iraq, and more enthusiastically among the Kurdish (non-Arab but Sunni) population of northern Iraq, this invasion was by no means the "liberation" that Bush had envisioned. Significant sections of the Iraqi public most especially in the so-called Sunni Triangle felt that this was an occupation and that their nation had been humiliated. Although Saddam Husayn, prior to the invasion, had called for suicide attacks against the U.S. forces, only four were carried out in this first phase of combat. By the beginning of the summer of 2003, it seemed that Iraq would accept the American presence.

However, this acceptance did not materialize. Starting gradually and then erupting ferociously, a combination of supporters of Saddam Husayn from the Ba'th Party, nationalists, Sunni Arab tribesmen, radical Muslims, al-Qa'ida, and Shi'ite radicals under the charismatic leadership of Muqtada al-Sadr have conducted a very powerful and sustained insurrection against the American and other foreign forces. The end result has been that Iraq has slipped over the past years into a state of chaos. Suicide attacks have been one of the primary tools used by the insurrection, especially by the radical Muslims among them, but most probably by others as well, and have contributed to the ungovernability into which Iraq has descended.[44]

Mohammed Hafez analyzed the primary groups conducting the Iraqi insurgency and came to the conclusion that they represent two basic tendencies. The first tendency is that of "system reintegration strategy," which includes attacks with Islamic and nationalist roots, by Sunni Arab tribesmen and especially former military personnel that was dismissed abruptly by the United States in 2003 and are frequently persecuted by the Shi`ite dominated regime or have no place in the new government. These people would like to negotiate the process of their reintegration into Iraqi society from a status of power; however, they have no grand religious goals and do not want to create an Islamic state. With these goals in mind, it is easy to see why this tendency will avoid the use of suicide attacks.[45]

The second tendency Hafez identifies, however, is the "system collapse strategy," which includes those groups such as the old Ba`thist party members, al-Qa`ida fi Bilad al-Rafidayn (al-Qa`ida in Mesopotamia, the group led by Abu Musa`b al-Zarqawi), and the Ansar al-Sunna that are mostly united under the leadership of the Majlis Shura al-Mujahidin (the Shura Council of the Mujahidin). These groups, because of their weakness, have every incentive to try to make the entire country of Iraq collapse. Without this collapse they will never attain their goals, which are much larger than Iraq, namely the foundation of an Islamic state that will have transnational goals. In order to accomplish this they employ a wide use suicide attacks.[46]

For the sake of convenience, one can divide the suicide attacks into several basic time periods; however, this should not be taken to mean that there are no other ways of interpreting the strategy of the insurgents or that their strategy at all times was coherent or unified:

1. *The initial phase until August 7, 2003*: This phase is characterized by military suicide attacks that were clearly inspired by the Saddam regime.

2. *Starting from August 7 until approximately mid-April*: During this period, there were major suicide attacks against the U.S. and international forces, Shi`ites, and foreign aid agencies, with something of a hiatus after the capture of Saddam Husayn on December 13, 2003. This quiet was broken by the spectacular suicide bombings of March 2, 2004 (below), and then by the insurrection starting in the Sunni town of Falluja.

3. *The Sunni-Shi`ite Insurrection, mid-April until approximately December 2004*: This period was characterized (at first) by a joint Sunni-Shi`ite insurrection triggered by the attempted American reoccupation of Falluja (April 2004) and by a significant lessening of the anti-Shi`ite violence on the part of Sunni radicals. Until the Shi`ite half of the insurrection, led by Muqtada al-Sadr, collapsed in August 2004, most of the violence in this period was directed against the U.S. and international forces. There was also

a pattern of kidnappings and beheadings of foreigners that were widely publicized on the Internet. During November 2004, the U.S. forces reoccupied Falluja and aggressively sought to pacify the Sunni Triangle.

4. *Attacks on the democratic process, approximately from December 2004 until January 2006*: For radical Sunni Muslims, the democratic process is fundamentally incompatible with the *shari`a* and is actually said to be a pagan religion (*dimuqratiyya din al-kufr*). For this reason they concentrated their attacks during this period on Shi`ites who were likely to benefit from the democratic process, Sunnis who wanted to participate in the vote, and any perceived collaborators with the Iraqi government (especially army or police recruits). The first election to the Iraqi National Assembly took place on January 30, 2005; most Sunnis boycotted it. However, the attacks on the political process continued as the new constitution needed to be ratified by a majority of the provinces, the ratification happened on October 14, 2005 (although not without some controversy; most Sunnis voted against it), and there was a further election on December 15, 2005 for the legislative assembly.

5. *From January 6 to June 9, 2006*: Starting on January 6, there has been a focus on suicide attacks on Shi`ite holy sites, which follows the pattern in Pakistan (of Sunni-Shi`ite desecration of holy sites), with the exception of the fact that Shi`ites have not responded with suicide attacks but apparently with death squads targeting Sunnis. Since the middle of fall 2005, there has been a significant decrease in support for al-Qa`ida among the Sunni population, although radical Islam overall remains attractive. This decrease in support heralded the killing of al-Zarqawi himself on June 9, 2006.

There have been so many attacks in Iraq that no writer or researcher can hope to cover them all. Although this study will focus more on the paradigmatic, spectacular attacks in which large numbers of people were killed or that had significant political or religious repercussions, one should not forget the large number of small, individual suicide attacks, in which occasionally merely a few people (one to three) are killed. Many of these small attacks are the ones that actually have either military significance, because they target American soldiers, or local significance, because they target some locally well-known figure and thereby maximize the terror for prominent figures in the community or political sphere. For the sake of analysis, six paradigmatic attacks will be examined here.

The first one was the attack on the Mosque of `Ali b. Abi Talib (fourth caliph of Islam, and one of the most highly revered figures in Shi`ite Islam) on August 29, 2003. Although this attack was not the first in phase 2 of the suicide attacks, it was the one that killed the most people (well over 80 up to 125), was the first that targeted a mosque, and used multiple car bombs in order to maximize the number of dead. The attack was also significant because it was apparently targeting just one man, Muhammad al-Baqir al-Hakim, who was at the time the dominant Shi'ite leader and thought to be quite pro-American. Interestingly, this attack, which was the largest bombing in the Middle East since the 1983 attack against the Marines in Beirut, was carried out by Yassin Jarrad, al-Zarqawi's father-in-law. This fact refutes those who claim that the *mujahidin* never send their close relatives or high members of their groups. Quite often they do, and one cannot accuse them of cowardice in this regard.[47]

The killing of al-Hakim was preceded and followed by a number of attacks designed to expel foreign aid agencies from Iraq (such as the August 19, 2003 attack on the U.N. office), but the dominant attacks throughout 2003 were on the U.S. forces and occasionally on Shi'ites. But on March 2, 2004, the date of the Shi'ite 'Ashura' period of mourning for Husayn, there was a paradigmatic series of suicide attacks that killed 181 people and wounded more than 500. Four suicide bombers were sent to the Shi'ite holy mosque of al-Kadhamiyya (burial site for the eighth Imam, Musa al-Kazim), of whom three managed to detonate their bombs; the fourth malfunctioned and was apprehended. At the same time at least nine suicide bombers attacked the holy city of Karbala (where Husayn was killed in 680), and others were apprehended in Basra and a number of other locations throughout Shi'ite Iraq. This was a well-coordinated operation, which, although many parts of it were aborted by the arrests of the suicide attackers, was by far the most spectacular and deadly operation that had occurred in Iraq until that time. Although no one took responsibility for the attacks, they seem to have the signature of al-Qa'ida on them.

Many suicide attacks have been designed to break any connection between the U.S. forces and the local Iraqis. As many times U.S. soldiers hand out sweets to Iraqi children, attacks upon this type of event are particularly gruesome. On July 13, 2005, as U.S. soldiers were driving up to a Shi'ite suburb of Baghdad on a community relations mission, a suicide bomber drove through the crowd of children surrounding the soldiers and exploded himself, killing at least 27 of them. Many other bombs have inadvertently (perhaps) killed large numbers of Iraqi children, but this one was clearly designed to punish the children who flock around Americans and teach others not to do so in the future. It is unclear which group was responsible for this operation.

As stated previously, the U.S. and international forces are the primary targets of the insurgents. But suicide attacks, their major spectacular weapon, are almost entirely ineffective against military targets, with a kill ratio of almost one killed for every attacker (in unusual circumstances it can be up to around four killed per attacker). This ratio is bad, even for a situation such as Iraq, where it seems that there is no lack of suicide attackers. However, there are unusual circumstances in which a suicide attacker, through careful reconnaissance can carry out a spectacular deadly operation against soldiers. Such an operation was carried out in Mosul (northern Iraq) on December 21, 2004. On that day a suicide attacker managed to slip through a wire fence guarding a U.S. Army base into a mess-hall to explode himself in the midst of a large number of soldiers, contractors, and local Iraqis who were dining, killing 22 (including 18 Americans). This operation was video-taped and widely distributed.[48] Most suicide bombings today are made effective by on-the-spot judgment on the part of the suicide attacker who might know of general opportunities that exist in a particular area and maximize them. The problem with this approach is the fact that many suicide attackers cannot maintain their cool under the pressure of knowing the deadly burden they carry, the equal pressure of wanting to find the optimal killing ground, and the fear of being caught. For this reason, it is best for those sending the suicide attacker to do the reconnaissance for him in advance and to make the time between his departure from that support network and the actual target as short as possible. This was indeed the case with the Mosul bombing.

But throughout the years of the U.S. occupation of Iraq, the primary targets of *suicide bombings* have been the Shi`ite population. Many times suicide attackers have targeted Shi`ites who were waiting in line at security points, at recruitment centers, or at vote-registering booths. The single most deadly attack against a recruitment center happened when Raed Albanna, a Jordanian lawyer, detonated himself with a car bomb in front of a health clinic in Hillah (south of Baghdad), where recruits to the Iraqi police had congregated, and killed 132 people. Albanna was identified only because stubs of his hands and forearms were found chained to the steering wheel of the car. This raises the question of whether suicide attackers can be actually coerced or forced to carry out their missions. Would chaining a man who (presumably) would know that his car was booby-trapped make it essential for him to carry out his mission in the optimum fashion? Or is it possible that Albanna himself asked to be chained in order to ensure that he would not be prey to any final doubts? It is our opinion that while there is no doubt that some psychological manipulation takes place in order to ensure that a suicide attacker carries out his or her mission, very few are actually coerced in the sense that they are either morally unwilling to do what they are about to do, or opposed to it. The waiting list of suicide attackers for operations in Iraq itself seems to militate against any coercion theory and highlights the importance of the operations. Suicide attacks have gained a high level of prestige throughout the Muslim world, especially the Arabic-speaking Muslim world; there is no need for Iraqi insurgents to rely upon half-hearted recruits.

Just as al-Qa`ida does in its operations throughout the world, radical Muslims and other insurgents rely on an image of heroism to convey their message. Videos that have wide distribution on the Internet, as well as occasionally on broader news agencies, portray them as "lions" going forth to battle. Al-Zarqawi's communiqués and other pronouncements produced by the Sunni Iraqi insurgency usually draw upon a wide range of Islamic and tribal Arab myths in order to present themselves in that heroic light. This propaganda sell is not always an easy one, especially since these suicide attackers are so often responsible for the mass killings of civilians. A large number of prominent radical Muslims, including al-Zarqawi's mentor Abu Muhammad al-Maqdisi and even Bin Laden's right-hand man Ayman al-Zawahiri (hardly known for being squeamish about blood-shedding) have protested against these tactics. Despite these protests, for many around the Arab world and the larger Muslim world the insurgency has a romantic appeal. Zarqawi and his associates have milked this appeal for all they can by focusing upon a few key themes: fighting the superpower, defending Sunnis against the Shi`ite traitors (Iranian agents), and emphasizing the innate appeal of martyrdom and marriage itself. Repeatedly, Zarqawi issued videos of "marriage ceremonies" in which the suicide attackers are promised to the black-eyed *houris* of paradise as a type of ritual or rite of passage that leads to redemption.

The effectiveness of these videos is revealed by the impressive numbers of Arab martyrdom seekers that come to Iraq. The number of foreigners carrying out suicide attacks versus Iraqis in Iraq is unclear, but Hafez details 101 who definitely come from other Arab countries or Europe.[49] The popularity of suicide attacks has also been heralded by the appearance of romantic martyrdoms, usually of a husband-wife team, but occasionally in other patterns as well. On the same day as another husband-wife team attacked the wedding celebration in Amman (November 9, 2005), Hisham Goris and his Belgian-born wife, Muriel Degauque, who was a convert to Islam, were to commit suicide. Her target was an Iraqi police patrol of whom she killed five. But because of a malfunction within the bomb she detonated, it took her hours to die in the crater she had created. A short time later her husband, who had been preparing a suicide attack of his own, was tracked down and killed by American forces.[50]

This type of romantic sacrifice was replayed in a different way in the case of the Saudi suicide attacker Abu Mu`awiya al-Shimali, known as "Fatima's fiancé." As a result of a letter that circulated from one "Fatima," who was purportedly a female prisoner at the Abu Ghraib prison in Iraq, al-Shimali was asked to become a martyr. He read how Fatima and the other women prisoners were repeatedly raped and degraded by the American soldiers, and longed to die. Al-Shimali's appeal is framed in terms of honor and shame.

> Like all of us, Abu Mu`awiya al-Shimali read the letter written by the sister in Abu Ghraib prison before she was martyred. He could not calm down, and resolved to avenge her death and the deaths of all free Muslim women. He could find nothing more precious than his own soul to sacrifice for the sake of Allah and to redeem the honor of his sisters. He asked Allah to accept him as a martyr and to marry him to this young woman.[51]

After some taunts toward Americans and the Saudi regime, in his video al-Shimali says: "Allah, marry me to the sister Fatima, who was killed in Abu Ghraib, and whose honor was defiled by tyrants and apostates, the off-spring of apes and pigs." The operation was against a roadblock manned by Americans and Iraqis, symbolic of the groups that al-Shimali held responsible for Fatima's violation.

Since the initial attack upon Muhammad al-Baqir al-Hakim in August 2003, there have been regular attacks on Shi`ite mosques and holy places. But since January 6, 2006, when suicide attackers targeted the holy city of Karbala as well as Sunnis in the insurgent-dominated town of Ramadi, killing a total of approximately 120, this cycle has become particularly vicious. Not all of the attacks have been suicide attacks (e.g., the attack on the Samarra Mosque of al-Askari on February 22, 2006), but many of them have been. It seems that the pattern behind these attacks is like that of Pakistan, in which the Sunnis and Shi`ites have also deliberately attacked each others' most holy places and events. On the Sunni side, however, it appears the goal is either to punish the Shi`ites for their support of the United States or in the case of al-Qa`ida to spark a civil war, while on the Shi`ite side the goal of militants (who have not employed suicide attacks) appears to be revenge.

Suicide attacks in Iraq show no sign of abating. Hafez details that the spikes in the number of suicide attacks are at the highest in the immediate wake of a major U.S. offensive (such as the Tell Afar offensive of 2005) and appear to be attempts to demonstrate that the radicals are still credible players.[52] It appears that the basic goal of the Sunni radical attackers is to create the conditions of a civil war in Iraq, or to make the country ungovernable so that the U.S. and other international forces will either withdraw or at least not be able to benefit at all from their occupation of Iraq. But in many cases listed above, there are more obviously religious goals that are being manifested: domination of Shi`ites or at least desecration of their sanctities, fulfillment of a deliberate separation between Muslims and non-Muslims, and in certain cases even a nihilistic love of destruction. It is significant that the Shi`ite population has almost completely abstained from suicide attacks during the U.S. occupation; as noted above, only al-Sadr threatened them when he was besieged in the holy city of Karbala during the spring and summer of 2004. It seems likely that this restraint will hold, except possibly if the Shi`ites begin to feel that they are in danger of losing power. For the Sunnis, it is unclear whether the numerous suicide attacks have obtained any of their political or religious goals, or whether prolonging the campaign may, at this point, be a goal in and of itself.

Western Europe and the United States

Iraq and its many suicide attacks do not exist in a vacuum. The war in Iraq has a powerful galvanizing effect upon the large Muslim population in western Europe, and it may be that the appearance of suicide attacks associated with radical Muslim elements in Europe is the result of the war. However, there were suicide attacks in Europe or attempted suicide attacks since mid-1990s. Already we have noted the failed GIA attempt to explode a plane over Paris in December 1994. Shortly after this, in Bosnia at the town of Rijeka, an Egyptian suicide attacker from EIJ exploded himself on October 22, 1995 as part of a protest against the peace agreement between the Bosnian government and the Serbs (the Dayton Agreement), and also in protest against the detainment of a radical Egyptian cleric (Abu Talal al-Qasimi).[53] Overall, the context was the fact that the *mujahidin* who joined the Bosnian Muslims in fighting the Serbs had begun to create a state within a state in Bosnia (in order to establish a radical Muslim society). As in Chechnya and other places where there was conflict between a Sufi local population and the radical Islamic fighters, there was social tension as a result of these attempts. The attack itself was fairly minor, took place outside a local police station, and killed only the suicide attacker himself. However, other suicide attacks might very well have been planned but stopped at the last moment.[54]

However, the most vulnerable countries for the appearance of suicide attacks were those, such as Turkey, that are majority Muslim or have large disaffected and radicalized Muslim populations, such as Britain and possibly France. (We are not referring to the likelihood of European converts to carry out suicide attacks, since these converts are taken from every country.) Turkey, although it is a secular country seeking entrance into the European Union, is quite vulnerable to the ideology of radical Islam. A large number of Turks appear among the volunteer martyrs of Afghanistan, Bosnia-Herzegovina, and Chechnya. In addition, in parts of the country there is a wide circulation of radical literature.[55] However, the suicide attacks of November 15 and 20, 2003 in Istanbul still came as a surprise to most Turks. These attacks, which like so many other al-Qa'ida-inspired suicide campaigns, were thematic and highly synchronized and aimed at typical targets: two synagogues on November 15 and the British Consulate and an HSBC bank on November 20, killing a total of 56 people. The bombings on November 15 were car bombings, neither of which succeeded to actually penetrate the synagogues they targeted (killing Turkish Muslims instead of their presumably Jewish targets), while those on November 20 were truck bombs. Prior to these attacks, Turks had known a number of suicide attacks associated with the Kurdish PKK (a Marxist group), but for the most part these attacks had been directed against the armed forces, the police, or other obvious governmental institutions. The 2003 Istanbul attacks were attributed to a group called the Great Eastern Raiders Front, which has been reported to have links to al-Qa'ida.

Many times during and since the mid-1990s Muslim radicals have threatened Western Europe. Whether because of Europe's affluence, its close ties to the United States, the relatively open policy of immigration and asylum (especially for former colonies) that enabled large communities of Muslims to create nonassimilating enclaves all over the region, or because of support for Israel, Europe is an obvious target. Large-scale attacks have occurred infrequently, such as the GIA bombing campaign in Paris during 1995 or the Madrid bombings of March 11, 2004 in which 192 people were killed by Muslim radicals from Morocco (and other places). However, none of these attacks were suicide attacks. On July 7, 2005 London was struck by a thematic series of four suicide bombings, which focused upon its transportation system and killed a total of 56 people. Three British Muslims of Pakistani origin and a West Indian convert to Islam all exploded themselves either on the Underground or on a bus. The three Underground bombings were coordinated to 8:50 a.m., while the bus bombing was later. This lack of coordination is thought to have been the result of a failed attempt to board another Underground line, and some possible panic on the part of the suicide attacker. Several weeks later on July 21 there was another series of four explosions that failed to detonate properly. It is as yet unclear what the relationship was between the two events.

Like so many of the other suicide attackers, the four British suicide bombers do not fit the traditional mold into which policymakers' attempt to put militants. None of them was of an economically deprived status, nor were they obviously traumatized or radicalized by some outwardly visible event. It is not even entirely clear what their connection was to the larger world of radical Islam, if there was one (their leader Muhammad Siddique Khan had visited Pakistan but his connections there did not seem to include al-Qa`ida links). The most plausible, if disturbing, conclusion to make about the London suicide attackers is that they represent the effectiveness of new recruitment and radicalization methods. No longer does radical Islam require any type of formal links in order to carry out successful operations. The principal paradigmatic operations are available to anyone with technical know-how and initiative. Apparently this type of cell is the one that will be the most immune to penetration by security forces because it is connected with the larger world only through the Internet or personal low-level religious and social contacts that are too broad and diffuse to be monitored.[56]

In reference to threats within the West, a final word must be said about the use of suicide attacks as an assassination method. Given the number of conflicts involving militant Islamic groups, there have been surprisingly few attempts by radical Muslim suicide attackers to assassinate prominent personalities, and of those the record of success is indifferent. President `Abdullahi Yusuf of Somalia barely escaped a suicide car that killed 11 people in the town of Baidoa on September 18, 2006.[57] Like Musharraf, Yusuf is loathed by the radical Muslims of Somalia and considered to be a secularist, although the militant Muslim leaders denied any involvement in this assassination attempt. Additionally, the assassination of Prime Minister Rafik Hariri of Lebanon (February 14, 2005) was probably accomplished by a suicide attacker,[58] although in both his assassination and the attempt upon Yusuf the perpetrators are unknown and might not have been associated with radical Islam.

Assassination attempts such as these are rarely used against Western leaders, unlike the aforementioned attacks in other conflicts and unlike the LTTE's strategy in Sri Lanka (not radical Muslim and therefore not further examined in this book), which seems to have perfected the ability to target heads of state and other prominent personalities in Sri Lanka and India. Radical Muslims, on the other hand, have tried fewer than six times to kill Muslim leaders using suicide attacks and have never made attempts on the lives of non-Muslim leaders they loath. Perhaps the logistics of organizing the massive bombs that were directed against Musharraf and killed Hariri is simply too much for European- and American-based radicals to attempt yet. But it is possible that suicide attacks will be adopted as an assassination technique in the future if Western militant groups are able to gain the logistical expertise required to successfully carry out such an attack.

Implications for the United States

Groups that al-Qa`ida has spawned, rather than the overarching group itself, will probably be the major danger to the interests of the United States. The justifications for suicide attacks that al-Qa`ida and its allies have created can and probably will in the future create groups that can be divorced from any central command and can perhaps engage in attacks without any advance warning. The two most urgent problems for the United States to confront are those of Muslims who suddenly turn to jihad without apparent reason or advance notice and of converts to Islam. Al-Qa`ida has done its best to ensure that the standard profile of the suicide attacker has become so broad as to make profiling meaningless. This is nowhere more evident than in those cases of suicide attackers who were apparently highly integrated into Western society and demonstrated no outward manifestations of religiosity. Rightly, prior to September 11, al-Qa`ida had already encouraged its operatives to shun obviously radical mosques and an obviously Muslim appearance.[59] Likewise, the four British suicide bombers of July 7, 2005 were not obviously connected to any radical group and had no evident Muslim manifestations (such as dress, beards, etc.).

Some highly successful suicide attackers are so completely outside of any profile that it might be almost impossible to distinguish them from the larger Muslim community. Probably the best examples of this are Ziad Jarrah (pilot of United flight 93, crashed in Pennsylvania on September 11), who was almost entirely secular in his upbringing and outlook. It is still neither clear how and why Jarrah decided to join the September 11 operation, nor more importantly why he carried through with it and did not betray it.[60] The case of Raed Albanna, the Jordanian lawyer who carried out one of the most deadly attacks in Iraq on February 28, 2005, killing 132 people (above), is a similar one. Albanna was an (apparently) entirely assimilated nonreligious Muslim who lived in California and enjoyed the good life. Although he apparently was very much against the radical Muslim attacks of September 11, during 2003–04, he gradually became more and more religious and apparently opened himself up to al-Qa`ida recruiters in Jordan.[61]

Unfortunately the pattern in these cases and those of many other suicide attackers is that there can be a sudden change in a Muslim's behavior— either suddenly becoming very religious for reasons that are not clear, or disappearing and losing contact with families—that preludes recruitment into the ranks of suicide attackers. This fact presents a very real problem for the United States in dealing with this phenomenon, since there are a large number of Muslim Americans and transients—usually students or workers resident for a short time—who can possibly fit into this category. For this reason, and for reasons of questionable effectiveness, we do not advocate profiling. Monitoring them at all times would be impossible and would infringe upon the rights of too many innocent people. To date, local nonradical Muslim groups have demonstrated little enthusiasm for such monitoring. But it is equally impossible not to make the attempt to cull out the problematic figures. (These problems are discussed more thoroughly in chapters 8 and 9.)

The other most dangerous group are the converts to militant radical Islam. It should be noted that the vast majority of converts to Islam convert through Sufism and are the natural opponents of the radical Muslim ideology. However, of those who convert through (or to) radical Islam, there are a significant number who convert (apparently) because they are attracted to the militant jihad aspect of radical Muslim movements and want to express their personal violence. Such converts are the most likely to be dangerous. To some degree, the categories of nonreligious assimilated Muslims who turn to radical Islam (e.g., Raed Albanna) and of the converts from outside the faith are the same.[62] Both are looking to fill a void in their lives, and both are attracted specifically to violent jihad and by extension to martyrdom operations.

Thus far the principal weakness of suicide attacks has been the fact that they kill Muslims and destroy the image of Islam in the world (in terms of religious prestige, likelihood to convert to Islam, etc.).[63] This is a consistent criticism that Muslims have leveled against the use of suicide attacks and has been the source of the loss of popularity for these types of attacks within the Muslim world. However, there are also other disturbing questions that come out of the Iraqi experience asking whether these suicide attacks are actually becoming nihilistic and transforming sections of the Muslim world into such a destructive ideology. With such a constant stream of adulation for suicide attackers, talk about martyrdom and its rewards, and other associated topics, there must be spillover effects as well. One of those is fairly obvious—the increased willingness of radical Muslims to actually commit suicide for no other reason than to avoid capture. Historically, Muslims have had a low suicide rate, and suicide merely to avoid capture was condemned. But a number of radicals take this step today.[64]

We can conclude that the tactic of martyrdom operations mixed with the ideology of radical Islam, in situations where there is occupation and/or perceived humiliation and a consequent need to fight for Islam, is extremely dangerous. It is of critical interest to know how this ideology spreads in contemporary media. Many will make exaggerated claims about the Western media's responsibility for the spread of martyrdom operations, and others will have exaggerated hopes for the media's role in winning the hearts and minds of Muslims worldwide from the lure of this ideology. The reality is more complex.

Chapter 6

Are Suicide Attacks "Catching"? Militant Media Organs' Publicity Efforts

The media and incitement failure of the jihadi groups is, practically speaking, the most obvious of their failures. They did not register even one success.

—Abu Musa`b al-Suri[1]

Whether it is the perception that "the media provides both an advertising and recruitment tool for terrorist groups,"[2] or that media coverage has caused or created more terrorists, the idea that media spreads or glorifies terrorism is taken as proven fact in policymaking circles. In this chapter, we will address the accusation that Western media spread terrorism, but scholars and politicians have turned their attention to Arab-language media, which they accuse of working with militants and popularizing suicide bombings. Many U.S. government officials, journalists, and policy organizations have misunderstood these new media, generalizing stations such as al-Jazeera (based in the Arabian Gulf state of Qatar) as being intricately linked with al-Qa`ida and other militant organizations.[3] In an extreme example, an al-Jazeera correspondent was barred from the floor of the New York Stock Exchange in 2003 after his station aired a video of U.S. soldiers.[4] Accusations that al-Jazeera and other Arab media spread suicide attacks should be evaluated in the context of the history of transnational Arab satellite broadcasting, of current Arab news coverage of suicide bombings. In many cases, in order to increase recruits, militant organizations work around these media outlets because of their dissatisfaction with them.

The Contagion Theory of Terrorism

The idea that media spread terrorism gained credence in the 1980s, when nationalist terrorists (such as the IRA) and Middle Eastern terrorists conducted numerous airline hijackings and bombings, and when suicide bombing was becoming a notorious and newly implemented technique. At that time, media scholars began to theorize that terrorists' tactics were spreading, and they believed this was primarily because of media coverage of terrorist attacks. Such attacks were designed to be extremely photogenic and media-friendly activities, especially the hostage crisis resulting from the hijacking of the TWA Flight 847 in June 1985. Journalists were criticized by groups such as the Heritage Foundation for not only accepting but aggressively pursuing hijackers' offers for interviews after the Iran hostage crisis (1979–81) and the TWA 847 hijacking.[5] ABC News correspondents were allowed to interview the crew while Shi'ite leader Nabih Berri held press conferences with the hostages. As a result of this, journalists were criticized around the world for consorting with terrorists and for making terrorist ideology available to the global public: "[b]y providing extensive coverage of incidents the media give the impression that they sympathize with the terrorist cause, thereby creating a climate congenial to further violence."[6]

Since that time, several Western journalists have interviewed public figures deemed "terrorist leaders"—most notably, the numerous journalists who have interviewed Usama Bin Laden.[7] These interviews were not "balanced" at all—bin Laden did not accept follow-up questions and demanded questions in advance, but bin Laden had no control over how the interviews would be edited before they were broadcast. Some of these interviews were not video-taped, and some were never aired in full. On the other hand, Arabic-language media is indeed more likely to interview militant leaders, with stations such as al-Jazeera allotting significant airtime to interviewing these figures or airing their statements. Nonetheless, numerous political and social figures opposed to these militant groups often offer contrasting opinions, criticizing the Arabic-language media. And despite bin Laden's stilted interview style, any interview may be better than the totally scripted videos that are the primary source of information at the time of writing. These interviews are inherently different from earlier hijacking and hostage situations, which lent themselves far more to media spectacle, because of their individuality. More importantly, because of suicide bombing's necessarily unpredictable nature, these attacks cannot constitute media spectacles on the same level as the hostage crises of the 1980s.

Despite its prevalence in discussions of media coverage of terrorism, the contagion theory is "fraught with conceptual and methodological difficulties"[8] and has not undergone serious testing in legitimate studies about the cause/effect nature of media coverage of terrorism.[9] Critics who say media glorifies or spreads terrorism hold the underlying but untenable assumption that there would be no terrorism if the media did not cover it. Ultimately, the contagion theory is propagated by Western scholars and directed primarily at denigrating Western media, which critics claim covers suicide bombings as much as possible, thereby undermining their home societies. Contrary to this criticism, Western media has largely ignored or not given prominence to many suicide bombing campaigns. There has been very little media coverage of suicide attacks in Afghanistan and Pakistan, and relatively little of terrorist attacks in Chechnya (see analysis of American media in chapter 7), Uzbekistan, POLISARIO in Western Sahara, and Yemeni uprisings, but these campaigns have continued.

Instead of asking "Why and how do global media spread suicide bombing?" it is more useful to examine where militant organizations look for legitimacy, how they communicate with their various audiences, whether they are satisfied with media coverage of their activities, how they use alternative strategies to distribute their message, and, finally, what biases are present in global media coverage of suicide bombing.

Those who criticize media in this way misunderstand not only the content of Western news—which will be discussed in the following chapters—but also how militant groups use the media, to be discussed in this chapter. Militant organizations, whose media operations are discussed in detail below, need first and foremost to legitimize their actions more to their own communities. These organizations' grassroots efforts are far more substantive and effective than their mass-media outreach, which both perpetuates the appealingly revolutionary feel to their communiqués (by undermining dominant media structures) and also gives them direct access to mass audiences already skeptical of and resistant to state and Western propaganda (maximizing possible recruits).

Strategy

Very little research has been conducted specifically about how militant organizations and suicide bombers relate to the media, although much has been written about media and terrorism in general. In general, scholars agree that terrorists have various audiences, to whom they release statements, and that they solicit media attention for their activities. Militant organizations have similarities with general terrorist organizations in media strategy, but some complications are unique to suicide bombing, stemming from the moral problems inherent to these attacks and the spontaneity that defines suicide bombings.

Militant organizations project their activities as "martyrdom operations" precisely because of the deep moral and religious problems with suicide bombing. Extraordinary justification is necessary to kill not only the (usually evil) enemy—a death easy to excuse—but also oneself. For a suicide-bombing campaign to continue, new recruits are necessary, and for this, a reverence for martyrdom must be established. Last, the ideology of martyrdom is not only power, on which most other terrorism focuses; suicide bombing is appealing for its religiously redemptive and posthumous heroism. Suicide bombing's religious aspect is usually discounted in political scientists' analyses of suicide bombing, but it is one that is significant for propaganda strategy. For these reasons, militant organizations must use media to address their sympathetic audiences at least as much as they present their grievances to their enemies.

In addition to religious and moral issues, spontaneity sets suicide bombings apart. Much media-and-terrorism research was conducted in the 1980s, when heavily covered terrorist attacks were frequently hijackings or standoffs, or even preplanned military offenses—events that lend themselves to media coverage. The very advantage of suicide bombers' "smart-bomb" nature is that the bomber chooses the best place to detonate the bomb, so once the organization dispatches a bomber, the organizers lose control of their bomb—hampering their ability to film or publicize the event. Only in exceptional cases such as the September 11 attacks can a suicide bomber count on spectacular real-time coverage. Although martyrdom operators have become more media-savvy, most suicide bombings can be filmed as they occur only from afar.[10] This fact (the lack of graphic news footage) significantly decreases their media value, although some of the videos are still featured in news stories around the world.

These facts separate suicide bombing from most other terrorist activities, but many strategic aspects remain the same, especially "public relations" and problems of differentiation between audiences. The audience question is crucial because terror "can only succeed if the act is conveyed to the audience whose behavior the terrorist is seeking to influence,"[11] as media scholar George Gerbner wrote. Scholars agree that, in general, terrorist attacks have multiple audiences and that their statements about attacks contain various messages to reach these audiences. There are, however, different ways of dividing the world into audiences. Some scholars find two audiences—generally split based on the inside/outside dichotomy.[12] The idea that there are only two audiences for any attack, however, is problematic because there are varying levels of "insiders" and "outsiders."

A clearer distinction between audiences is a tripartite explanation: (1) organization members (or strong ideological supporters of the organization), (2) sympathetic publics (including potential recruits), and (3) unsympathetic publics (enemies). This formulation borrows from analysis that divides audiences into the terrorist group's own members, its supporters outside the group or neutral publics, and adversaries (who are grouped in their theory with "other observers").[13] This tripartite audience definition is most useful when evaluating the violent and attack footage, such as that surrounding suicide attacks, because these attacks do not usually attempt to convert non-Muslims (unlike other radical groups' messages, which address more neutral audience[14]), instead focusing on glorifying those who choose to fight. The group of "neutral publics" is still important in suicide-attack videos because this audience may be less sympathetic to long-term fighting against militant groups, possibly losing its patience with heavy-handed "counterterrorism" measures if victory is not easily obtained. In other words, these "neutral publics" can dictate a large portion of policymaking in a free/democratic society, if they tire of a conflict and demand an end to a struggle.

Nonetheless, the three-audience view is the most useful way to examine suicide-attack media releases because unlike in videos calling for converts to Islam, the neutral audience is not directly addressed in such videos. Still, numerous questions remain about the three-audience explanation. The idea of who the intended "audience" might be for any given attack can only be a purely theoretical one and, to some extent, our tripartite breakdown quantifies only general global audiences for any political event. These three groups are, essentially, the reality of global communications: Either a person watches and is a member of the acting group, sympathizes with the action, or opposes the action, although neutral bystanders exist to varyng degrees. Militant groups must choose which audience(s) they are addressing and distribute the communication properly to assure it reaches the intended audience. It must be noted, however, that due to the 24-hour news cycle and Internet, these three audiences are not distinct and no organization— political, military, or other—can separate their messages to each group into distinct communications.

There are clues, however, for identifying an operation's or bomber's intended audience, contained in their statements; martyrs' wills provide an excellent repository of audience formulation.[15] Most of the videos contain an address to an audience, but the audience varies widely from video to video. In 2005, Zarqawi directly addressed bin Laden, in the statement "A Message from a Soldier to His Emir,"[16] the Muhammad Siddique Khan video, released after the July 7 London bombings, addresses as "you" the West, referring to "your democratically elected governments." This statement is an effective method of both identifying with the West (speaking in English) and distancing from its form of government and culture. A Saudi Arabian suicide bomber addressed young Muslim men in his will encouraging them to enlist in jihad: "O young men of this Islamic nation, be strong and enlist in the cause of Allah so that the Islamic nation will be relieved of its current crisis."[17] Clearly, these wills and videos do not directly address all three audiences in each communiqué. On the other hand, just because a single video or statement does not specifically address all audiences does not mean that the message is not intended for all audiences. The example of Zarqawi's letter to bin Laden serves as an example of a message to the world, in the guise of a one-to-one letter; if that message had not been intended for public consumption, it would not have been released in such a public way. Many wills are distributed to mainstream Arabic-language and Western media outlets, as well as duplicated for public consumption, proving there is a wider audience than is immediately clear from the literal words in the statements.

Despite these problems, examining ongoing suicide-bombing campaigns proves that the three-audience view is the best way to formulate attacks' audiences. The example of Palestinian suicide bombing organizations is a useful model: Their first audience is made of active supporters and recruits. The second audience is a moderately sympathetic population that in theory agrees with the ultimate outcome of martyrdom operations' goals (ending Israeli occupation), and this group may provide future recruits. Finally there is a hostile (Israeli and Western) audience. Iraq provides a similar breakdown: first, actors and organization members; second, enabling segments of the population; and, third, sectarian enemies, American/European militaries and their constituent publics.

The second problem—planning public relations for three simultaneous audiences—is more complicated. Suicide bombers and militant organizations deal with each of these audiences in different ways. As discussed above, most of their statements to the Arab press are intended to address the first two audiences—the active supporters and the sympathetic publics (although because once a statement is released the organization has no control over it, all statements must be understood to speak to all audiences). This is particularly true in light of the fact that many, if not most, Muslim countries are sympathetic to at least some of al-Qa'ida's goals, and often their actions.[18] This data does not mean that all Arabs or Muslims support suicide bombing but rather indicates a degree of ideological sympathy regarding opposition to the United States and the West in general, such that anti-Western terrorist groups address these publics differently than they address American or European publics.

To reach these first two sympathetic audiences, martyrdom-operation leaders produce and distribute wills and testaments of suicide bombers, hailing them as "martyrs." This is true not only in the Middle East but also in most instances of suicide-bombing around the world. Most of these hagiographical documents, videos, and audio tapes (discussed further below) are distributed primarily to the first audience—to those who are already members—and to the second audience—those who are potential members. The phenomenon of militant organizations filming their activities is well-engrained and unlikely to change. Terrorism expert Bruce Hoffman wrote about al-Qa'ida: "Given the long-established sophistication of bin Laden and al-Qa'ida's propaganda efforts...it is likely that this message will be peddled with increasing fervor for its intended motivational and recruitment value."[19] Even if, as we have argued in other parts of this book, al-Qa'ida is not the sole expression of militant Islam, the organization is often first to utilize powerful new technologies and often sets trends in martyrdom operations. Between al-Qa'ida's propagation of its martyr's wills and the widely circulated Palestinian suicide bombers' wills, suicide bombers almost always produce video or written wills (with the notable exceptions of Afghanistani and Pakistani attackers).[20]

Militant organizations use selective distribution methods to avoid detection and punishment in many places, out of necessity. This strategy of selective distribution is necessary not only because of the legitimization problem for suicide bombing discussed above, but also because of the crackdown that exists on such ideas in many countries with significant Muslim populations. Political alliances with the United States and fears of religious uprisings have prompted many Muslim countries' governments to monitor and/or punish radical Muslim ideas (i.e., in Egypt, Morocco, Uzbekistan, Pakistan, and numerous others). Because of fears of punishment or detection, much of the martyrdom material has been taken off the conventional and subject-to-search bookshelves and moved to the more-anonymous Internet or personal distribution. In other cases, they are available in markets but are still hidden below innocuous religious tracts or available only upon request.[21] Even in Syria, one of the countries least open to cooperation with the United States, pro-martyrdom pamphlets are rarely seen or available even upon request,[22] despite the fact that few people in that country view these attacks as terrorist (although low percentages called al-Qa'ida a resistance organization).[23]

Even in places where one can obtain militant materials, in many places distribution and possession of such materials has often been harshly punished. A more anonymous forum has become desirable, and the Internet has provided just such a forum. First, printed propaganda must be produced in quantities large enough to distribute to a mass audience; this is difficult to do without attracting attention in societies where printing presses are often controlled by government figures. An email need only be written once and forwarded infinitely; a web page can be created, moved and recreated an infinite number of times simply by cutting and pasting text. In fact, forwarding and cutting-and-pasting tactics are encouraged by organizations spreading the message of suicide bombing: "We expect our web-site to be opened and closed continuously," admitted the Azzam Publications site (the most important outlet for jihad propaganda in English prior to September 11) in November 2001.

> Therefore, we urgently recommend any Muslims that are interested in our material to copy all the articles from our site and disseminate them through their own web-sites, discussion boards and e-mail lists. This is something that any Muslim can participate in, easily, including sisters. This way, even if our sites are closed down, the material will live on with the Grace of Allah.[24]

The implications of such Web sites are discussed below.

The ideological spread of martyrdom culture to sympathetic audiences has been quite successful, and hundreds of martyrs' wills, statements, support documents, and other propaganda efforts exist from campaigns around the world. The fact that these are difficult for outsiders to find in printed form does not negate their prevalence or power. In countries where one newspaper is passed around to several people each day (a phenomenon called "pass-along readership" in marketing and media studies), a single martyrdom-praising tract, cassette, or, especially, Web site can reach a huge audience, magnifying militant organizations' already monumental propaganda efforts toward sympathetic audiences.

Tactics

Because pro-martyrdom (and, indeed, much of radical Muslim) propaganda has such an informal distributional structure and the material so varied by organizational goals, it can be difficult to track down and quantify specific propaganda tactics used by all or most militant organizations. There are across-the-board methods of reaching these target audiences, however. Unlike other terrorist organizations, a vast majority of propaganda efforts must take place *after* suicide bombings because of the inability to predict them and for recruitment purposes—therefore, militant organizations' tactics have focused on the video and text statements mentioned above and on claiming responsibility for attacks, often in competition with other martyrdom organizations.

Militant organizations have established savvy media organs for addressing the two more sympathetic audiences. These media organs have become increasingly important in gaining legitimacy—al-Qa`ida has at least two if not several separate production houses, but unlike other militant organizations such as Hamas or Hezbollah, al-Qa`ida does not have an official Web site, since the Al-Nida site (alneda.com) went down in 2003. Two media houses specifically named in various al-Qa`ida communiqués are Global Islamic Media Front[25] and Al-Sahab Productions.[26] These media arms are the source of the information making up most Americans' knowledge about these groups; media arms significantly target both the second and third audiences—the outsider audiences, both sympathetic and unsympathetic. The same can be said of the media arms of the al-Qa`ida in Mesopotamia group (formerly headed by Zarqawi), Hamas, and dozens of other groups employing suicide bombing. Notable exceptions are the Pakistani sectarian suicide attackers and Afghanistani attacks associated with the resurgence of the Taliban.

Militant organizations use these production houses to produce recruitment video and audio tapes supporting martyrdom, such as the one produced as early as March 2002, seized in the spring of 2002. It should be noted that, in views propagated by these organizations, "martyrdom" is not limited to suicide bombing but could be any death occurring during fighting (see chapter 1). These tapes not only recruit more fighters and suicide bombers but also work to foster a culture of reverence for martyrdom.[27] Almost all martyrdom videos contain Qur'anic verses or hadith about martyrdom because glorifying martyrdom is the primary goal of such videos. Regardless of the global (unsympathetic) audience, video producers are correctly convinced that sympathetic viewers will also watch the video and may also be convinced to participate in an operation, or to support them financially.

Typically, such videos end with contact information or a logo of the organization that organized the attack(s)—an indication of the increased "branding" of such organizations.[28] Claiming responsibility for attacks is also an important propaganda technique. This idea is important for Mia Bloom's "outbidding" thesis, and she postulates that militant organizations use suicide bombing to get more publicity and to stake a claim in producing martyrs. In other words, the more a group participates in suicide bombing, the more support such a group has. Although there have been several critiques of this thesis, the idea is that a certain amount of branding and name-recognition occurs when a group publicizes itself through suicide attacks on the enemy. Bloom writes that there is such intense competition within these "markets," groups "prove themselves" using martyrdom as the ultimate proof of commitment to the struggle. She points to statements by the Al-Aqsa Martyrs Brigades: "Martyr Hashaika, member of al-Aqsa Martyrs' Brigades, *proved that our Brigades are leading the path of Jihad*" [emphasis added by Bloom].[29]

Such competitiveness could indicate a crisis of legitimacy for competing militant organizations, and in many cases, this crisis may lead to the proliferation of suicide attacks. The competition is most likely to be worst among Palestinian groups, several of which are vying for influence in the political sphere (especially in the power vacuum following the arrest of some members of the elected Hamas government in spring 2006). To gain power, these groups may choose the cheapest and most easily available weapon they have, namely suicide bombing. A similar situation exists in Iraq, where groups are competing for name recognition, recruits, and "enemy killed." The situation in Iraq differs, however, because here the militant groups have a wide variety of weapons, of which suicide bombing is only one of the many tactics, the other means include inter alia traditional bombings, mortar attacks, hand-to-hand fighting, roadside bombs.[30]

The media strategies for promoting suicide bombing attacks on U.S. troops, therefore, are largely the same as the media strategies for all such guerilla-military attacks. According to an August 2004 *Christian Science Monitor* article, the Iraqi Shi'ite leader Muqtada al-Sadr's Mahdi Militia has a media department that claims to film whenever they go out on the battlefield; competing groups are likely to similarly attempt to publicize.[31] Although at the time of writing, al-Sadr's organization had not employed suicide bombings, these same media strategies have been adopted by groups that do carry out suicide bombings. On the Internet, videos on attacks on U.S. troops in Iraq abound, traded and viewed hundreds (even thousands) of times on video-trading sites such as YouTube (discussed below). It should be noted that at the time of writing, videos of suicide bombings against religious, sectarian sites had not been distributed (this is, recently, a far more common use of suicide bombings, as discussed in chapter 5). The need to have community approval for such attacks is obvious in the fact that, at the time of writing, we knew of no videos showing the targeting of sectarian targets (Shi'ite mosques, etc.),[32] although a few videos showed cars exploding in the distance, aimed at unnamed targets. Not naming targets at times can also indicate the savviness of militant media releases because killing other Muslims—even across a major sectarian divide—is far less permissible than the targeting of U.S. convoys, in the minds of many radical Muslims.

The question of when to claim responsibility for suicide attacks is often a more difficult one than for claiming traditional attacks because not all propaganda is good propaganda for militant organizations.[33] Groups sometimes claim responsibility for an attack and sometimes do not, and analyzing their decision to claim attacks is complicated. At times, multiple groups will claim responsibility for a single attack, contradicting each other,[34] and at other times, no group will claim responsibility for an attack. Sometimes groups claim joint responsibility for attacks, as other scholars have noted.[35] Gabriel Weimann's paper on the subject explains one reason for this phenomenon, stating that "even if they expound at length on the moral and legal basis of the legitimacy of the use of violence, most [terrorist] sites refrain from referring to the terrorists' violent actions or their fatal consequences."[36] Although Weimann is discussing only general terrorist groups' "PR" sites, this reasoning— the espousal of violence and support thereof but a reticence to be culpable—illustrates a fence-walking attitude terrorist groups utilize to brand themselves as revolutionaries without making public blood-stained appearances. Suicide bombing groups are often subject to precisely these pressures because of the grisly nature of their operations.

There are other dilemmas for suicide-bombing groups—namely, the moral issues involved because of deliberate suicide and because many suicide attacks kill many Muslims. In a dramatic turnaround, the Taliban apologized for civilian casualties incurred by its suicide bombings in Afghanistan; this move was likely intended to curtail local dissatisfaction over a bombing that killed 17 and wounded at least 47.[37] Days before, the Taliban issued a statement distancing itself from recent suicide bombings in general, claiming they were due to a breakaway faction's alliances with "foreigners."[38]

Weimann names two exceptions, Hamas and Hezbollah, whose Web sites keep detailed accounts of claimed victims. The same can be said for some insurgent groups in Iraq, which send out violent videos of their fights with U.S. soldiers, some of which show killings and hostage situations. This is likely because of the high degree of legitimacy of these particular campaigns, which are viewed as "counter-occupational" guerilla warfare rather than as terrorism in most of the Arab world.[39] Bloom notes that "[v]iolence has become *the* source of all honor among Palestinians,"[40] and the same could be said about Iraq. However, even these organizations do not claim responsibility for all the attacks scholars studying terrorism attribute to them. Many suicide bombings in Israel and Iraq remain unclaimed or claimed by several organizations, and there are divergent interpretations of this fact. (Some academics have claimed that these multiple claims of responsibility indicate competition, while others claim this fact indicates increasing cooperation between groups.)

Some militant organizations have vehemently denied terrorist attacks when journalists have attributed attacks to them, including attacks that are part of "legitimate" campaigns. Al-Zarqawi's al-Qaʿida in Iraq has renounced reports of at least one attack in March 2005. Most notably, al-Zarqawi's statement denying the attack names only al-Jazeera, although "the report [attributing the attack to al-Qaʿida in Iraq] was additionally aired by Reuters and other news agencies."[41] While this could indicate al-Zarqawi's ignorance about what Western stations are airing, it also indicates a significant concern about the Arab world's public opinion about his group, a question that became especially relevant after the harsh criticisms he received in the wake of the November 9, 2005 Jordan bombing. In fact, al-Zarqawi's group has even distanced itself from threats supposedly issued on behalf of them in 2005, and they suggested that supporters to only "acknowledge 'authentic' news."[42]

Leaders of militant organizations aim all of these tactics at controlling what information comes out about their organization. They cannot, however, control how global media redesign their information, or excerpt from these press releases and videos. Most frustrating for these militant leaders are the very groups they think should help their cause—that is, the Arabic-language media that does not live up to their expectations; these leaders reserve harsh criticism for media in Muslim countries.

How Organization Leaders Evaluate Their Success

When Peter Arnett interviewed bin Laden in March 1997 and asked him about future terrorist attacks, bin Laden answered, "You'll see them and hear about them in the media, God willing."[43] Obviously, al-Qaʿida and other terrorist group leaders recognize the importance of propaganda, and they know their attacks will receive media coverage. Most references to the importance of propaganda occurs in the context of Muslim leaders criticizing terrorist organizations' public relations efforts. Abu Musʿab al-Suri addressed media relations in his lengthy book, *Daʿwat al-muqawama al-Islamiyya al-ʿalamiyya* (A Call for Worldwide Islamic Revolution), a book detailing post-Afghanistan jihadi strategy that has been discussed widely in jihadist circles.[44] "The media and incitement failure of the jihadi groups is the most obvious of their failures in practice," he wrote. "They did not register even one success."[45] Al-Suri suggests terrorists begin using the most basic public relations rule: "The message should be much simpler."[46] Al-Suri strongly criticizes international media and jihadi public relations equally, believing that attackers and organizations should work harder to be portrayed more in line with their goals. Many of his criticisms relate to suicide bombings and suicide-bombing campaigns, which will be discussed below.

This failure may be seen as unimportant by some leaders, including bin Laden, who believes the media—in Muslim and non-Muslim countries— are political mouthpieces, so such leaders are not surprised by the media failure to properly report their goals. For bin Laden, Arab media falls in the "same category" as corrupt Arab governments, more interested in Westernization than Islamization. In one interview, bin Laden said the media sector "strives to beatify persons of the leaders, to sedate the community, and to fulfill the plans of the enemies through keeping the people occupied with minor matters, and to stir their emotions and desires until corruption becomes widespread amongst the believers." Applying these words to the Arab media environment, his words hold true for state-owned media, with their lengthy descriptions of official visits and statements, or for al-Jazeera's brand of often-sensationalistic talk shows. In global media terms, his words could be applied to Western news channels' brand of "infotainment." Although Arabic-language media often gives far more information about the motivations of the suicide bombers and the militant organizations' goals, compared to American media (which is discussed in the following chapter),[47] giving backgrounds on suicide bombers' personal history does not necessarily equate propagandizing suicide bombings. Indeed, militant organizations would prefer not to have their suicide bombers' personal pasts and motivations (often containing perceived moral corruption) revealed to the public.

Because of the strong link between corrupt Arab governments and national media outlets, most leaders' statements focus on how they are covered by the leading Arab satellite station, al-Jazeera. Al-Jazeera has revolutionized Arab media by providing lively talk shows and factual reporting at a much more comprehensive level than any national Arab media outlet.[48] Despite repeated Western accusations that al-Jazeera supports terrorism and spreads terrorist propaganda, attack organizers themselves criticize the channel more often than they praise it. Al-Suri falls outside this pattern, writing that al-Jazeera's September 11 coverage was "a contributing factor in the jihadi message reaching hundreds of millions of Muslim viewers in the world, and this contributed to the renewal of the jihadi factor inside the world."[49] (Nonetheless, he criticizes al-Jazeera coverage elsewhere.) In an essay called "The 11 September Raid: The Impossible Becomes Possible," al-Qa'ida ideologue Abu Ubeid al-Qureshi wrote, "Al-Jazeera's exclusive videotape of Shaykh Usama [bin Laden] and other leaders brought the network worldwide notoriety and carried the voices of the *mujahidin* to the Islamic community and the entire world at no cost."[50]

Militants' criticisms of al-Jazeera are stronger than their commendations, and a significant body of writing and statements prove this. Of the numerous examples, we will discuss only criticisms of how Arab media covered suicide-attack campaigns. One basic problem for "effective" coverage of suicide bombing is the application of the term "martyr" to suicide bombers. Because these attacks require significant moral justification and cultural complicity, media participation in creating the martyrdom culture is required. Contrary to perceptions in the West, calling suicide bombers "martyrs" is not universal; it is, in fact, a complicated issue.

So far, militant groups and radical Muslim writers have focused much less attention on other, increasingly popular Arab stations such as al-Arabiya (a station to which the U.S. government has taken a greater liking), which has close ties to Saudi Arabia, probably because al-Jazeera remains the most independent of their funders and therefore others are perceived as having more bias.

In Yemen—a country known for its conservative brand of Islam and its citizenry's long history of participation in martyrdom attacks—the matter of pronouncing martyrdom is complicated. The Aden-based thrice-weekly independent newspaper, *Al-Ayyam*, received numerous letters from readers after editors labeled a suicide bomber a shahid (martyr) in the caption of a picture, which "created a problem," international news editor Basha Basrahil said in an interview. He said, after a three-week conversation that took place in the pages of the newspaper in 2004, the editorial department decided to only use the term "suicide bombing." He noted that most other Yemeni newspapers did not have editorial policies on the use of the word "martyr," and the use of this word depended on the writer's personal stance on the issue. But calling the attackers "suicide bombers" does not mean the newspaper also labels them "terrorists," a term that makes readers suspicious: "My readers would not believe me—they would say this comes from America."[51]

Journalists elsewhere in the Arab world are similarly selective. Muhammad Agha, editor of the Syrian English-language newspaper *Syria Times*, admits that his country's pro-Palestinian and promartyrdom attack stance influences his editorial policies, given Syria's low level of press freedom. Nonetheless, he does not universally call suicide bombers "martyrs," and neither do other newspapers in Syria, he said. In a conversation attempting to find the dividing lines between "martyrs" and "suicide bombers," he said that an Iraqi suicide bomber attacking a densely populated area or against Iraqi police would be a suicide attacker, but "when they fight foreign occupiers, they are *shahid*." Perhaps a suicide car bomber would be a *shahid* if it was in a marketplace, but perhaps not; Agha said he would have to know the full situation. Palestinians are basically always martyrs, but Chechen suicide bombers are rarely called martyrs because they attack civilian areas such as schools and marketplaces (although these targets are acceptable in Israel, he said).[52] But, like the Yemeni newspaper editor, he said his newspaper never calls anyone a terrorist. All of these varying standards points to a still ongoing discussion of who exactly is a martyr—and to a political ramification of the martyr label. (Syria has long had strong political ties with Russia and it may be politically expedient for them to ignore this conflict, even if jihad-fighters view this as another front of liberation.)

Al-Jazeera, which originally called suicide bombers "martyrs" regularly, is also reconsidering its stance. During the more recent past, al-Jazeera stopped using the word *shahid* without attribution in its news broadcasts, although they still use quoted statements from others employing this word. This has divided opinion within the station; Syrian al-Jazeera correspondent Dr. Fuad Sharbaji said he disagrees with the policy change because the word *shahid* is a good one, and when journalists use it, "people will think it's a good work." He said he believes it should be used especially in reference the Palestinian suicide bombings: "I don't agree [with the station's policy] because he's a *shahid* . . . I think we must name him *shahid* because he does not have anything in life except his death, so he presents what he has, his death." In the case of Iraq, he said he believes the media should work toward creating peace, so they should not present violence in Iraq as resistance; they still view the American government as occupiers, so some of the suicide attackers are still martyrs.[53]

Despite these complicated terminological and ideological discussions of suicide bombing, much of martyrdom supporters' criticism of Arab media coverage fits into certain patterns. Paradigmatic of criticisms of suicide-bombing coverage are discussions of the September 11–attack media coverage and coverage of the various suicide attacks in Sinai, Egypt. These attacks have been called media and propaganda failures, particularly because of organizational leaders' disgust with how al-Jazeera and other Arab media covered them. These criticisms relate to both how the media covered these attacks, many of whom criticized the attacks, and the attackers' media statements themselves. Suicide-bombing proponents' condemnations of the Arab media fall into two categories:

1 *Defending the suicide bombings themselves*: The defense arguments are often criticized on Arab media for ineffectiveness, the response to which is to say the media miss the point of the attack; or

2 *Critiquing the martyrdom operations themselves for lacking clear messages*: Proponents' criticisms, which take into account both the methodology and goals of news media, are justified because transnational media outlet rarely gives totally sympathetic coverage to suicide bombing.

Scholars and terrorist organizations alike view the September 11 attacks as model attacks, and the September 11 attacks continue to have high levels of support among militant supporters of suicide attacks (although the September 11 attacks do not have the same level of legitimacy as suicide bombing operations in Israel). Most Western media discussions have focused on these attacks as examples of careful propaganda planning, noting that they were planned for early morning, giving the possibility of a full news day's coverage (in the United States, but not in the Middle East, where it would be afternoon or evening). Despite all this careful news-related planning, supporters of the attacks have criticized the coverage of these same attacks, usually focusing on the lack of ideological coverage in Arab media. (Such supporters of martyrdom operations believe that the Arab media should wholeheartedly support their operations as the path to liberation.)

The al-Qaʿida ideologue Abu Iman al-Hilali critiqued Arab media's coverage of the September 11 attacks, pointing out specific al-Jazeera journalists who criticized the attacks. One journalist states that the September 11 attacks had no political or religious justification because no military or strategic goals were fulfilled; al-Hilali disagrees. Al-Hilali also criticized a Kuwaiti journalist who said it detracted world attention from the Palestinian issue, with which Al-Hilali also disagrees. He also singles out pubic figures who had said the release of the cassette of the bombers' statements to Western news was humiliating because European opinion would turn against Muslims.[54]

Al-Hilali was particularly disappointed in what he called al-Jazeera's stubborn shying "away from the content of the cassette," which was a discussion of the will of the martyr. "Instead they completely ignored the causes and goals and a study of the motives of the martyr, despite the fact that they knew this was the first and primary cassette coming out of the groups that initiated [September 11]."[55] In other words, in Al-Hilali's opinion, "effective" media coverage is that which examines the motivations of attackers—making attackers more understandable and more likely to become heroes. As will be discussed in the next chapter, his goals are even more thwarted by Western media coverage, which ignores attackers' motivations almost entirely.

Speaking summarily, al-Hilali criticizes al-Jazeera's coverage of the September 11 attacks because the journalists failed to understand the purpose of the attacks and because they failed to give the full message of the martyrdom videos left by the attackers. When al-Jazeera could have examined the religious necessity of attacking the United States in such a way, the channel chose to show only brief, sensationalistic snippets of the video wills—disappointingly so, for al-Hilali and other proponents of the attacks.

The coverage of suicide attacks in Sinai resort areas, carried out October 7, 2004 (Taba) and July 23, 2005, was attacked for reasons more related to insufficient legitimacy for the attacks themselves; this is a problem for many attacks occurring outside Iraq and Israel. Some leaders, while supporting suicide bombing as a tactic, do not think it is effective everywhere; such leaders believe, as Kuwaiti journalist Mohammad al-Awady believed about the September 11 attacks, that other suicide bombings distract media attention from suicide bombings that are legitimately fighting real occupations—that is, bombings organized by the Palestinians.

Another al-Qa`ida ideologue, also named Abu Muhammad al-Hilali[56] criticized the Sinai attacks of 2004 and 2005 because the attacks had no clear message. And not only did they not have a clear message, but these attacks should have also had different messages to different audiences—domestic and foreign. Israeli counterterrorism scholar Reuven Paz explains:

> A message, he believed, should have been published for two audiences: the civilian tourists and the Egyptian government. Al-Hilali believes that the Mujahidin should have sent a clear message to the tourists, saying that these operations were a result of their governments' support for the campaign against the Muslims. The tourists should therefore return to their countries and borders, and stay there.[57]

Al-Hilali also criticized the lack of effective propaganda about the attacks, calling it "a defiance of the order of Allah, who commands 'and you should incite the believers.' "[58] Given the frustration these and other figures have with mass-media coverage of martyrdom operations, it is not surprising that they have chosen to work around mainstream coverage using grassroots and informal Internet mechanisms.

Working around Mainstream Media

Militant organizers and their supporters feel seriously dissatisfied with the attention they get on Arab media. They completely dismiss Arab countries' internal media and have been disillusioned by the lack of discussion on the main regional television channels (al-Jazeera, Al-Arabiya, Abu Dhabi TV, and several others). Such regional media outlets have even refused material from terrorist/insurgent groups, as one Iraqi insurgent complained:

> "I went to Al Jazeera and Al Arabiya with this video, but nobody accepted the film," complains Mujtaba. "So then we invited them to come to Sadr City and film the fighting themselves, but they also refused that offer. It is not just me who thinks the TV channels are liars, it is the whole world."
>
> Mahdi [Army] filmmakers say the Arab news media may be afraid to broadcast such videos because they could face official backlash from Iraqi authorities. Last month, the Iraqi government closed the Baghdad bureau of Qatar-based Al Jazeera. Prime Minister Iyad Al-Alawi accused the station of inciting racial and religious hatred by airing footage of kidnappings and fighting.[59]

While this statement does not refer to suicide bombings specifically, problems of getting raw video footage aired on television (which relies on such footage) astounds and disappoints terrorist and martyrdom operations. Other books attempting to vindicate al-Jazeera in the wake of American criticisms have cited the numerous times al-Jazeera has possessed terrorist statements and refused to air them, even citing a time in 2002 when CNN aired an interview al-Jazeera conducted with bin Laden, which al-Jazeera claims CNN obtained without authorization. Al-Jazeera had decided not to air the interview, saying it lacked news value.[60]

Al-Arabiya editor Nabil Khatib proudly told Western journalists in 2005 of the station's "decision to no longer air the anonymous tapes of Iraqi insurgents, believing they gave groups of questionable credibility an unwarranted platform."[61] This summary rejection is problematic for groups that need to publicize and validate their activities in the Arab media's public sphere. Still, these organizations' footage ends up more often on transnational Arabic-language channels than on hostile countries' media; even Chechen groups send their videos to al-Jazeera instead of Russian media.[62] An important but substantial research task that could not be completed for this book remains the examination and changes in Arab news coverage of suicide attacks.

Al-Suri was so dissatisfied with these aspects that when he made media recommendations for how to deliver the jihad message to the public, he completely left out "mainstream" media outlets such as television or newspaper, focusing on word-of-mouth communication such as preaching, text-messaging, and Internet sites.[63] Accordingly, the number of jihadist propaganda sites has increased from 14 in 2000 to more than 4,000 in 2005.[64]

The Internet has been an active forum of discussion and promotion of terrorist ideology because of the difficulties of policing and tracking materials. In addition, many extremist groups have found the Internet to be a place where, unlike in the formal media, their ideologies will not be hampered by the confines of a "dialogue." Although the Internet provides the possibility of meaningful dialogue by providing the ability to freely, and usually anonymously, gather information, another outcome of such a vast information storehouse is the ability to avoid dialogue altogether. Terrorist groups can communicate instantly and freely about jihad recruitment and can easily send messages about upcoming terrorist activities, and a person susceptible to radical ideology could find plenty of recruitment propaganda. The Global Islamic Media Front (GIMF) wrote that the "Allah has enlisted [the internet] in the service of jihad and of the mujahidin, which has come to serve your interests—given that half the battle of the mujahidin is being waged on the pages of the internet."[65]

Groups supporting martyrdom operations have recognized this and use this fact to their advantage: "Usama bin Laden and his followers concentrate their propaganda efforts on the Internet, where visitors to al Qa'ida's numerous Web sites and to the sites of sympathetic, aboveground organizations can access prerecorded videotapes and audiotapes, CD-ROMs,

DVDs, photographs, and announcements."[66] The phenomenon is so widespread that jihadi messageboards appeal even to Muslims who do not speak or read Arabic by posting the news of events and messages in other languages.[67] Given that there is a lack of Western intelligence and security analysts who know Arabic—despite its status as one of the most common languages—communication in other languages such as Urdu is probably not closely monitored. In the words of Reuven Paz, these Web sites "have replaced the old Madrassa [Islamic school] as a tool of recruiting...The Internet in fact, became one global madrassa."[68] While this may be an over-generalization, insofar as one can still find diversity of opinions and many Westerners criticize the participants in such jihadi forums, Paz's statement that the Internet is where training is now occurring is accurate.

Even in countries with relatively little Internet infrastructure or at-home computer use (as in many Middle-Eastern countries), information read on the Internet has been rumored to be relayed to several people per Internet user by word-of-mouth (similar to pass-along readership). On the other hand, an organization propagandizing on the Internet loses control of its message once it releases it; in the so-called remix culture of the Internet,[69] the message can be manipulated, changed, or even turned against the original organization. Web sites such as Google Video, Yahoo Video, and YouTube now provide infinite possibilities for the mass distribution of these videos. On these sites, members (and membership is free) can post any type of video and tag the videos with key terms such as "shaheed" or "martyr" or names of organizations. From that point, these videos are available to anyone who searches for or stumbles upon them—unless they are reported as contrary to YouTube's "terms of use."[70] YouTube, when made aware of the postings of such videos, removed "dozens" of anti-U.S. videos in September 2006.[71]

A search for "Iraq" and "insurgents" conducted in August 2006, before YouTube removed many videos, returned more than 500 results, most of which were pro-insurgent video clips. Similarly, a search at the same time about the Israeli-Palestinian conflict returned hundreds of results, some of them pro-Palestinian. There are dozens of suicide bombing videos on YouTube (more than 100 results for the search term "suicide bombing," when we originally searched for these terms in August 2006),[72] and count-less more videos of other militant attacks. The remix culture allows these videos to be reclaimed by opponents of suicide bombing and ridiculed, but this same remix culture allows proponents of suicide bombing to also sub-mit typical BBC or CNN videos as "victory" videos. YouTube also provides a list of sites that link to the YouTube video in question, so YouTube browsers could be directed to a pro-suicide-bombing Web site easily if it fea-tures the clip—and, likewise, to an anti-suicide-bombing site. The com-ments area for these suicide-bombing videos proves that both proponents and opponents of suicide bombing are accessing these videos,[73] but it is unclear how many undecided or vaguely sympathetic viewers access them. Many of the videos had been accessed thousands of times by August 2006—and that is just for one copy of a single video (of which there may be several copies on YouTube). At the time of writing, it appears these videos had been reported to YouTube because most of the videos accessed previously had been removed, and the users who had posted them had their profile deleted.

There is extensive research into the potential threat posed by cyber-terrorism, a high-tech issue, whereby terrorist groups could hack into crucial government or business servers and wreak economic or political havoc. But Weimann's article points out that a more present danger is the widespread use of the Internet as a means of recruiting and creating terrorists—and this is certainly relevant for facing suicide bombing and, especially so in Iraq, a place to which fighters and suicide bombers travel long distances and a place where such fighters have advanced technological capabilities. More attention has been paid to radical Web sites, as there are various attitudes toward such sites. Many experts advocate deleting and removing these sites to stop the spread of the ideas, but other experts have advocated simply monitoring the sites, so as to learn more about the organizations they serve. Either way, much valuable information about ideologies can be gained on sites propagating or promoting suicide bombings.

Implications for the United States

This extensive use of the Internet opens up a new issue for the United States. The internet is making inroads almost everywhere in the world. On one hand, this means the United States has an (almost entirely unused) opportunity to reach these audiences with Arabic-language Internet content. There are options available with a far lower cost than the costly American-run TV station Al-Hurra and radio station Radio Sawa, both of which have very low ratings and low levels of public trust in the Middle East. Web material can be far less transparent, sponsored by various different organizations not seemingly connected with the American government, whereas most people in the region know that Al-Hurra is a propaganda mouthpiece for the U.S. government. Production of short, anti-suicide-bombing videos, or catchy videos discouraging other militant activities, which could be distributed on chat boards and the video-swapping sites such as YouTube and Google Video, could also potentially reach a wide audience and prompt debate.

On the other hand, Internet sources are more prone to appeal to certain target groups. Bloggers and especially Internet-based forums/chatboards can be extremely one-sided, appealing primarily to followers of radical groups. While these sites often have serious debates on organizations' political tactics (beheading, participation in elections, etc.), these sites do not usually question the legitimacy of suicide attacks performed against an "occupation." If a more neutral person is curious about the legitimacy of martyrdom operations, s/he may encounter many persuasive arguments in support of mainstream attacks that contain no acknowledgment of contrasting opinions in online forums. Furthermore, in countries with both tightly controlled official media and radical Muslim groups (including Saudi Arabia, Egypt, Sudan, Morocco, and some of the former USSR), these pro-suicide attack opinions could magnetically draw new recruits for martyrdom because of their subversive appeal.

Some experts argue that jihadists circulate these materials on the Internet in order to indoctrinate their own constituencies and followers, but these sites may not be readily available to Muslims in the developing world or may be difficult to find (with the exception of a few well-known sites). Therefore, they may lack mass audiences in Africa, the Middle East, or Asia (although they certainly do have substantial audiences there), outside of capital cities. Because of this fact, it is difficult to judge what the intended audience is (European, American, Middle-Eastern, African, or Asian; convert or those born Muslim) and whether these sites are the most effective way of reaching those audiences. Regardless of the intended audience segment, militant leaders are looking to expand: to address an increased marginalization in mainstream media, leaders are looking to widen their video distribution.[74] Rather than shutting these sites down, prompting the posters and discussors to move to other sites (which, as stated above, is not necessarily the stated U.S. policy stance on this issue), a better approach may be to inject discussions that *are* exceedingly one-sided with dissenting opinions, to get a more valid debate and possibly to inject doubt into the discussion.

These sites can have mass appeal among Arabic-speaking youths and, in some cases, among converts in Europe and the United States (even those who know little or no Arabic, because many sites have translated sections). Appealing to these groups may be more dangerous than appealing to the "Arab street" because global travel is far easier for them, while appealing to Arabs in the Middle East could be more effective for recruiting suicide bombers for the Iraq or Afghanistan campaigns, where blending in would be important. Regardless, it may be unlikely that parties totally uninterested in learning about jihad would just stumble upon some of these sites without already having some idea that they were looking for a jihad site (especially among Western audiences, which may be unfamiliar with martyrdom operations' names).

The Western media provides a largely violence-free narrative of the wars in Afghanistan and Iraq, while on many militant Islamic sites, every kill is documented in text and, increasingly, in video. Among radical Muslim—or potentially radical Muslim—populations, the Western media's silence on the violent reality of war has driven audiences to disregard Western media as filtered propaganda, and the jihad sites as revelations of a secret truth. It is difficult to solve this, however, without advocating for more violence on the evening news—something few believe would have a positive social impact.

While the U.S. government cannot engage in dialogue with such sites, there remains an open opportunity to dialogue on satellite media, especially Arabic-language media. In the past, state-controlled media messages could be manipulated by powerful governments through a diplomatic process, but this has changed dramatically with the advent of al-Jazeera and subsequently with other transnational satellite channels, and through small democratic shifts around the world. "Political change in some parts of the world has opened up channels of communication that were controlled and censored in the past by autocratic governments. As a result, mass-mediated terrorism has become a more attractive weapon."[75] Examples of cases abound—from the Middle East to Central Asia—when, at the beginning of a national or international crisis, state-owned television plays traditional music concerts or conservative programming. These countries had the greatest possible control on potential political messages resulting from attacks, and this power has gone. With that comes the sometimes organic, sometimes top-down discussions of radical ideas—understanding who a martyr is, and whether suicide bombing is justified. Al-Jazeera and al-Arabiya—stations with major ideological impact in the Middle East— have invited and hosted U.S. officials and spokespeople in debates on policy issues, and these appearances can be expanded.

U.S. officials have been criticizing the Arab press on the basis of "bias" for years, but this criticism is an overreaction. In January 2006, President Bush continued his tradition of criticizing the Arab media, saying "Arabic TV does not do our country justice."[76] This type of criticism is not helpful for policymaking and ignores the fact that the United States has not actually tried to engage the Arabic television audience. Rather than idly saying that Arab media unfairly portray the United States, public diplomacy efforts should focus on engaging the Muslim audience in its cultural comfort zone. The plan to set up al-Hurra and Radio Sawa was criticized by experts on the Middle East and public diplomacy before it was carried out,[77] and since its establishment, the stations have received extremely low ratings.[78] As mentioned above, however, public diplomacy has improved under the new under secretary for public diplomacy and public affairs, Karen Hughes, but a vast number of options remain unused.

The time has long passed when the U.S. government could open a media outlet in a hostile country and have such a station believed to be objective. As recommended in the report *Changing Minds; Winning Peace*, the U.S. image would likely be better served by unscripted appearances on popular Arab channels or, at minimum, recording programs and airing them on stations that already have an audience. This tactic was briefly explored in 2006, when an anti-suicide-bombing public service announcement (PSA) was filmed for an Iraqi audience. It was, however, only to be played on the post-Saddam Iraqi Media Network, but many Iraqis have viewed this network as pure U.S. propaganda, preferring satellite television.[79] Still, such material is a step forward in spreading more antimilitant messages to a grassroots audience.

The debates on the legitimacy of suicide bombings present an opportunity for our most virulent critics to speak against our policies, but they also represent an opportunity for more moderate and sometimes even U.S. voices to speak to these audiences in ways they previously could not. The uncertainty about which bombers are martyrs and which are suicide bombers points to an opportunity for Western governments to inject more doubt into the discourse. If such a tactic is used, the emphasis should not be on using the word "terrorist," which is a problematic and politically charged concept for many audiences. The emphasis should be on injecting doubt about the religious justification of suicide bombing itself, and on the many Muslims who are dying as a result of these attacks, among other things. While further discussion of how the United States can use this opportunity to its advantage are explored in chapter 9, it must be emphasized that the culture of hopelessness about suicide bombing attacks has kept the United States from effectively addressing global audiences on this topic.

Chapter 7

Success of Terrorist Messages in the American Media

> *If terrorism is ultimately a battle for the hearts*
> *and minds... it seems that the press is neither a totally*
> *reliable nor a totally effective weapon.*[1]

As shown in the previous chapter, policymakers and Western publics have vastly misunderstood how Arabic-language media covers these attacks and how militant radical Muslims actually distribute information. This misunderstanding is based on the complicated nature of communicating with the various "sympathetic" (and "neutral") audiences. But Western policymakers have also misunderstood how they should communicate with their home audiences such that they counter militant organizations' considerably more straightforward goals in communicating with enemy publics: Suicide attackers and their organizers undoubtedly intend to terrorize enemy publics through these actions, and sometimes to convey a rebuking message. Bombers and organizations fulfill these intentions by using strongly worded, threatening, and often apocalyptic statements addressed to enemy publics. Western news coverage of suicide bombings falls into two basic categories: coverage of the violent actions themselves, and background coverage of the forces and motivations driving these actions. The trauma effect of repetitive media coverage of suicide bombings has been studied and found to be potentially significant, as noted in many media studies—especially those about September 11.[2] The news media are unwilling or inadvertent accomplices in this traumatic effect, but the trauma does not come from news organizations' giving credence to the violent *ideologies* they are covering. In fact, very little of suicide bombers' ideological statements or views makes it into Western news.

Reliance on policymakers' statements is an essential part of Western news media, and this fact is unlikely to change. But, as will be shown in this chapter's content analysis of CNN, this reliance on policymakers' priorities has allowed several misperceptions about suicide attacks and policymaking priorities to dominate the news agenda, such that Western governments (especially the U.S. government) are, to some degree, discredited because of an informational gap. The lack of ideological statements, on one hand, is understandable because of a desire to keep enemy propaganda silent. The wide gap between how militant leaders are portrayed in Western media and what their statements actually say, however, may contribute to the recruiting of future bombers. It should be noted that we do not advocate censorship or specific terminology for media coverage; media organizations may take the shortcomings discussed in this chapter as suggestions for further angles to pursue, but we do not advocate anyone *controlling* how these attacks are covered. This chapter is primarily designed, however, to show the shortfalls of information that appears in mainstream news coverage in order to help those responding to the attacks craft better statements.

Understanding how Western news has covered these attacks is necessary to prove the misperceptions and defeatist attitudes in the current policy debate on suicide attacks, which are discussed in the following chapter. As this chapter will prove, it is not just the policymaking world that has been infused with these problematic ideas about suicide attacks, but because of reliance on statements from official sources, Western media coverage has become similarly infused with such ideas.

Militants' Limitations in Addressing Western Media

Compared to the variety of ways terrorists address their followers and potentially sympathetic publics, their possible outlets for addressing this unsympathetic audience are limited, especially by language. Most martyrdom leaders and proponents make statements in Arabic or local languages. There are, however, suicide-bombing recruits from the United Kingdom that bridge that barrier, including the London bomber Muhammad Siddique Khan, who recorded video wills in England.

A second limitation is a format problem: Attackers' martyrdom wills and leaders' videos are often much longer than a standard "sound byte" on Western news, often lasting at least 30 minutes and contain verbose language difficult to force into a 30-second sound-byte. So far, radical jihad leaders— including martyrdom operation leaders—have shown little interest in crafting shorter statements that explain their missions and goals in a more media-friendly style; instead, these leaders later criticize media outlets for "missing the point" of their statements. Western recruits such as the London bombers and the September 11 planners may have understood this cultural divide more, as their statements were considerably shorter: London bombing ringleader Muhammad Siddique Khan's video will, released eight weeks after the July 7, 2005 bombings, was recorded in English but paired with a statement from al-Qa`ida leader Ayman al-Zawahri and totaled only 15 minutes.

Still, an additional, considerably longer, Khan statement was released in November 2005. And there are exceptions: Adam Gadahn's ("Azzam the American") joint statement with al-Qa`ida leader Ayman Zawahiri released in September 2006 was almost an hour long.

Another limitation is that Western news outlets have been admonished not to air statements directly from militant leaders, in case they contain coded messages. Then-U.S. national security adviser Condoleeza Rice propagated this idea in October 2001, when she warned news outlets of the "possible risks of broadcasting messages from al-Qa`ida, which the administration believes may contain imbedded messages to followers of Mr. bin Laden."[3] In the wake of the request, many U.S. news outlets aired only clips of the statement, and NBC News' Nightly News decided not to air it. Since then, however, most international televisions networks have aired bin Laden's statements, or at least clips of or quotes from them. Even so, they rarely air suicide bombers' wills, usually opting only for statements of major al-Qa`ida leaders; this could be a decision based on time constraints, given the limited amount of time devoted to any subject on TV news, and given the high number of suicide bombers in the past several years. On the other hand, this could be a resolute decision to block militants' propaganda channels to Western audiences. Whatever the reasons, networks are not airing as much primary material about suicide bombing as they could.

Yet another issue affecting how militant statements are distributed is that, unlike in the past, militant organization leaders no longer view CNN as the only vehicle for spreading their message to the world in general, to the Western world, or even to U.S. audiences. Before Arab stations such as al-Jazeera and al-`Arabiya existed, CNN was the only transnational vehicle for getting statements to either a sympathetic or unsympathetic audience. While militant groups could communicate with their *members* using various means, for years many Arabs relied on American satellite news for timely reports about international conflicts. This provided an extensive censorship mechanism that kept undesirable voices from speaking to these potentially sympathetic publics. Media scholar Robert Picard wrote that in the 1980s, there was no format for Yasir Arafat (late leader of the PLO) or George Habash (leader of the Palestinian radical faction PFLP) to express their viewpoints, which denied them "the element of legitimacy they seek [to] air issues" without resorting to violence.[4] This has changed because Western media is no longer the only way to reach this audience. Many militant leaders view stations such as CNN and BBC as less important for reaching potential audiences. Indeed, these leaders view Western channels such as BBC and CNN as tainted by what they view as reliance on their respective governments.

Despite these problems, many observers believe that Western news media's focus on violent activity and that repetitive airing of terrorist-attack footage leads to disproportionate attention to small militant groups.

Intensive media coverage attributed to terrorist attacks does appear to give terrorists power that is disproportionate to their actual military strength, as one study of Western elite press pointed out: "In sheer military terms the terrorist group is in most cases a miniscule force; its tactical strength, however, derives from its ability to attract publicity for its cause."[5] In other words, a small group of terrorists can wreak major havoc with a single attack and by appearing on the airwaves, and if suicide bombings are ubiquitous on television, viewers may believe suicide bombers are everywhere.

Due to the limitations discussed above, few messages that promote suicide bombing are spread through English-language television news. To date, the only significant past content-analysis research on terrorist attacks' portrayal in Western news outlets dates from the 1980s, with the notable exception of the significant analysis of the coverage of the September 11 attacks. Studies from the 1980s found that, although terrorist actions are covered extensively in Western media, very little terrorist *ideology* is discussed in these reports. A 1980s study of *The New York Times* and *The Times* of London—two top elite newspapers—found that media coverage of terrorism appears to be "sapping terrorism of its political content." The findings included that more than 40 percent of transnational terrorist attacks in the 1980s were ignored by both newspapers, that the number of people killed in a terrorist attack was the most important factor determining whether the newspaper covered it, that each newspaper had a definite regional bias, and that there was very little explanation of what was happening and why.[6]

Since the 1980s, the news environment has shifted dramatically. U.S. newspapers and wire services have closed or cut back on foreign bureaus, diminishing their ability to cover international news.[7] Furthermore, television news has become the overwhelming first media choice for most of the West, and television's programming contains less depth and more "sound bytes" than are found in "elite" newspapers. Therefore, decades-old findings are not only still relevant, but one would expect that these findings would be even more apparent in contemporary television news coverage of attacks because of the shrinking-sound byte. Because no one has studied how English-language television media cover suicide bombings, it is necessary to examine these issues here.

In order to show how media coverage of terrorism affects and perpetuates policymakers' misinterpretations of the suicide-attack phenomenon, we will examine global media coverage of suicide bombing to determine ideological and technical trends. Evening news programs on any of the three major networks (ABC, CBS, NBC) get higher ratings than either CNN or Fox News, but CNN has a global reach that is significant in determining its influence. Therefore, this analysis will compare CNN's coverage with that of NBC, the network with the highest evening-news ratings since 1998. For discussion of ideological issues, we focused on CNN's coverage of suicide bombing between 1996 and 2006,[8] because of its standing in the global political dialogue and greater perceived neutrality. Following examination of these U.S. networks' coverage, BBC was also examined, albeit less thoroughly, and BBC coverage is discussed following the discussion of U.S. media trends. For background and anecdotal information, we read hundreds of articles (news and opinion) in various American and international newspapers, especially from those countries where suicide bombings have occurred, such as Russia/Central Asia, Africa, Turkey, and Southeast Asia.

Tendencies in U.S. Coverage of Suicide Bombings

Quantitative Analysis

In-depth exploration of CNN's and NBC's suicide–bombing coverage shows several basic trends: More news value was assigned to suicide bombing after September 11, and there is a heavy regional bias in suicide bombing, as the 1980s study concluded. Suicide bombings were considered to have greater news value when Americans were victims, when the number of casualties was relatively higher, or when American "strategic" or foreign-policy allies were targeted (i.e., Saudi Arabia and Israel); suicide bombings in Chechnya and Sri Lanka were given relatively little coverage, almost always in very short segments, despite the frequency of attacks and the high number of casualties of some attacks. Suicide-bombing coverage has a heavy regional bias, and sensationalistic elements are given more prominence in news reports about suicide bombing.

To analyze percentages of suicide bombings covered by CNN and NBC, we used Robert Pape's list of suicide bombings between 1995 and 2003,[9] published in his book *Dying to Win*. As would be expected, CNN gave more coverage to suicide bombings after the September 11 attacks, the first suicide/martyrdom attack on American soil targeting American civilians (See table 7.1). Before the September 11 attacks, the percent of suicide bombings covered by CNN during the evening news was 25.6 percent, and after the September 11 attacks, the percentage of total suicide bombings covered jumped to 61.1 percent. NBC Evening News' jump was slightly more dramatic—from 23.9 percent to 62.7 percent. This indicates that, following the September 11 attacks, American news channels began assigning a per se news value to suicide bombings.

Table 7.1
Percentages of suicide bombings covered, 1995–2003

Network	Before September 11	After September 11
CNN	25.6	61.1
NBC	23.9	62.7

Not all suicide bombings had the same amount of news value for these networks, however. The 1980s news analysis found that the key factor in determining whether a terrorist attack would be covered was the number of people killed—that there was a correlation between the number of people killed and whether it was covered. This concept is expressed in the journalism adage, "If it bleeds, it leads," meaning traumatic events are more likely to make front-page news. In this analysis of CNN and NBC evening news, the correlation between numbers of casualties and news coverage was not completely confirmed and, at times, the number of casualties was less important than prioritization of regions or conflicts perceived to be important to American interests.

There was only weak correlation between suicide-attacks' fatality rates and the length of their coverage, once the September 11 attack (which got extremely high amounts of coverage because it happened in the United States and also had the most fatalities—and therefore it is a unique example within the category of suicide bombings) was removed from the sample.[10] Even limiting the data points to only suicide bombings covered on each network and excluding those ignored, there is only a weak correlation between length of coverage and numbers of fatalities.[11] Therefore, the previous finding that news organizations cover terrorist attacks based on casualties does not hold true in this instance, so other news values must be considered.

CNN and NBC both covered suicide bombings with significant regional *or* political bias, and this bias was largely consistent with American foreign policy priorities. A simple regional analysis is problematic because al-Qa`ida has carried out suicide bombings in various countries, especially against American targets, which get extremely high amounts of coverage. Analyzing the data only by region, then, it would apear that CNN and NBC news values place Africa over Israel for policy importance, since the major African suicide bombings (Kenya twice, Tanzania, Morocco, Tunisia) were organized by al-Qa`ida or groups very closely associated with it. Therefore, al-Qa`ida-organized attacks are given their own category. Table 7.2 shows the percentage of bombings covered in each category.

These percentages clearly show that the regional conflicts in Sri Lanka, Turkey, and India-Kashmir have significantly less news value, despite the fact that Sri Lankan suicide bombings have been numerous and at times produced high fatality figures. (NBC's regional bias was slightly stronger—NBC did not cover Sri Lankan suicide bombings at all in the data for this period.) These networks' lack of coverage reflects the fact that these suicide-bombing campaigns rarely target American or Western interests, so they are unlikely to directly affect most Americans; they have not been thoroughly analyzed in this book for the same reason. The Chechen suicide bombings carried out in Russia were, however, covered significantly more, although it too is more of a regional conflict than an international one. Russian-American relations are extremely important, and influencing the decision to cover these suicide

Table 7.2
Regional percentages of suicide bombings covered by CNN and NBC, 1995–2003*

Region/organization	CNN	NBC
Al-Qa`ida	72.73	77.27
Iraq	61.9	71.43
Israel-Palestine	69.44	70.37
Russia/Chechnya	42.11	36.84
Sri Lanka	11.67	0
Turkey**	6.67	0
India/Kashmir***	0	50

Notes:
  * There are several important omissions in this data: Neither the Pape list nor the news media covered suicide bombings in Pakistan or Afghanistan during this period (approximately a dozen), so we have not analyzed this data because either way, it would find that none of such suicide bombings had been covered.
  ** These are PKK-organized suicide bombings, not the May 2003 al-Qa`ida suicide bombings in Istanbul.
  *** This is extremely small sample of four suicide bombings.

bombings is the perception that Russians are fighting the same radical Islamic enemy as that of the United States. This is a glaring example of how proximity and political news judgments trump casualty figures. All the rest of the suicide-bombing figures—for al-Qa`ida, Iraq, and the Israel-Palestinian conflict—follow expected norms of political prioritization.

Coverage of Palestinian suicide bombings and al-Qa`ida suicide bombings has low length-fatality correlation. NBC's coverage of Palestinian suicide bombings has a length-fatality correlation of about 0 (no correlation), although its al-Qa`ida length-fatality correlation is about 0.5, meaning it could be said to be correlated. CNN's Palestinian length-fatality correlation is higher, but its al-Qa`ida length-fatality correlation is quite low. The suicide-bombing campaigns with the highest correlation between coverage and fatalities are precisely those that the networks cover least—especially Sri Lanka and Russia. Based on this, one could surmise a rule: The length-fatality correlation matters most in campaigns that do not have predetermined political importance.

One exception to this is the attention suicide bombings in Afghanistan and Pakistan get. For an area of the world considered by most to be on the "front lines" of the "War on Terror," these areas get disproportionately little media attention. Of all the al-Qa`ida-organized or -related suicide bombings around the world, the ones least likely to get any coverage on either or both networks are those in Afghanistan and Pakistan, which often have low casualty rates, so this represents an entirely overlooked but important battlefield, especially considering the Western troop presence in

Afghanistan. This reflects the lack of attention these conflicts get overall both in the media and, because of news channels' reliance on official sources, in the policymaking world.

Thus, coverage of suicide bombing in the U.S. media, like its relative importance in the Western policymaking world, is linked not only to the likelihood of facilities among American soldiers or American citizens (or Western citizens). Coverage of Afghanistan's suicide bombings—which often target and kill Americans—is very scarce, despite the American foreign policy interest in the area. When Afghanistan's suicide bombings are mentioned on the networks, they are usually reported on during news-brief segments and are rarely the subject of a full story. It should be noted, however that coverage of suicide bombings in Afghanistan received increased attention at the end of 2006, when suicide bombers increased. Likewise, suicide bombings in Iraq that target American *soldiers* are covered in less detail than suicide bombings targeting other Iraqis.[12] News channels may have made a determined or inadvertent decision to consider these attacks to be part of the basic strategy of the enemy in these wars, and to therefore give them only as much coverage as a rocket attack would get (i.e., not much). Policymakers, similarly, have ignored the enormity of the suicide-attack phenomenon in Afghanistan and Iraq. As discussed in the following chapter, treating suicide bombing as "just another weapon" is dangerous because of its nihilistic undertones and because it requires so little preparation or weaponry and therefore is difficult to protect against.

While it would be undesirable and difficult (if not impossible) to cover all the suicide bombings in these areas, the lack of coverage of these suicide bombings gives credence to militant organizations' statements pointing out U.S. media's ignoring successful attacks on U.S. troops. On the other hand, the lack of coverage is understandable because attacks against U.S. troops rarely kill many soldiers (with the exception of the bombing of a mess hall in Mosul, Iraq), while bombings targeting civilians, often carried out in large crowds, frequently kill dozens.

Qualitative Analysis of U.S. Media

Beyond these statistical findings underscoring political prioritization in news coverage, there are many observations to be made based on *how* news organizations cover suicide bombings—what they say, what they include, and what they exclude. As in the case of our quantitative analysis, no significant examination of this subject has occurred in other studies of suicide bombing or in recent studies of terrorism in general, but such an analysis is essential for evaluating and correcting the public discourse on this phenomenon. The content analysis in this section will rely heavily on CNN's coverage of suicide bombing but will draw from a variety of American news sources; it will not be limited to the 1995 to 2003 range but instead will draw on media coverage through mid-2006. All of this research points to the fact that not only is there no sympathy for suicide attacks expressed in mainstream American news but there is very little explanation of the phenomenon and very little productive dialogue on policy responses to suicide bombing. Furthermore, many prominent misperceptions (which we address in the following chapter) are frequently cited in news coverage of these attacks, and for effective debate on the topic, these misperceptions should be corrected by policymakers.

First, there are very few explanations of why the suicide attacks happened—contrary to earlier research. The earlier studies cited above found that, if any explanations were given, they were overwhelmingly personal—rather than ideological or political—in nature. We too found very few explanations given for suicide attacks, but we found fewer personal motivations than political. Often, political motivations were given or assumed but these motivations were rarely based on any communication from terrorist groups or from the bombers themselves; they were usually based on speculation or sound-bytes from "policy experts" invited to speak on the topic. These experts were invited back repeatedly and they often offered the same explanations each time. Explanations given by newscasters and political experts included "plans to disrupt the peace process,"[13] "using suicide attacks as a tool of diplomacy,"[14] Palestinian leaders' demands that they stop the bombings,[15] Israeli violations of the peace "roadmap," destabilization,[16] and "maximum impact on [a country's] elections or peace 'roadmap.' "[17] Other explanations were less sophisticated and more circumstantial or emotional, such as "anger" or "frustration,"[18] upcoming elections in the United States or anywhere in the region,[19] or a desire to demonstrate occupiers' weaknesses (especially in Iraq).[20] As sectarian violence increased in Iraq, sectarian reasons were increasingly cited instead of goals of political legitimacy.[21] One of the most coherent explanations of a terrorist group's goals referred to the little-covered Sri Lankan bombings, about which a newscaster said that the Tamil Tigers guerilla group "wants to establish its own homeland in Sri Lanka." A similar explanation was given on March 10, 2000 coverage, and in reference to Chechan rebels in a minute-long segment about a December 5, 2003 suicide boming in Russia.

In other cases, terrorist political reasoning is inferred when facts are stated in proximity with each other. In the November 19, 1995 coverage of the suicide bombing of the Egyptian embassy in Islamabad, Pakistan, there was no direct explanation given, but the newscaster mentioned the upcoming Egyptian elections. In the context of a 15-second news clip, such a reference almost constitutes a directly causative statement. For instance, a much longer news segment (five minutes) on August 14, 2001 that mentioned an aside about Israeli "violent" actions against Palestinians in Jenin did not have the same causative feeling. These insinuated reasons, and their political nature, actually shore up the organizational reputation of militant groups by giving them loftier goals than the personal goals many attackers have (see chapter 8).

Very rarely are reasons such as "revenge" given—possibly because these would imply an initial action that necessitated revenge. "Revenge" explanations for suicide bombings are most often mentioned in the aftermath of an Israeli "targeted assassination" of people deemed either "terrorists" or, more neutrally, "activists."[22] The revenge explanation was also mentioned when Israelis attacked usually "civilian" areas, such as refugee camps.[23] These vengeful and other, more personal motivations explored in chapter 8 are extremely important for drafting official responses to militants' statements regarding their attacks because it can help to undermine the lofty political goals these groups claim to have.

In 2002, CNN began exploring the possibility that suicide bombers were performing publicity stunts. This could have been a response to post–September 11 criticisms that terrorists were achieving their terrorizing goals by using the media, who repeatedly showed the violent, shocking images from the September 11 attacks. Many politicians and policy groups noted that terrorist activity is propagandistic in nature, so CNN and other media outlets began self-consciously discussing whether suicide bombings were an attempt to garner media attention. Caught between much analyses that said the September 11 attackers had timed the attack for optimal U.S. media coverage and a need to cover the news in the most riveting way, U.S. television media became very self-conscious about how they might be manipulated. On March 2, 2002 a CNN newscaster said the timing and location of a Jerusalem bombing "seemed calculated not only for casualties but also for world attention." News organizations also began using the caveat, when airing videos from al-Qa'ida leaders, that they did not know if the material was "authentic." Regardless of this self-consciousness, the media did not, of course, stop covering suicide bombings.

Around the same time in 2002, CNN began giving far more narrative explanations of difficulties Palestinians were facing as a result of Israeli policy. On March 21, 2002, CNN not only quotes an Israeli talking about Palestinians' mythologization of their homeland,[24] but they also talk extensively about Israeli settlements and Israelis acting as if "they had no intention to leave." Israelis are also interviewed, saying that Palestinians are being treated as an invisible people. The same segment concludes with a quote from former *New York Times* reporter David Shipler saying there is a conscience in Israel, but Palestinians are unable to see it "beyond the brutality." By May 2002, explanations became more neutral—newscasters still recognized Palestinian suffering, but expert Diana Butto explained it by stating that Israeli prime minister Ariel Sharon has terrorized a civilian population in the hope of ending suicide bombing: "There is a direct link between terrorism and Palestinians' lack of freedom."[25]

The primary sources for quotes and information in the news segments under consideration were official sources—usually from Western or Western-oriented countries, but in some cases members of the official

Palestinian leadership. Under this structure, and given the wealth of press releases and statements that militant organizations release, CNN could have contrasted these Western official voices with their opponents' in order to provide a more coherent or accurate explanation for these attacks. CNN, however, aired statements from militant leaders only on a few occasions. On March 22, 2002, CNN showed footage of an Al-Aqsa member saying, "We are willing to give more martyrs in order to defeat injustice and oppression." On April 29, 2003, the newscaster read portions of Islamic Jihad and Hamas statements saying they rejected the new Palestinian government. On April 17, 2004, a Palestinian Liberation Organization (PLO) spokesman was interviewed on reasons to approve of suicide attacks, citing babies killed at Israeli checkpoints and Palestinian civilians killed in several attacks. A video from Iraq aired December 26, 2004 stated the point was to terrorize "the occupiers" (Americans).

Most often newscasters express total confusion as to the possible motivations for committing a suicide attack, so they speculate about the reasons. This is particularly salient in one newscaster's comment about Iraq in 2003, when suicide bombings were becoming frequent: "The bomber or bombers created a scene of enormous human suffering in the name of something, we don't yet know who they are or what that something is, but we'll explore the possibilities tonight."[26] There were no reasons given later in the broadcast.

As stated above, attackers' personal motivations were also explored only in exceptional cases. The only time a young male's personal explanation for suicide bombing was explored in depth was March 31, 1997, when CNN featured an interview several minutes long with a Palestinian would-be suicide bomber, who had changed his mind. The would-be bomber, Mousah Ziadah, was 16 years old, and in the interview he said, "I wanted to die, to become a martyr, away from the tragic life I had lived on the Palestinian streets among my family and friends."[27] While this segment is vaguely Palestinian-apologetic in nature (it discusses refugee camps and a Palestinian mental health specialist's statement that Hamas "offers hope and moral victory over humiliation and desperation"[28]), the piece does not really offer any insight into terrorists' mindset or ideology. It is the wrong "conversion" story, focusing on the conversion *from* militant interests, rather than attempting to explain why someone would turn *to* militancy. Similarly, a March 27, 2004 report explores the reasons a 16-year-old, such as the one caught that month with an explosive belt at an Israeli checkpoint, would attempt to become a suicide bomber. The newscaster calls children "easy prey" for those with violent intentions because of the "glorification of martyrdom."[29]

Female bombers' personal motivations were covered more often on CNN than males'. Female suicide bombers have been somewhat of a news fixation in media around the world, and it is revealing that the only personal revenge motivation mentioned in the universe of coverage studied was the explanation given for an October 2003 female bomber, whose brother and cousin were assassinated by Israelis earlier that year.[30] For U.S. journalists covering suicide bombers, the "redemptive" suicide-bombing motivation—discussed in chapters 3 and 5—appears more operative for female attackers than for male.

The question of why radical groups would allow women to participate in resistance, and why women would take part in violence mystifies journalists and writers alike, and the topic has attracted numerous books. As Zedalis claims in her book *Female Suicide Bombers*, women who perform suicide attacks are more able to "capitalize on the sensationalism."[31] Zedalis cites analyst Melanie Reid as saying, "Women are hot news. It is a reaction that knows no state or religious boundaries." Women's martyr videos are more frequently aired: Of the four martyr video segments CNN aired during the course of this survey, three were taken from women bombers' videos. One CNN-aired martyrdom video shows a female Palestinian bomber, whose name (Dareen Abu Aysheh) was not given in the news segment, reciting the lines translated on air as saying, "Because a body and soul are all that we have, so I give them to God as an explosion to burn the Israelis and destroy the legend of the chosen people."[32] Despite this more visible role in daily news coverage, female suicide bombers receive neither more time nor more frequent coverage than males, on average.

Thus, rather than increasing sympathy or aiming to increase sympathy for suicide bombers, this type of coverage tends to focus more on "exotic" cultural aspects. Segments involving female suicide bombers tend to mention personal details such as marital status or family trauma—almost exclusively asking why the woman was suicidal, while segments involving male bombers focus on military preparedness or links to major terrorist groups—almost exclusively asking who trained the man. While these personally traumatic stories about female suicide bombers are compelling for viewers, they do not help to increase knowledge of martyrdom operations and does not help to inform the policy discussion on suicide bombings. Such "exotic" coverage also obfuscates the reasons why *ordinary* people can be drawn to or support suicide attacks, leading to further misunderstanding of the phenomenon.

The only sympathetic coverage a suicide bomber received on CNN was through the airing of statement from Palestinian Council member Hannan Ashrawi. On February 28, 2002, Ashrawi expressed the idea that the suicide bomber is a pawn of bigger organizations, so s/he too is a victim, and "in his victimization" also victimizes innocent people. This is not an overly sympathetic statement, however, and it does not express any opinion that a suicide bomber's actions are "understandable."

After the criticism television media received for airing interviews with Usama bin Laden or statements from al-Qa`ida leaders in the wake of the September 11 attacks, U.S. news organizations' reluctance to publicize average radical Islamic video materials is understandable. If they vet the al-Qaʻida leaders' statements with clauses disavowing the materials' authenticity, they would almost never air films from typical fighters in Iraq. Airing fighters' materials would likely give militants more solidified military status in U.S. media by showing they are capable of carrying out coordinated attacks, as opposed to their current portrayal as small bands of untrained militants. This untrained-militant framing perpetuates the idea that U.S. troops are vastly superior to these militants in Iraq and Afghanistan.

CNN could and likely does, therefore, obtain many more videos than it airs; the fact that it rarely shows clips of insurgent videos represents an editorial choice on the part of CNN. CNN and other Western media outlets appear to air such videos when they meet standard news values such as timeliness, proximity, impact, and prominence; the most prominent other instances are in specialized, "feature" documentaries on militant groups, such as the CNN documentary "Terror on Tape." Likewise, although radical groups have videotaped some suicide bombings themselves and circulated such material widely on the Internet, CNN only rarely aired footage taken by terrorist groups *during* a suicide bombing (as opposed to footage of the aftermath of a bombing). In the wake of the December 2004 suicide bombing of a Coalition Forces mess hall in Mosul, Iraq,[33] CNN aired footage of the attack that showed the explosion shooting through the roof, recorded from a distance. This video material was aired only after strong statements warning that the veracity of the footage was unknown. In December 2005, an in-depth CNN study of insurgent use of "homemade bombs" aired two videos of suicide car bombings at security checkpoints, taken from the Web site Ogrish.com. No audio of the attack was played.[34]

Some journalists claim these warnings are necessary so they are not blamed for broadcasting radical messages. This is an idea that bin Laden himself has found humorous, but it is also extremely unlikely for objective reasons: Many martyrdom videos contain standard prepared texts and suras from the Qur'an, so U.S. media could air these segments without passing along coded messages or could air the footage in the background for visual effect without playing any of the audio (as BBC does—see below). Ideological reasoning—namely, that the U.S. news media should not help distribute these videos—is the reason for this refusal. Nonetheless, this decision makes the dialogue considerably more stilted and uninformed, based on a lack of understanding about both the nature of the enemy against which U.S. troops are fighting and about the technological capabilities of such groups.

So far we have shown that news reports on suicide bombings lack explanation as to why suicide bombings occur and why people choose to kill themselves to terrorize others. Both of these problems are issues that, as discussed throughout this book, paralyze decision- and policymakers addressing this topic. In addition to these problems, news reports contributed to the wide circulation of the idea that suicide bombings are impossible to prevent, stop, or contain. This entire book is an attempt to refute this idea, but the idea that suicide bombings are a tactic that is impossible to prevent or stop has been a salient feature of the media discussion of suicide bombing for years. On several occasions, CNN guests and news anchors have expressed this idea:

> Look, when you have fanatical young men who are prepared to commit suicide and they're strapping dynamite to themselves, there's very little you can do about it.[35]
>
> So a sense that if you have a suicide bomber, there's virtually nothing that can be done to protect against this? CNN Anchor Judy Woodruff.
>
> In a way that's absolutely true, provided they can get into Israel or if they were inside Jerusalem already, that's largely true, yes...But you're right, if the suicide bombers are determined to get through, then it's sure to do so.[36]
>
> Of course, it is a reminder that whatever the plan or process the White House envisions for the Middle East, someone or some group can and probably will try and stop it.[37] CNN Correspondent Jerrold Kessel

In addition to these telling quotes, an expert interviewed on May 7, 2002 essentially ceded all power in the negotiations to extreme groups performing suicide attacks: "There is a message here, and the message is extreme groups can derail even a minimal peace process." This adds heavily to an atmosphere of hopelessness and inertia so prominent in the U.S. media discussion of suicide bombing. BBC has employed similar language at times (see below).

Although the imagery of hopelessness dropped off after 2002, newscasters also began to refer to suicide bombings—especially Palestinian and, recently, in Iraq—as "more of the same."[38] CNN anchor Aaron Brown called the aftermath as a "familiar scene of destruction" on February 16, 2002. Similar statements were made about the long spate of insurgent suicide bombings in Iraq.[39] CNN and other mainstream news outlets rely heavily on official viewpoints, usually American experts or politicians, rather than an average Palestinian, Israeli, or Iraq citizen. Still, despite this, no significant statements were made by any U.S. leader or expert who said suicide bombing was possible to deal with from a policy standpoint. Most official and expert statements mimicked the widespread opinion that there is "nothing we can do" about suicide bombing. This hardly seems like the type of attitude officials would want to exhibit to their publics and the world about this phenomenon.

BBC Coverage of Suicide Bombings

While our analysis of BBC coverage is less extensive than that of U.S. network news, we chose to analyze BBC coverage of the following bombings in order to compare its content with that of CNN: August 8, 1998 (Kenya and Tanzania); October 12, 2002 (Indonesia); June 1, 2001 (Israel); August 19, 2003 (Iraq, Israel); and July 7, 2005 (United Kingdom). For each day, the main BBC1 evening news segments (9/10 p.m. 30-minute slots) were analyzed for consistency with the U.S. news samples. As we show below, the BBC coverage contains similar content-related mistakes that serve to disrupt productive policy debate on suicide attacks.

Like the U.S. media, the BBC did not refer to the Kenyan, Tanzanian, or Indonesian bombings as suicide bombings in the news segments we studied. (Given the initial lack of information about these bombings, it is likely that information was not yet publicly available.) Similar to CNN, which called the United States' record of prosecuting attackers "mixed," BBC was skeptical of then-president Bill Clinton's ability to punish those responsible: "The U.S. monitors groups it thinks are suspicious, but that doesn't mean it will be easy for Clinton to make good on his promise to punish those responsible," the anchor stated.[40]

These segments also offer no explanation—political or religious—for the bombings in Africa, which generally received less coverage than the other bombings studied. The Indonesian bombings received more significant coverage on BBC than they did in the United States because of the number of British (and Australian) tourists who were vacationing in Indonesia at the time. For the Indonesian bombings, many explanations were given: radical Islam, desire to establish a "Taliban lifestyle,"[41] that Bali was a Hindu island,[42] and to target tourists.[43]

The June 1, 2001 suicide bombing in Israel received no explanation. Unlike the U.S. coverage, which focused heavily on the details of how the suicide bomber killed youth outside a nightclub, the BBC coverage focused almost entirely on political mechanations, saying "Islamic extremists say they have more suicide bombers ready to strike" and the Israeli public wants their "government to strike back, hard."[44] Similarly, for the August 19, 2003 suicide bombing in Israel the only explanation was that it was Hamas extremism.[45]

On the same day, the U.N. building in Baghdad, Iraq, was bombed, and BBC again offered only assumed political explanations. On the first day, an anchor called it a "deliberate assassination" and showed a U.S. coalition adviser saying that the bombing was done by "people who don't want this to succeed."[46] The second day's explanations were similar: that it was done by people attempting to get "world attention," cause devastation and doubt in the coalition—one person interviewed said, "It causes the world to wonder, I'm sure, my gosh, is Iraq so unsafe?"[47]

Like with the September 11 attacks in the United States, the July 7, 2005 attacks in London dominated the news coverage for days, so several hours of coverage were examined. Previous footage of suicide bombings had not discussed whether suicide attacks could be prevented, but the July 7 news repeatedly implied the attacks had been "inevitable." A newscaster called them "not just inevitable but predicted," and in an interview asked Member of Parliament Charles Clarke, "Realistically, it's almost impossible to stop this kind of attack in a society like ours, isn't it?" Unlike U.S. politicians and experts, who stated that these attacks *are* impossible to prevent,[48] Clarke had a vaguer but hopeful answer: "If we're an open society, and I think it's an important part of our democracy that we are an open society, people can exploit that. But we try and protect ourselves in a variety of ways, sometimes publicly controversial ways, and I think that's what we have to try and continue to do."[49] The July 7 coverage also included another anomaly, in contrast to the lack of direct militant statements aired in evening news, that day's news featured a direct quotation from the Egyptian cleric al-Qaradawi justifying suicide bombings: "It's not suicide, it's martyrdom in the name of God," the quote dubbed over a video said.[50]

Unlike its U.S. counterparts, BBC has editorial guides publicly available on its Web site, and these guidelines have recently been both criticized and praised widely for their mandate to avoid the word "terrorism":

> The word "terrorist" itself can be a barrier rather than an aid to understanding. We should try to avoid the term, without attribution. ...We should use words which specifically describe the perpetrator such as "bomber," "attacker," "gunman," "kidnapper," "insurgent," and "militant." Our responsibility is to remain objective and report in ways that enable our audiences to make their own assessments about who is doing what to whom.[51]

These editorial guidelines were adopted in June 2005, a little over a week before their first major test—the July 7 London bombings. (The term "terrorist" was somewhat pervasive in its pre-2005 coverage.) Regardless of the merit of avoiding the word "terrorist," BBC's July 7 bombing coverage proved that adhering to that standard is extremely difficult. The news organization responded to reports that it had removed the word "terrorist" from news stories about the bombings. BBC chairman Michael Grade said that "the word terrorist was not banned and that it was up to individual editors to decide when and where to use it." Furthermore, he said the bombers were terrorists and that "the BBC's coverage has used the word(s) 'terror', 'terrorism', 'terrorist' very, very freely."[52] In the three days' evening news coverage we studied (totaling three hours), the words "terror," "terrorize," "terrorist," or "terrorism" were used by correspondents and anchors three times and quoted directly or indirectly five times.

Finally, the BBC relied extremely heavily on a single "terrorism expert," M.J. Gohel, for its analysis, like CNN and NBC tended to do. This is a common flaw in Western newsgathering because of journalists' need to have experts whom they can call in a time crunch (which they obviously have because they repeatedly go to the same experts), but also because of the imperative to get a variety of opinions (which they usually failed in doing, according to our findings). Gohel's opinions always attempted to discuss al-Qa`ida and attempted to make an al-Qa`ida connection, even when it was tenuous: "A lot of these groups are actually autonomous and they have semi-autonomous cells themselves. The way they're linked to the al-Qa`ida network is that they all share a common philosophy and that philosophy is to create a Taliban-style lifestyle for the entire world."[53] Constantly quoting from such experts is inflammatory and potentially irresponsible reporting, especially because there is some evidence that the Bali bombings were not carried out by al-Qa`ida; the overemphasis on al-Qa`ida is a barrier to truly understanding militant organizations.

Implications for the United States

The question of what is interesting to a television audience and what is useful for informing the public is the quintessential one in discussing media's influence on the political discourse. The evolution toward "infotainment," with its increasingly brief sound bytes and emphasis on visual material contrasting with "hard news," has put journalists in a "quasi-symbiotic relationship" with terrorists, some experts claim, by driving them further and further in pursuit of drama, tragedy, and panic.[54] This is an overly harsh criticism: The specter of suicide bombing looms large on Americans' television screens and in American news, but that specter is not well-understood or well-explained. American media has not been sympathetic to terrorist goals—indeed, it has refused to use suicide bombers' own words in explaining their goals, relying on American experts and politicans instead, potentially to the detriment of public understanding of militant organiztaions. And, like most media in the world, U.S. and British media rely heavily on official go-betweens, rather than on original-source material. When quoting from martyrdom operation leaders, the only statements mentioned are exclusively those of the highest powers of the operations, rather than individual suicide bombers' wills or statements.

As media coverage is now, suicide-bombing coverage generally tends to depersonalize the attackers by blocking their statements and wills, which could help to shore up support for the American "War on Terror." Up to this point, existing research has ignored "the institutional power derived from responding to terrorism and the degree to which the dominant ideology is reflected and reconstructed in news coverage of terrorism."[55] The impact of depersonalized and hierarchically oriented news coverage on perceptions of the enemy in the "War on Terror" is a topic that should be explored further.

Furthermore, this tendency represents either a misunderstanding of the nature of suicide-bombing organizations or an attempt to make these organizations appear more hierarchical—to make them seem more like an organized military than an array of small, loosely organized cells. Some experts on media coverage of terrorism have also noted the American media's tendency to focus on technologically advanced terrorist threats—weapons of mass destruction and nuclear proliferation, for instance—and while these issues are important, a more subtle threat to Americans and Europeans comes from these disorganized groups of suicide bombers, who craft their weapons from basic materials available anywhere.[56] Suicide-bombing organizations have various organizational makeups, depending on where they operate and whose organization they are from, but none of them are organized in top-down military structures. The difference between leaders and attackers in militant organizations will be discussed in the following chapter, but overall, American news' emphasis on higher-ups in militant organizations is misleading. On one hand, excessive use of individual wills and statements might increase sympathy for bombers and could personalize bombers. On the other hand, without these statements, the organizations' disorganized, cell structure is obfuscated for American viewers, who come to perceive Al-Qa`ida as a military organization such as the army, with Usama Bin Laden as a general, ordering all terrorist attacks in the world.

The fact that traumatic images or facts of terrorist attacks are reaching American viewers is unquestionable. This does not, however, mean the media is symbiotically working with suicide bombers, and it does not mean that CNN's coverage increases sympathy for suicide bombers. As mentioned in the previous chapter, this divide between what terrorists say and how they are presented on the media is wide; it is wide in the Arab media and far wider in U.S. and British media. The proliferation of Internet technologies discussed in the previous chapter is a result of this divide, complicating the ability to research the relationship between militant leaders and attackers.

Overall, the U.S. media has largely supported official depictions of the War on Terror (by focusing on technologically advanced weapons and relaying official views of organizational structures, rather than emphasizing the flexibility of the cell structure). On the other hand, while Western media *quoted* sources draw heavily from official statements, politicians' statements are rarely accompanied by pictures. Visually jarring imagery of suicide bombing thwarts official claims that the world is getting safer; the best footage results from action, and in action, terrorist organizations have the upper hand. By contrast, counterterrorist efforts are secret and classified and frequently span months or years, and counterterrorist "victories" are alluded to but rarely detailed for the public (with some notable exceptions such as the Miami-Chicago group arrested in June 2006, the British liquid explosive plot detected in August 2006, Moussaoui, etc.). Counterterrorism's successes may be secret, but its failures are vivid, bloody, and seemingly ubiquitous. Officials have done too little to make statements about successful counterterrorist activities, so to a television-news viewer, terrorist attacks appear more successful than official counterterrorist activity.

Several officials' statements have even described suicide bombing attacks as having been "successful" (e.g., the Jerusalem attack of August 9, 2001). To overcome such defeatism, officials should avoid applying words such as "success" to their enemies—at least when making public statements. This hopeless defeatism, and other similarly damaging mistakes discussed in the next chapter, should be corrected, if the United States is to defeat the tactic of suicide bombing.

Chapter 8

Correcting the Suicide-Bombing Discourse

*The enemy can be patient, but not for a lengthy time. But we
with our faith and creed and desire to meet Allah can
be patient for a lengthy time until the enemy collapses,
even if that takes decades or generations. We are obligated
to fight them—whether to victory or to martyrdom.*

—The Abu Hafs al-Masri Brigades[1]

No single study of suicide bombing has proposed a compelling model for evaluating those suicide bombings most likely to affect the West and especially the United States. Existing studies have failed to combat the misperceptions in the policy debate, and they have failed to formulate a compelling model that combines organizational and personal motivations for suicide attacks with explanations for why suicide bombings are used and religiously justified in some conflicts and not others. This chapter addresses these deficiencies in the policy debate by formulating models for understanding what conflicts are likely to produce suicide bombers (especially bombers bent on attacking Western targets).

Before describing our model for understanding suicide bombings, some important misperceptions about suicide bombing that hamper the debate should be discussed. The most important incorrect assumptions about suicide bombings and suicide bombers are:

1. Suicide bombers are poor and/or have no hope and no other choice;
2. Most suicide bombers are not religious;
3. The ideology of suicide bombing has not spread everywhere and can be stopped; and
4. The specter of suicide bombing is monolithic and is the same in every place and in every conflict.

First, the poverty explanation for suicide bombings is flawed. From initial discussion of Palestinian suicide bombing, and the images of Palestinians living in poverty and displaced from their homes broadcast, this explanation may have got a long-lasting foothold in discussing legitimacy of suicide bombings in this conflict. Academic publications on suicide bombing have roundly critiqued this thesis, showing that suicide bombers are not usually in the lower classes of their nations or societies.[2] Furthermore, the countries that have produced the most suicide bombers are not the poorest countries in their regions. Even in the Palestinian conflict, the explanation does not stand up to data on suicide bombers' economic backgrounds.

Somehow, though, the idea still abounds in media reports and policy recommendations that suicide bombing is something that can be limited first and foremost by alleviating poverty within a given country or region. This is something propagated continually by various organizations. The European Union's main Web site states, "Although political grievance can be a more immediate motivator for terrorists, poverty can contribute to radicalisation as young men—and increasingly women—lose hope in their future."[3] Similarly, the Association of Southeast Asian Nations (ASEAN), which has made many statements about counterterrorism, declares in several places that fighting the "root causes" of terrorism (i.e., poverty, economic development, education, and human security issues) is a central way to stop terrorist organizations.[4] While bodies such as the EU and ASEAN have also pursued more concrete methods of fighting terrorism—financial and security cooperation, namely—their statements prove the poverty explanation still holds a prominent place in the antiterrorism dialogue.

Debra Zedalis wrote in a book about Palestinian female suicide bombers that suicide bombing is "abnormal," and if normal conditions returned to a society, the suicide bombings would stop.[5] What defines "normal" conditions and how to make normal conditions return are topics that the author does not discuss. In the same way, methods for distributing international aid in such a way that it would reach potential suicide bombers are rarely detailed. A large number of suicide bombers in Iraq are from Saudi Arabia or Morocco, which are definitely not their respective regions' poorest or least-developed countries.[6] Indeed, because suicide-attack recruits do not come from the poorest countries, international aid designed to specifically combat suicide attacks would require reallocation of aid from those poorest countries to countries that may not be interested in American aid organizations opening within their borders. (Saudi Arabia and Syria are paradigmatic examples.) The EU Web site cited above, written in response to the Madrid bombings, names international humanitarian aid as an important counterterrorism component, but the site has no specific instructions on distribution or how it would have prevented those bombings.[7]

Suicide bombing has proven to appeal increasingly to Western converts, a group that international humanitarian aid is unlikely to reach. On the other hand, factors such as poor job prospects, low education levels, and unemployment in some cases contribute to the appeal of militant Islam, as cited by studies of U.K. converts.[8] These socioeconomic factors explain why, seeking a stronger sense of belonging, some people turn to militant Islam or volunteer for suicide operations; nonetheless, unemployment or low education levels of certain groups does not provide a coherent explanation of suicide attacks in general.

More important than individual or collective economic difficulty is perceived victimization—whether actual or mythologized—which is discussed extensively in chapter 1. "Perceived victimization" refers to discursive tendencies that accuse the West of occupations, wars, and economic exploitation—sometimes with factual and logical backing, sometimes using the conspiracy theories so pervasive in many Muslim countries.[9] Victimization narratives have great social and political force in much of the developing world and within Muslim leaders' teachings. Palestinian suicide bombers, for instance, often say in their wills that they have nothing but their bodies or lives as weapons, thereby "justifying" their actions. Rationalizations of suicide bombings against U.S. military targets elsewhere cite the inability to fight American occupations with conventional weapons because of the United States' superior military might or military oppression. Another example of the internalization of perceived victimization is the communal nature of Mohammad Siddique Khan's statement, released after his carrying out the July 7 London bombings. In this statement, he frequently refers to the "subjugation of 'my people' and 'my Muslim brothers and sisters' as being principle amongst his grievances."[10] In the Palestinian and Chechen conflicts, personal victimization has performed a similar function—as in the case of the Chechen Black Widow suicide bombers (women whose husbands have been killed by Russians).

Contrary to the second misperception, attackers carrying out suicide bombings against the West have been usually religiously motivated. Unfortunately, large portions of political analysis spend significant time and effort trying to make suicide bombing less religious: Some say that suicide bombers are not religious because suicide-bombing campaigns are organized through secular organizations. This may be arguably true for suicide attacks before September 11, 2001, but it is no longer factual, useful, or true. Other analysts say suicide bombers are not religious because they are motivated by political struggle—often against an occupation. In this case, the combination of the religious and the political in justifying suicide attacks does not eliminate the importance of religion, as many have argued, but it rather underscores religiosity's importance in these conflicts. Leaders, whether religious or cynical, appeal to recruits and followers by justifying these actions with a higher law (a religious law), and these justifications themselves—prevalant in the Muslim world—must be considered and dealt with in devising a policy for dealing with these attacks.

Militant operations utilize a hierarchical motivational structure, as we will discuss in greater detail below. The motivation for a person *organizing* suicide bombings may be more political than religious (i.e., to gain support for his operation, to gain territory from occupiers, etc.), but an individual suicide bomber often relies on a religious or, at least, cultural guarantee of immortality. Where suicide itself is explicitly forbidden by the religious doctrine, permissive attitudes toward suicide bombing are not an act of rejection of the religion but a manipulation of religious norms. In order to actively kill oneself in a political or religious cause, the suicide attacker must believe his/her sacrifice will be honored after death, and for this reason, martyrs are given socioreligious guarantees of a place in heaven or rewards after death.[11] Discussions of altruistic suicide partially describe this phenomenon—the suicide bomber believes s/he is helping the community,[12] and in most places suicide bombers produce martyrdom statements or wills to perpetuate the impact of their deed. These will help to motivate a new generation of recruits and solicit popular legitimization of the suicide attacks.

More concretely, data on attackers' religiosity has been stated differently in different sources. Pape found that only 43 percent of Palestinian suicide attackers for whom data is available between 1980 and 2003 were religious.[13] Other analyses of suicide bombers' backgrounds, however, had different results: One study found that Palestinian suicide-bombers were "far more likely to have received a religious education (over 82 percent versus slightly more than 36 percent for conventional terrorists)."[14] Depending on the data used, the source of the data, and the indicator, obviously these numbers can vary widely. Therefore, we will not attempt to add another number into the mix but will instead stop at highlighting the problematic nature of such statistics when attempting to *disprove* the religiosity of something that is otherwise cloaked in heavily religious terminology and characteristics.

As we pointed out in chapter 3, none of the Palestinian suicide bombers are Christian (although there were Christian suicide attackers in Lebanon against the United States and Israel in the 1980s), and most of the martyrologies appeal to Muslims by using Qur'anic verses. Chechen martyrologies also use Qur'anic verses, even though (as stated in chapter 3) their statements are far less religious than those eminating from other conflicts. Therefore, the argument that Palestinian or other suicide attackers are not motivated by or attune to religious justifications is not a compelling one, if for no other reason than that religion is so often cited in the literature on suicide bombing.

Emphasizing the importance of religion does not mean implying that the phenomenon of suicide bombing is exclusive to one religion or that all Muslims are potential suicide attackers simply because some Muslims perform suicide bombings. This book does not seek to take a "clash of civilizations" view—the view that these attacks and behaviors are exclusively culturally based.[15] We do, however, emphasize that suicide bombing has thus far required a strong belief system and a presupposed acceptance by a community and/or a god because of the attack's deliberate nature and finality. Too many academic studies of suicide bombing ignore or attempt to deflect this issue. The martyrdom-glorification culture, because it is most open to manipulation by martyrdom-operation leaders, could be important in addressing through policies, which will be discussed in the following chapter. The more common the acceptance of suicide bombing as a political or religious action, the less it will require such a martyrdom culture and at that point, the phenomenon of suicide bombing will be far more difficult to stop because there will be no ideological basis on which to fight. It is important to deal with this phenomenon now, before it reaches this point.

A third misperception frequently stated in policy recommendations is that the United States and Europe, through public diplomacy or ideology, can stop the spread of the suicide-bombing idea. The idea that suicide bombers could be martyrs is diffuse throughout the world, and no U.S. public diplomacy tactic is going to stop the spread of the idea. People all over the world—particularly in Muslim countries—have heard about suicide bombings in the Israeli-Palestinian conflict, in Iraq, in Chechnya, and elsewhere. People around the world have heard these bombers called "martyrs," whether the audience agrees with this or not. The United States cannot stop this potential message from being spread. No amount of public diplomacy can counter statements objecting to foreign presence on Iraqi soil, not to mention United States' political dealings with other Middle Eastern, Arab, and African countries. These are, as scholars such as Pape mention, not just "ideas" that can be explained away through official statements.

On the other hand, although many radical Muslim statements object specifically to U.S. military presence on the Arabian Peninsula and specifically in Saudi Arabia, viewed as an occupation of land surrounding Mecca (which Muhammad forbade[16]), attacks have continued past the U.S. troop redeployment from Saudi Arabia to Qatar in August 2003.[17] For radical Muslims, the term "occupation" can be applied to any foreign presence in the Middle East, and specifically the Arabian Peninsula, so foreigners left in the region after the troop redeployment are considered "legitimate" targets. The reality is that there are and will probably continue to be foreigners in these places, so the ideology of fighting such troop presences may not be possible to stop. In other words, "legitimate" targets (by radical Muslim definition) will continue to exist in the region, almost regardless of what the United States does. The only solution, then, is to confront the religious and social nature of the justifications given for these suicide bombings, as we suggest below and in chapter 9, rather than hoping that small appeasements will nullify the justifications for attacks, or hoping that the these justifications can be contained.

A final misperception lies in the U.S. political establishment's tendency to explain all suicide bombings in the same way. Although it may be expedient in the short term to call any suicide bombing not related to a territorial occupation an al-Qa`ida-orchestrated attack, as Pape does, this is not necessarily accurate. Chapter 4 details operations that we view to be organized by al-Qa`ida, but suicide attacks in Indonesia and Morocco, and some of the attacks in Afghanistan and Pakistan, are likely not al-Qa`ida-organized. Some of these may have been perpetrated by groups affiliated with al-Qa`ida, but as stated above, we have found that al-Qa`ida plans major, paradigmatic operations, as opposed to smaller, national-scale operations.

Many different groups and different people can use suicide bombing for a variety of reasons. Suicide bombings are not exclusively international nor exclusively nationalistic; they are not always internally organized or always externally planned. There are suicide bombings that fall into each of these categories, and ignoring the roots of suicide bombings organized within a country is as dangerous as ignoring steps leading up to an international suicide attack. Some reports have stressed the importance of such a division, which is especially important when referring to suicide bombings in Uzbekistan, Indonesia, Morocco, and Pakistan. The use of the tactic itself does not necessarily imply al-Qa`ida's role in the planning, and dynamics of individual conflicts must be examined. Even in places where outside fighters have come to wage war, local grievances give them the mobilization power and legitimacy they could not have simply relying on their globalist Islamic worldview. About Indonesian Mujahidin networks, the International Crisis Group report wrote:

> Until now, attention to Maluku and Poso in the context of Indonesian terrorism has focused on the degree to which jihadist groups such as JI [Jama`a Islamiyya] were able to exploit anger generated by attacks on Muslims to promote their own agenda. But an equally important dynamic is the degree to which outside fighters adopted local agendas as their own and helped plan and implement attacks which make little sense in the context of international terrorism but much more as responses to local grievances.[18]

In other words, in Indonesia, the local grievances played a dual role—at first, they were "exploited" by jihadist groups, but eventually local grievances became primary concerns in planning attacks at a local level, thereby dominating the jihad agenda. National and local motivations are also important in the 2004 Uzbekistan suicide bombings, discussed in chapter 5. The targets in those attacks were far more "local" in nature (i.e., policemen—symbols of local corruption) than international. In these conflicts, even if international Muslim groups are promoting the suicide-bombing tactic, the enabling factor is not only a strong base of militant Islamic leadership but also localized anger and dangerous political radicalization.

The tendency of U.S. policymakers to group all "terror threats" together as being the same impedes intelligent and productive thought on these problems. Suicide bombers, for instance, emerge because of complex factors, and often because of local grievances as much as international goals. Because of the problems associated with drafting appropriate counterterror measures dealing with the vast array of local conflicts, from which an attacker may appear, policymakers have instead focused on major international/transnational threats, such as al-Qaida. While international financing of major organizations and cross-border migration for terrorist purposes are major problems, many potential suicide-attack threats will be locally based and locally motivated in the future and therefore cannot be stopped by these technical measures.

Up to this point, we have critiqued other academics' models of suicide-attack analysis, but the remainder of this book is aimed at proposing our own models and suggestions. In order to rectify the misconceptions laid out earlier in this chapter, and in order to compose working policy recommendations, we propose models for addressing threats leading to suicide-attacks, first within Western countries and second from conflicts in the Muslim world where instability causes some to turn to violent anti-U.S. action. First, we discuss potential external sources of suicide attackers. Examples exist of both successful and unsuccessful suicide-attack campaigns in the Muslim world, and the success of suicide attacks in local conflicts shores up global support for the tactic of suicide attacks in general. We discuss these with the goal of formulating policy recommendations to minimize "successful" attacks and thus reduce the numbers of people opting to carry out such attacks. Next, we discuss an internal threat—the phenomena of radical conversion and religious intensification, acknowledging that suicide attackers targeting targets on U.S. and European soil are most likely to come from within our societies. From there, we propose a hierarchical model of organizations' and attackers' motivations for carrying out suicide attacks—a model that is true for all militant organizations employing suicide attacks, locally and internationally—and the as-yet-unused possibilities for countering justification of suicide attacks using this model.

Successful and Unsuccessful Bombings

If, as we are arguing, a central problem for policymakers in dealing with suicide attacks is dealing with the ideology and legitimization of suicide attacks, then local conflicts, in which suicide attacks are viewed as successful, are as important for dealing with this ideology as international ones.

Suicide bombings do not occur in all conflicts, as we have shown in previous chapters, and not all organizations want to or are able to carry out long suicide-bombing campaigns. In evaluating why groups continue carrying out these attacks—or why they begin them—it is necessary to understand the idea of a "successful attack." Drafting a policy to stop the spread of suicide bombings is intimately related to finding a way to curb the perceived success of these early attacks. In examining past conflicts producing suicide bombings, we found that if an initial attack does not achieve the intended goal, the likelihood of a second attack drops dramatically (e.g., attacks in Morocco and Bangladesh[19]). To examine this, it is first necessary to quantify which conflicts and situations are likely to produce suicide bombings and then to determine how potential audiences and organizers evaluate the "success" of a suicide bombing—for the more "successful" campaigns there are, the more suicide attacks will be accepted on the basis of strategic necessity and political justification.

Pape argued that suicide bombings have been used most often and effectively against democracies occupying other countries, and when the occupations have a religious difference (i.e., the Israeli occupation of Palestinian territories, Russian-Chechen war, and U.S. troop presence in the Middle East, especially Iraq). We found this to be generally true for those suicide-bombing campaigns strictly based on an occupation, and these are the suicide-bombing campaigns most likely to be successful because, as Pape notes, they have a strategic logic.

By overlooking sectarian-religious and local-political suicide bombings, however, this theory misses a huge component of global anti-Western suicide bombing. Pakistan, Algeria, Indonesia, Egypt, Morocco, Uzbekistan, and possibly Sudan have all had local-political or religious-sectarian suicide bombings. There are two questions that arise in studying these locally motivated suicide bombings: First, why have these countries had such suicide bombings and not other countries with similar conflicts? Second, why do suicide bombings take different trajectories in different countries after—either producing long strings of suicide bombings or not? That is, why haven't there been more suicide bombings in Morocco or Algeria, whereas Egypt and Pakistan have had numerous instances, and Indonesia and Uzbekistan have experienced only a few highly coordinated attacks?

We found that if occupation-related suicide bombings are effective against democratic governments, then suicide bombings about local or national grievances are usually carried out in nondemocratic or dictatorial states (with varying levels of success). These attacks are generally against other civilians (Pakistan), a political rival (Sudan, Somalia) or a government that is perceived as stifling radical Muslims (Uzbekistan, Egypt, Morocco, Algeria, Bangladesh). These are no less important than "al-Qa`ida attacks," particularly because the use of suicide bombing has now spread far outside the exclusive realm of the few major groups well-known in the West, such as Hamas and al-Qa`ida. While U.S. policymakers are often willing or eager to dismiss these suicide bombings as unrelated because these are not directed against Western targets, it is the very fact of legitimizing suicide bombings in general we should hope to contain, and to do this, all local-religious antecedents should be taken into consideration.

The umbrella term "nondemocratic or dictatorial" is, of course, difficult to quantify and somewhat relative, and it includes a great many countries. Many, or most, of these "nondemocratic or dictatorial" governments have yet to face such an attack. On one hand, this means that this model's net is still cast too wide for prediction of future suicide bombings; on the other hand, this means many countries that have not yet experienced such an attack may face one in the future.

From our observation, we believe that, within the subgroup of dictatorial countries, suicide bombing is most likely to occur in those nondemocratic countries where individual citizens perceive themselves as having low prospects for change. Revolutionary or critical groups attempting to change the political institutions are attractive in these countries. When these revolutionary groups fail, citizens usually face mass arrests and harsh governmental crackdowns. (This has been true in all the above mentioned countries; even China has faced several suicide bombings related to citizen despair.[20]) At that point, citizens will believe they cannot change their situation by nonviolent means, and thus they are likely to be open to using extremely violent or self-sacrificial means. Those imprisoned may become more radicalized while in prisons, not only because of the outrage of being arrested for religious beliefs but also because such prisons house other like-minded, radical Muslims. For example, a 2004 Human Rights Watch report on Uzbekistan cited jailed Muslims' increased fervor as a primary consequence of the religious crackdown instigated by Uzbekistani president Islam Karimov, especially because radical ideologies were spreading fastest in prisons.[21] Many countries, including Egypt and Saudi Arabia, arrest radical Muslims regularly, which means prisons may be the easiest place to meet radical Muslims. (This is true closer to home, as well: One foiled attack on Los Angeles, detected in 2005, was planned at least partially by inmates of a U.S. prison.[22]) For those left on the outside of prisons, desperation may prompt them to also resort to drastic antistate measures, due to a feeling that they have nothing else to lose. But whether these desperate suicide bombings turn into lengthy campaigns depends on how successful the organizers view their first attempt(s) to have been.

In many locally motivated conflicts (more than in international conflicts), body counts do not define the success of a suicide attack. Suicide bombers, rather than attacking mass numbers of civilians and aiming for mass casualties, sometimes target symbols or citizens of their home country. Generally, when a group organizes a suicide bombing, the suicide bombing must have a clearly symbolic target and be accepted within the group's constituency. Some radical Indonesian Muslims too have accepted the Bali bombings as legitimate—and the targets have been highly symbolic, focusing on tourists, as in the numerous suicide bombings in markets and resorts in Egypt. These attacks, focusing on tourists, are usually accepted as "successful" only if they do not kill large numbers of local Muslims.[23] Uzbekistan's suicide bombings in April 2004 targeted police—viewed as instruments of oppression in the harsh political culture—and therefore had widespread grassroots support; these attacks have been chalked up to radical Islam by official narratives, but a political explanation may be equally compelling.[24]

Especially in countries where the majority of the population is Muslim, the number of casualties may actually detract from the main measure of success for an attack: Whether the home population accepts the attack's legitimacy, whether the attack's organizers are able to create positive publicity to capitalize on the attack, and whether the organizers remain able to carry out further attacks. Regarding the first characteristic, as stated in chapters 4 and 5, and in other places,[25] one of the major reasons radical Muslim groups fighting Arab governments in the 1990s failed was because of the mass Muslim casualties caused by the fighting. On the other hand, there are some suicide-bombing campaigns that have specifically targeted mass civilian casualties, like the sectarian conflicts in Iraq and Pakistan. Still, even when aiming for mass casualties, the targets tend to be symbolic, usually either an "other" figure or a governmental figure. Some Pakistani Sunni groups condone sectarian attacks on Shi'ite mosques because they view Shi'ites as infidels. All of these indicators are components of the measures of success, stated above.

The methods for achieving the second characteristic of a "successful" attack—publicity—are addressed in chapter 6. But simply because an organization runs heavy publicity campaigns to attempt to legitimize their attacks does not mean the population will accept them; examples in which the population has dismissed the legitimacy of the attack include Jordan and, to some extent, Morocco. The third component—the organizers' own ability to produce another attack—also fell short in Morocco, where the planners died in the attack and therefore would be unable to perform further attacks. This is increasingly true for those suicide attackers who volunteer for attacks without clear organizational recruiting or encouragement. The fact that the acceptance of these attacks has become so widespread in militant radical Muslim circles means that predicting whether a "suicide campaign" will continue or not has become harder, and will continue to get more difficult. Indeed, in some contemporary cases, including Iraq but also including European recruits, "suicide campaigns" no longer exist, with individuals planning their own attacks. [26]

It may appear that these suicide-bombing campaigns with local motivations are irrelevant to U.S. and European policy interests, but Western policymakers should note the tendency of local conflicts to escalate or of organizations' desire to target foreigners in order to draw attention to their cause. The processes of legitimization of suicide attacks—whether in local or international conflicts—are the same, and, as stated above, it is the legitimization itself that is dangerous for the West. Past experience has proven that when fewer people accept these attacks, societies will be more likely to report plans of such attacks to authorities, as has been the case in Morocco since the 2003 bombings there.[27] Therefore, reducing local complicity in and acceptance of such attacks is crucial to stopping transnational threats.

Converts and Religious Intensification

As stated in chapter 5, there are two large groups of people who pose the most serious threat as potential attackers, and they can be found anywhere: (1) recent converts, and (2) Muslims (especially those living in the West) who have suddenly taken an interest in militant jihad. It should be noted again that a vast majority of Western converts to Islam convert through Sufism, and not through radical Islam, so the statements in this section do not apply to *all* converts to Islam—indeed, they apply only to a small number of converts. For the most part, members of these groups are the most likely potential suicide attackers from within Western societies. Their absorbtion of and perception of Muslim humiliation or anti-Muslim racism can mix rapidly with circulating radical Muslim ideology to create the threat of difficult-to-detect, spontaneous attacks in Europe and the United States—as they have, indeed, already done.

Not all converts to Islam, and not even all converts to radical Islam, are likely suicide bombers; indeed, very few are drawn to violent, anti-Western action. Similarly, many Muslims who experience an intensified interest in their religion do not become violent. Akil Awan, studying British Muslim converts, theorizes that it is not simply converts or Muslims who intensify or change their religious practices who are the problem. Awan found that many of the British Muslims involved in militant organizations had transition/intensification experiences resulting in what he calls "contextual disjuncture"—that is, a break with their previous life and often even their families.

Most of the European converts to Islam who have been involved in potential or actual suicide attacks have fit the "contextual disjuncture" formulation.[28] Muriel Degauque, the Belgian suicide bomber who attacked a U.S. convoy in Iraq, had been involved with drugs and had had a tumultuous love life before she met an Algerian man and began to drift into radical Islam.[29] Although at the time of writing there was little information on the three British converts allegedly involved in the liquid-explosive plot foiled in the United Kingdom, at least one of them was described as forging a kind of "break" with his past life: Ibrahim (Oliver) Savant was described as "increasingly isolated from his neighbors" as he became more religious.[30] The July 7, 2005 bomber Abdullah Shaheed Jamal (Germaine Lindsay) was reported to have had "confrontations" with his preconversion friends.[31]

Richard Reid (the "shoe bomber" apprehended in December 2001) converted to Islam while in prison for a string of muggings, and upon release was eventually drawn to a more militant mosque. He reportedly went to Pakistan in 1998 and communicated with friends in Arabic but lost contact with his mother, according to a BBC article: "He reportedly sent several letters written in Arabic to friends in London...But mother and son eventually lost contact and in summer 2001 Ms. Hughes telephoned Brixton Mosque seeking news."[32] In Russia, two ethnic Russian females who considered suicide bombings to help the Chechens said they were attracted to Chechens' "pride" and "courage," qualities they did not see Russians as having. These females, in an interview, stated that they abandoned relationships with their families in favor of newfound Chechen friends.[33] The Russian/Ossetian involved in the 2004 Beslan hostage crisis, Abdullah (Vladimir) Khodov, was in prison for a murder when he converted to Islam (and his brother converted a short time later) and following that experienced increasing estrangement from his family. He was later accused of rape and virtually disappeared, only reappearing to take his brother's body from a Christian funeral and bury it in Muslim style.[34] There have been other ethnic Russian Muslim converts involved in suicide attacks, such as Sergey Dmitriev and Aleksandr Alekseev (June 2000 attack in Grozny, Chechnya)[35] and Pavel Kosolapov, but little information about these figures are available in either Russian or in English.

There is a clear difference between radically changing a lifestyle—especially one marred by crime, hopelessness, or substance abuse—through religion, and rejecting one's family, friends, and all neighbors. This distinction is vital to forming a model of "dangerous" conversion patterns. Of the two other Briton plotters in the liquid-explosive plot—Abdul Waheed (Don Stewart-Whyte) and Umar Islam (Brian Young)—the latter is reported to have "turned his back on a life of drink and drugs when he converted."[36] The British press, in the aftermath of the discovery of the plot, did not attempt to prove what those arrested had become but instead overwhelmingly described their clothes and beards. These characteristics (growing beards and quitting alcohol or drugs) do *not necessarily* indicate terrorists-in-the-making, and we have no intention of implying that.

Defining policy recommendations based on this information, therefore, is a difficult task because a government cannot simply monitor all Muslims with an intensified religious fervor; we do not advocate racial or religious profiling. Casting such a wide net would violate numerous civil rights and freedom of expression principles, not to mention the massive amounts of data it would produce. There may be some way to predict, for instance, which Muslims with interests in jihad are most susceptible to the perceived humiliation of their ethnic or religious groups, but currently just identifying those Muslims with renewed interest in their religion is not a sustainable policy. It would be foolish to propose to monitor all Muslims with intensified religious interests to see if they have broken with their previous lifestyle; such a suggestion is dangerous and insulting to Muslims, as well as impossible to carry out. An obvious point of observation is that there are a few known radical mosques that do attract these types of Muslim converts, those who regularly attend these types of mosques are more likely to be attracted to violent action promoted by leaders in such a mosque than those who attend irregularly. But, again, proposing a policy based on this obvious observation is problematic because the most radical figures are likely to be aware that such mosques are being monitored and will likely avoid these mosques. In addition, because of the Internet-as-*madrasa* problem explored in chapter 6 (that the Internet may now serve as a more important training site for radical Muslims than does a radical mosque), it is unclear whether radicalized converts are associating heavily with people at mosques for ideological purposes. At this point, the ideology is so widespread, especially on the Internet, there may be no reason to risk association with a radical mosque. Most signs in the U.K. liquid-explosive plot foiled in August 2006 indicate the plotters did not attend the same mosque.[37] Richard Reid, traveling for years around the Muslim world, did not have strong mosque-based ties but instead corresponded with European supporters using email.[38]

There are converts and religiously reinvigorated Muslims all over the world, and very few of them are dangerous. But so far, these groups have produced the suicide attackers *inside* Western countries—their familiarity with both Western lifestyles and Muslims' feelings of humiliation have proved lethal especially in the London and Spain attacks, although Mussaoui also fit the patterns outlined in this section. In terms of external threats, national and transnational conflicts that have already produced one or more suicide bombings, or that are likely to produce suicide attacks, should also be analyzed. We can use some of these as examples to learn which societies around the world are potentially vulnerable to suicide attacks and propose some ways to deal with this specific type of attack.

Motivation Model

Our top-down motivation model is designed to contrast the goals of organizers with those of individual bombers. For leaders of militant organizations, goals are most often religious (i.e., establishing the caliphate), national or global aspirations (territorial aspirations, world order change), and strategic issues. These are the reasons most often stated in statements and press releases because organizations—not individuals—release these materials; therefore, these are the ones most likely to be cited in analyses.

The organizational goals are those discussed in earlier chapters. In general, for al-Qa`ida, the establishment of a caliphate, as discussed in chapter 3, is the major institutional-organizational goal. For Palestinian organizations,

Motivations of Attack Organizers and Bombers

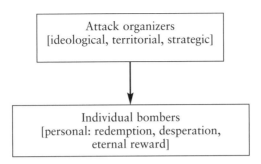

there are nationalistic goals, such as the destruction of the state of Israel. Al-Qa`ida and Iraqi suicide bombing groups—and most other militant Islamic groups—also claim to be working to end U.S. occupation of Arab land. A 2006 study by Robert Brym and Bader Araj found that the following were organizational rationales for Palestinian suicide bombings stated in Arabic-language media and organizational statements:

1. Desire for revenge or retaliation for an Israeli attack on the organization.
2. Desire for national revenge or retaliation.
3. Desire to achieve specific, short-term political goal (disrupting security cooperation between Israeli and Palestinian authorities).
4. Desire to achieve long-term, strategic goal.
5. Desire to achieve religious goal[39].

All or most of these reasons are usually given in martyrdom videos when they are distributed—because such propaganda videos are more useful for the organizations than for the individual bombers.

Personal considerations are more likely to be stated as an individual attacker's reasons for choosing to perform a suicide bombing. While a suicide bomber usually also states national, global, or religious goals, s/he rarely states a strategic goal (winning a certain campaign) and almost never refers to the caliphate. These goals are more functional and more specific, and organizers are able to plan for them when numerous suicide bombers have carried out their actions. This division is logical: the individual attackers will die immediately, so they usually require personal motivations beyond long-term goals, which they will not live to see come to fruition. For bombers, personal reasons are sometimes cited, especially those motivations related to personal revenge (if a family member has been killed, etc.). Sometimes, though, the personal reasons are covered up to maintain the dignity of the cause—such motivations can include vengeance, social honor/redemption (religious or personal), local military or political problems, and revolutionary-participatory goals (being involved in a movement or revolution bigger than themselves).

The individual motivations are rarely discussed in martyrologies produced by suicide-bombing organizations, for the obvious reason that it would detract from the saintliness they intend to create. Martyrologies are discussed in detail in chapters 3 and 5, but these motivational factors are almost always omitted. The Araj/Brym study cited above also found that the following were major motivations for individual suicide bombers: desire for personal or national revenge, religious revenge, regaining reputation after engaging in shameful behavior, and desire to achieve religious goals such as the spread of Islam.[40] The majority of the female Palestinian suicide bombers, for instance, were sexually or morally compromised (as discussed in chapter 3). For them, a martyrdom operation may be a good way to overcome the stigma of this status. One Chechen suicide-bomber, Zulikhan Elikhadjieva, wrote a letter to the man she had been living with—another jihadist planner—which was found in her pocket after her death. Indicating her feelings of guilt and abandonment, she wrote, after he left: "I have no one besides you on this earth and because of that I went to become a shahid in the path of Allah . . . We touched each other in hell, and for that we are going to heaven."[41] Vengeance—for loved ones killed or for general aggressions—is also a known motivation factor for individual suicide bombings.[42]

These personal motivations—which could be perceived by radical Muslims as less pious or appropriate than the higher organizational goals—are rarely stated in martyrdom videos and only emerge through examining suicide bombers' backgrounds. Therefore, obtaining detailed personal backgrounds has so far been difficult, especially in the case of Iraq. Suicide bombings occur almost daily in Iraq (sometimes several a day); even in an environment with good access to information, researching all these bombers' histories would be difficult. Given that even the nationalities of the bombers are not always publicized, and that they have jihad names that can differ from their given names, research on these bombers is extremely difficult. In Pakistan and Afghanistan, where martyrdom wills are produced very rarely and names of bombers are rarely released—either by militant groups or governments—research on motivations and socioeconomic profiles is virtually impossible.

The existence of these personal motivations provides a good opportunity to distribute alternative narratives to those offered by jihad groups. Total disinformation campaigns would not be necessary or useful in this case, but giving more information on the bombers' less-than-wholesome background could be both a deterrent to potential suicide bombers (who may not want their shameful histories or real motivations revealed) and an information campaign to make some audiences cynical about the purity of these movements. If not performed correctly, however, informational tactics such as this one could backfire, making martyrdom *more* attractive to people because of this perceived redemptive aspect.

A related tactic that could be gleaned from this motivational duality is the spreading of the idea that suicide bombers are manipulated or coerced by their organizations to carry out their missions. Already widely circulated in Western media narratives of suicide bombers (possibly too widely circulated), this idea may not be believable to Arab or Muslim audiences. But emphasizing this divide between suicide bombers' motivations and organizational goals could be helpful in discrediting the bomber and/or the organizations.

This hierarchical motivational divide may be partially true for all organizations carrying out militant attacks, not just suicide bombings. But this motivational divide is important when discussing suicide attacks because of the element of legitimization and the importance of communicating the benefits of becoming a martyr—with both the personal benefits (the afterlife, etc.) and the posthumous fame. By recognizing the religious and social aspects essential for recruiting for such attacks, which we outline above, policymakers can take the first step toward creative and effective policymaking that addresses the root causes of the suicide-attack phenomenon.

Chapter 9

Fighting Suicide Bombing and the Culture of Martyrdom

When we talk with him in the name of God...
and tell him what he wants to do is religiously prohibited,
we block the martyrdom operations.[1]

Most policy studies about terrorism and/or suicide bombing base their observations and recommendations on traditional counterterrorism methods such as border control, financial transaction restrictions, and surveillance procedures.[2] We are not experts in these fields, and these types of policies have already been proposed by experts all over the world. Many laws exist on such technical aspects, but while such laws are important for cutting off organizational mobility and financial means to carry out attacks, these laws do nothing to stop the spread of the ideas that condone—indeed, promote—suicide attacks as a desirable method of opposing Western policies.

In the previous chapter, we observed that much of the discourse thus far on suicide bombings has been flawed in ways that have crippled the discourse itself. We therefore made the following corrective observations:

1. Suicide bombers are not usually poor, within regional or national standards.
2. The creation of a martyrdom culture usually requires religious sanction and an element of religious justification/reward.
3. Pro-suicide-bombing ideology is diffuse in the world, so attempting to cut off outlets propagating it is a moot effort.
4. The specter of suicide bombing is not monolithic.

Resulting from these observations and our research presented in previous chapters, we explained a dualistic motivational model showing the differences between organizational goals for suicide bombings and individual suicide bombers' goals. We also observed that suicide bombings are occurring in conflicts unrelated to occupying powers. While Pape's theory applies to suicide bombings targeting occupations, it does not apply to the increasing use of suicide bombing in local and national conflicts, which could lead to a harder-to-combat, nihilistic use of the these attacks. Therefore, it is necessary to combat the ideology promoting suicide bombing and to create a dialectical space where opposition to suicide bombings is accepted or, ideally, encouraged. We propose the following recommendations:

1. *Hold clerics who incite suicide bombings accountable for their statements*: When Muslim clerics issue a fatwa promoting suicide bombings, this is an act, within Muslim communities, that is not simply like condoning suicide bombings or approving of them. Because of the heirarchical structure of the `ulama*, a statement inciting suicide bombings (saying they should happen) is essentially tantamount to actually organizing a suicide bombing. Hizbullah leader Hasan Nasrallah has repeatedly called on clerics to issue fatwas encouraging suicide attacks, saying, "When we come to tell him [a prospective suicide bomber] that this act is religiously prohibited or that it is a sin or suicide, he will never move one step forward. No one will manage to push him one step forward. When we talk with him in the name of God... and tell him what he wants to do is religiously prohibited, we block the martyrdom operations."[3] The international community should take greater steps to deal with the importance of not only the justifications of these attacks but also the incitement to such actions.

Muslim clerics inciting suicide bombings should be held accountable for this incitement and participation in suicide bombing. The United Kingdom adopted a new Terrorism Act on March 30, 2006, meant to modify the previous antiterror laws that punished international terrorism occurring in the United Kingdom (2003). The 2006 law makes punishable acts "preparatory to terrorism," encouragement to terrorism (defining it as a "terrorist offence"), dissemination of terrorist publications, and terrorist training.[4] Such a policy recommendation may run into problems with free-speech advocates, as indeed the U.K. Anti-Terrorism bill has,[5] but it should be clear that there is a difference between an individual person approving of suicide bombing and a cleric—someone with authority—calling for suicide bombings. To avoid potential rights abuses, the emphasis must be placed on incitement *to action*, and legislation on incitement must focus on incitement that specifically encourages particular attacks.

Our intention is not to recommend that every country adopt a law akin to the U.K. law on terrorism. Indeed, the most compelling critique of this law lies in the fact that it contains no new criminal actions, and that the actions it is used to prevent were illegal in existing codes and laws in the United Kingdom and other countries.[6] Laws already exist in most countries to prevent the transfer of money to militant antistate groups (or groups defined as "terrorist"), and material or even moral support has been outlawed; antidefamation laws and hate-crime laws can be used to deal with incitement.

Therefore this recommendation does not require drafting an entirely new policy but instead enforcing and applying those laws to what are, indeed, criminal actions—namely, planning with and actively encouraging others to commit criminal or murderous *actions*.

Arresting these figures, however, could cause several practical problems, in addition to the obvious problems of rights violations if clerics were punished for *words* instead of involvement in *actions*. Practically speaking, the figures' persuasive powers make arrests and enforcement more difficult because of the phenomenon of non-Muslims converted or Muslims radicalized while in prison (discussion in chapter 8). Furthermore, large-scale arrests could contribute to claims of rights abuses and therefore justification of the very attacks such silencing would attempt to stop. Therefore, the United States and Western countries should carefully consider their approach on how to deal with religiously related incitement to such attacks. Finally, the most authoritative scholars on these topics are often not actually located in Western countries, so holding such figures accountable would require cooperation with many other countries, not all of which could be counted on to act on this recommendation without corruption, major human-rights abuses (this recommendation should not be seen as a license for such abuses), or high-profile failures.

2. *Identify potential suicide-bombing recruits by focusing on converts and newly radicalized Muslims' communication*: One of the best ways to isolate people who could fall into both the convert and the newly radicalized Muslim groups is to monitor discussion sites where jihad is propagated or discussed. There are some policymakers who would prefer to shut down such sites immediately, before the ideology on them spreads further. Some Web sites promote this idea, posting names and screen-shots from radical Muslim sites, urging readers to hack into or disable them (or servers to remove their accounts).[7]

Others argue that these radical sites should be kept open so that they can be more easily monitored. An ideal approach may include some elements of both arguments. So far, however, we have no indication that there is a stated "policy" of shutting down such sites. Sites that publicize radical sites' servers and names do not appear to be sanctioned by any defense department or intelligence agency, so this activity may not be state-sponsored or may not be "officially" state-sponsored. Thus, a standardized policy about what types of sites are shut down is lacking; if none exists (and we have not heard of one), it is difficult to perceive who benefits from the shutting down of such sites. As stated in the previous chapter, monitoring these fora is likely to produce far more information and be far less controversial than systematic monitoring of radical mosques.

We do not mean to imply that all converts are suicide bombers or are in favor of the use of suicide attacks. As we stated earlier in the book, the vast majority of Western converts come to Islam through Sufism, and even those who are attracted to radical Islam are not necessarily drawn to *militant* radical Islam. Among converts and nonconverts alike, radical Muslims are very rarely militant. But for the foreseeable future, there is likely to be a stream of Muslims who are interested in suicide attacks and who do carry them out for the various reasons discussed throughout this book. Among converts to Islam, some will be open to performing suicide attacks—ones such as Richard Reid, Germaine Lindsay, and Muriel Degauque (discussed in chapter 8).

We do not advocate using this information for profiling purposes because profiling is unlikely to be effective, would threaten citizens' civil rights, and would produce far too much data to be useful. Furthermore, it could increase radicalization in targeted groups and thereby defeat the purpose of a logical counterterror policy. On the other hand, groups that are more likely to be drawn to militant attacks, if properly analyzed, could provide clues for how to best combat the ideology promoting such attacks. If such recruits receive their information or militant messages from certain sources, opposing opinions and public diplomacy campaigns should also address these audiences in similar ways.

3. *Engage the Muslim discourse on suicide bombing on its own terms*: The United States cannot continue the pure informational isolationism it has attempted through the time of this writing. Instead of addressing mass audiences, the U.S. government has set up its own station, which has abysmal ratings. Instead of making arguments on Arab TV stations such al-Jazeera or al-Arabiya (a potentially friendlier station), which discuss the more problematic aspects of suicide bombings, few attempts have been made to address the already-existent public sphere formed by these transnational stations. When U.S. officials address Arab audiences, with few exceptions, they do it in the form of a Donald Rumsfeld or former national security adviser Condoleeza Rice[8] interview with al-Jazeera.[9] While these get official U.S. messages out, they are not as useful as interviews with officials such as former ambassador to Syria Christopher Ross, who speaks fluent Arabic and has appeared on al-Jazeera several times since 2002. More recently, State Department official Alberto Fernandez (a fluent Arabic speaker) has appeared on Arab media hundreds of times and was praised throughout the media for these appearances[10] until his October 2006 statement that the U.S. government had acted with "arrogance" and "stupidity" in Iraq.[11] These statements, although they reflected legitimate opinions held in parts of the political and public establishment, were harshly criticized, and Fernandez quickly withdrew them, which may have harmed the U.S. government's efforts at "candid" public diplomacy. Other groups that should be sought for public diplomacy efforts include Muslims from the United States and Europe—especially those with some religious education, and, ideally, experience in the Middle East. This recommendation has been stated in numerous public-diplomacy reports[12] but so far has not been followed enough. If they are to be given platforms to

speak to Arab and Muslim populations, there will likely be more of Fernandez-style criticism, however, so the U.S. government should weigh these considerations.

The recently produced public-service announcement (PSA) for Iraqi audiences attempts to argue against suicide bombing by emphasizing the dramatic human cost of a suicide bombing.[13] While this is a potentially positive first step, it does not counter any of the arguments Muslims may have *for* suicide bombing. A better anti-suicide-bombing PSA could focus more on religious clerics arguing about the human cost or about the religious legitimacy of such attacks. Given the backlash against U.S. covert efforts to place anti-terrorism items in Iraqi media, these PSAs and announcements should not attempt to conceal their origins. It could be better, however, if the United States gave competitive grants to filmmakers to produce these themselves— thereby sidestepping some of the issues of direct U.S. involvement.

4. *Encourage (moderate) discussion about suicide bombings that focuses specifically on religious problems with suicide bombing*: Many have suggested co-opting moderate Muslims or finding Muslim clerics who would be willing to take an anti-suicide-bombing stance. Indeed, Shaul Shay wrote that although most other studies of suicide bombers come to the conclusion that what is needed is a high-ranking cleric to issue a fatwa against suicide bombings, "attempts made over the years to implement this conclusion did not meet with any success."[14] Given the anti-Americanism levels and the amount of damage that collaboration with the United States can cause for Muslim leaders, it is difficult to say how to encourage moderates to speak out without actively paying them, making them objects of ridicule or targets for treason.

Several Muslim groups have issued fatwas against suicide attacks, but while such prohibitive fatwas are numerous, they come from groups of Muslim leaders in Pakistan, Saudi Arabia, the United States, and Europe.[15] Muslim leaders in these areas are usually considered by radical Muslims to be co-opted by the (corrupt) states in which they are located.

Currently, even a well-respected Muslim leader issuing an anti-suicide-attack fatwa would likely be dismissed immediately by his intended audience or have no effect. Radical Islam has been promoted by many with no impressive religious education, which has eroded the traditionally hierarchal structure of religious leadership in Islam. More effective than a single high-ranking cleric releasing a fatwa against suicide bombing would be a campaign of publicizing religious arguments against killing and against suicide, especially a campaign that emphasizes the desperation of some of the attackers (because some Muslim scholars have claimed that "desperation" is what separates "normal" suicide from suicide-attack "martyrdom," so an attack done in desperate situations could be judged only as suicide—a Muslim taboo). Concerted efforts in this fashion in Saudi Arabia have had some success.[16]

5. *Address perceived humiliation by combating its logical roots*: Work on combatting myths in perceived-humiliation narratives is necessary. Many of the texts and myths propagated by radical Muslim groups are based on irrational "facts" and conspiracy theories, which could be combatted through counterpropaganda, especially if spread by rival groups.

Some of the publications, however, can be said to focus largely on real injustices, such as Abu Ghraib prison abuse or U.S. torture practices, in addition to fact-based objections to U.S. and European foreign policy.[17] For obvious reasons, such objections will continue to exist as long as such practices and policies are in place. The damage that has been done to the United States' and Europe's reputations, in terms of ability to spread human rights and other democratic values, is difficult to overstate. On the other hand, governments' ceasing to use blatantly unjust or illegal practices is unlikely to immediately stop the anti-Western sentiment or the perceived humiliation. Unless the United States does more to address these real injustices, there will be endless fodder for even the more rational publications addressing this humiliation.

These (real) injustices are usually expanded in radical publications to fit greater, conspiratorial worldviews. The prevalence of conspiracy theories in the Muslim world has been noted elsewhere,[18] but its importance would be hard for a U.S. audience to understand. Collecting more concrete information on the phenomenon, however, is necessary and a topic that should be researched further in the future.

Humiliation narratives are also strengthened when the United States attempts to stop the flow of terrorist financing a crackdown that has the effect of closing down the Islamic charities run by the same organizations. These charities, while drumming up support for radical Islamic groups, also provided real services to poorer segments of society, and the abrupt end of those services creates the feeling that the United States has targeted civilian Muslim populations.[19] Although the poverty explanation of suicide bombing has been proven to be false, there is little arguing with a person who no longer has food to eat because the United States shut down the Islamic charity that fed him or his family. The United States should work harder to address these social gaps left by its closure of such organizations, and in appropriate contexts even encourage American Muslim groups to operate new charities in these areas.

In combination with social support in areas most affected by the shutting down of Islamic charities, U.S. financial assistance to Muslim countries' militaries should be properly monitored to be sure it does not lead to human rights abuse; provisions for such oversight exist in laws but a recent government report indicated that such procedures are not being followed thoroughly.[20] This military aid should be monitored closely, in order to prevent increasing fodder for conspiracy theories and anti-Americanism.

Pape's recommendation that the United States and other democracies alter occupational strategies would likely help in the short-term solve those conflicts that are revolving around perceived or real "occupations," but it assumes that suicide bombing would end if the U.S. occupation ended. Not only is the total abolition of a U.S. troop presence on Arab or Muslim soil unlikely, but this assumption ignores radical Muslim definitions of "occupation," which, as discussed above, include all foreign presence in the Arabian peninsula (not just U.S. presence and not just military). This suggestion also ignores globalist aspirations that are common to many radical Muslim groups. Their intention is not only to end the U.S. occupation but also to establish a caliphate and to establish *shari'a* law in all places with significant Muslim populations (not just countries containing a Muslim majority).

Nonetheless, the belief in the necessity of violent action to achieve these global goals is not as widespread as radical Muslims' domination of the discourse warrants. For this reason, and because of the vulnerability of Islamic reasoning condoning suicide bombing discussed in this book, we believe that the defeatism expressed in policy papers and news reports on suicide bombing is completely misplaced. Most previous policy discussions have focused on financial or security measures, but these do not address the most unique aspect of contemporary suicide bombing. Suicide attacks inherently require a great deal of justification, primarily religious justification, because they involve killing oneself. Thus far, no major policy study has highlighted this issue or identified it as a weakness in the West's discourse on the topic. We believe, however, that this most sensitive aspect of these attacks would not stand up to serious ideological confrontation if religiously based opposition to these attacks existed in the open. Without confronting these religious justifications and these specific facts of suicide bombing as a militant tactic, policymakers and governments will find themselves increasingly unable to deal with this threat.

Notes

Chapter 1

1. Summarized from *Report of the Department of Defense Commission on the Beirut International Airport Terrorist Act, Oct. 23, 1983* (from December 20, 1983); see also Sa'd Abu Diya, *Dirasa tahliliyya fi al-'amaliyyat al-istishhadiyya fi janub Lubnan*, pp. 35–43.

2. Noted by Asaf Moghadam, *Suicide Bombings in the Israeli-Palestinian Conflict: A Conceptual Framework*, pp. 27–28, although the discourse of humiliation continues far beyond the Israeli-Palestinian conflict.

3. Some examples: Usama b. Laden, *Messages to the World*, p. 60 (Declaration of the World Islamic Front, February 23, 1998), p. 104 (statement of October 7, 2001); statement of Ahmad al-Haznawi (one of the September 11 attackers), "....the time of humiliation and enslavement is over..." at news.awse.com (April 16, 2002); and Takruri, *al-'Amaliyyat al-istishhadiyya fi al-mizan al-fiqhi*, pp. 12–13 (preface by Muhammad al-Zuhayli), pp. 18–19 (preface by Ahmad al-Khatib), pp. 140–41 and ff.

4. See the full discussion of Muhammad Khayr Haykal, *al-Jihad wa-l-qital fi al-siyasa al-shara'iyya* (3 vols.).

5. Such as Yusuf al-Qaradawi (based in Qatar) who is associated with the Muslim Brotherhood and a well-known media figure.

6. This list can change; for example in the late 1980s according to 'Abdallah 'Azzam, *al-Difa' 'an aradi al-Muslimin*, appendix the emphasis was upon Burma, the Philippines, Bulgaria, and Uganda.

7. See Etan Kohlberg, "Martyrdom and Self-Sacrifice in Classical Islam," *Pe'amim* 75 (1998), pp. 5–26 (in Hebrew); Kohlberg, "Medieval Muslim Views on Martyrdom," *Mededelingen der Koninklijke Nederlandse Akademie van Wetenschappen* 60 (1997), pp. 281–307; Kohlberg, *Encyclopedia of Islam*[2] s.v. "*shahid*"; and Cook, *Martyrdom in Islam* (forthcoming).

8. Ibn al-Mubarak, *Jihad*, pp. 63–64 (no. 68); also al-Bukhari, *Sahih*, iii, p. 278 (nos. 2829–30); Muslim, *Sahih*, vi, 51; and al-Suyuti, *Abwab al-sa'ada*, pp. 36–37 (no. 2).

9. Al-Tirmidhi, *Sunan*, iii, p. 106 (no. 1712); see also Ibn Maja, *Sunan*, ii, p. 1452 (no. 4337); and al-Hindi, *Kanz al-'ummal*, iv, pp. 397–98, who cites many similar traditions from the entire *hadith* literature.

10. The question of intercession for friends and relatives of a martyr is a problematic one in Islam, and the idea of intercession is by no means universally accepted.

11. See 'Abd al-Jabbar 'Adwan, *al-Shuhada'*, for discussion.

12. For historical antecedents, see Scott Atran, "Genesis of Suicide Terrorism," *Science* 299 (March 7, 2003), pp. 1534–39; Pape, *Dying to Kill*, pp. 11–16.

13. This book is widely circulated among radical Muslims, cited by them frequently, and has been translated by them into Urdu and Uzbek.

14. Ibn al-Nahhas, *Mashari` al-ashwaq fi masari` al-`ushshaq*, i, pp. 557–60.

15. Chris Quillen, "A Historical Analysis of Mass-Casualty Bombings," *Studies in Conflict and Terrorism* 25 (2002), pp. 279–92.

16. Stephen Dale, "Religious Suicide in Islamic Asia: Anti-Colonial Terrorism in India, Indonesia and the Philippines," *Journal of Conflict Resolution* 32 (1988), pp. 33–59; another example of this would be the suicidal charge of the Hindu nobility of Denpasar, Bali, in 1904 against the Dutch.

17. Statistics and dates are from Pape, *Dying to Win*, pp. 252–63 (Appendix 1).

18. Bloom, *Dying to Kill*, pp. 134–35.

19. Because a fatwa is a solicited legal opinion theoretically there is no limit to the number that could be produced on the subject of suicide attacks. Therefore, we cannot say that the list is complete; merely that the number is sufficient to have a sense of the breadth of the support for suicide attacks within the Muslim religious establishment.

20. "The Islamic Legitimacy of Martyrdom Operations: Did Hawa Barayev Commit Suicide?" from the Arabic *Hal intaharat hawa Barayav?* (at tawhed.ws) penned by Yusuf al-`Ayyiri of the Saudi Arabian branch of al-Qa`ida, which has been summarized by a number of other articles, e.g., Abu Ruqaiyah, "The Islamic Legitimacy of the Martyrdom Operations," *Nida' al-Islam* (January 1996–97), at ict.org.il.; and Yahya Hashim Hasan Firghal, *Kashf al-tawiyya fi al-`amaliyyat al-istishhadiyya* at tawhed.ws.

21. Forsan.net (August 18, 2002); the *hadith* citation is from Abu Da'ud, *Sunan*, iii, p. 10 (no. 2504).

22. See Cook, "The Implications of 'Martyrdom Operations' for Contemporary Islam," *Journal of Religious Ethics* 32 (2004), pp. 129–51, especially pp. 132–33.

23. For example, after the Riyad bombings of May 2003, see "Saudi Press: Initial Reactions to the Riyadh Bombings" at memri.org, Special Dispatch no. 505 May 15, 2003); and "A Statement from the Committee of Senior Scholars...Concerning the Riyadh Explosions" at islamica.com.

24. For example, both the Palestinian and Chechen suicide attacks have been critiqued in this manner: "A Palestinian Communiqué against Martyrdom Attacks" at memri.org, Special Dispatch no. 393 (June 25, 2002); "Egyptian Opposition Daily Condemns Suicide Martyrdom Operations" no. 474 (February 25, 2003); "Arab and Muslim Reactions to the Terrorist Attack in Beslan, Russia" no. 780 (September 8, 2004).

25. Ibn Mar`i, *Ahkam al-mujahid bi-l-nafs*, ii, pp. 397–99.

26. al-Takruri, `*Amaliyyat al-istishhadiyya*, pp. 105–07; on the issue of suicide see Franz Rosenthal, "On Suicide in Islam," *Journal of the American Oriental Society* 66 (1946), pp. 239–59.

27. `Abd al-Qadir b. `Abd al-`Aziz, *Risalat al-`umda li-jihad fi sabil Allah*, pp. 353–58.

28. For example, Ibn al-`Arabi, *Ahkam al-Qur'an*, iv, pp. 1800–01; al-Qurtubi, *al-Jami` li-ahkam al-Qur'an*, xviii, pp. 73–74.

29. hammad Tu`mat al-Qudat, *al-Mughamara bi-l-nafs fi al-qital wa-hukmuha fi al-Islam*, p. 37.

30. For example, Ergun Çapan, *Terror and Suicide Attacks: An Islamic Perspective* is a good start (although much of the booklet is wasted on irrelevancies), and his own article (pp. 102–18) is the only one known to me by a Muslim who details problems with the traditions cited by the radicals. Unfortunately he

undermines his own argument by citing an example of the Armenians (massacred by the Turks in 1915–22) on p. 116.

31. An example of this is the handbook of Ahmad b. Salim al-Misri, *Fatawa al-`ulama' al-kibar fi al-irhab wa-l-tadmir wa-dawabit al-jihad wa-l-takfir wa-mu`amalat al-kuffar* (2006). Although this book is a good start, too many of the `ulama' in it are complicit with the process of justifying suicide attacks. For a great many of the fatwas listed in it one can easily find counter-fatwas from the same person (usually justifying suicide attacks against Israel). Additionally, there is no serious confrontation of or serious knowledge of the extremely wide-spread arguments in favor of suicide attacks.

32. At the time of this writing (Summer 2006) the LTTE had begun to use suicide attacks again.

33. See the comments of Pape, *Dying to Win*, pp. 166–67, 241–43; Bloom, *Dying to Kill*, pp. 2–3, 133.

34. See James Piazza, "Rooted in Poverty: Terrorism, Poor Economic Development and Social Cleavages," *Terrorism and Political Violence* 18 (2006), pp. 159–75; Alan Richards, "Socio-Economic Roots of Radicalism," at globalsecurity.org; "Terrorists Are Motivated by Cultural and Religious Factors, not Poverty," at memri.org, Special Dispatch no. 853 (January 26, 2005).

35. A good example is Jalal `Alam's book, *Qadat al-gharb yaquluna: dammiru al-Islam, ubidu ahlahu* (*Western Leaders are saying: Destroy Islam, Annihilate All of Its People*) first published in 1976.

36. Under the Bush administration conspiracy theories have focused upon his supposed responsibility for the September 11 attacks and collusion between his administration and Islamic radicals; while accusations against the Clinton administration focused upon the supposedly Jewish domination of his administration and his frequent attacks upon Iraq.

Chapter 2

1. Muhammad Fanish, "Concerning the Resistance and the Martyrdom Spirit" (`An al-muqawama wa-l-ruh al-istishhadiyya*) (April 18, 1992), in *Hizbullah: al-muqawama wa-l-tahrir*, i, p. 65.

2. There are a few exceptions to this rule, for example, both the Russian and the Indian militaries have proven quite vulnerable to attacks by suicide attackers and seem to resist learning the lessons of previous attacks.

3. Etan Kohlberg, "The Development of the Imami Shi`i Doctrine of Jihad," *Zeitschrift der Deutschen Morgenländischen Gesellschaft* 126 (1976), pp. 64–86.

4. For discussion see Mahmoud Ayoub, *Redemptive Suffering in Islam*, pp. 120–21; and Joseph Alagha, "Hizbullah and Martyrdom," *Orient* 45:1 (2004), pp. 47–74.

5. For full discussion of the range of views, see Yotam Feldner, "Debating the Religious, Political and Moral Legitimacy of Suicide Bombings," at memri.org "Inquiry and Analysis" nos. 53–54, 65–66 (May 2–3, 2001, July 26–27, 2001); "Suicide, Martyrdom, Terrorist Attacks or Homocide: A Debate in the Arab Media," at memri.org, Special Dispatch no. 378 (May 12, 2002); "Palestinian Debate over Martyrdom Operations," memri.org, Inquiry and Analysis nos. 100–01 (July 4–5, 2002).

6. For example, `Azzam, *Ithaf al-`ibad fi fada'il al-jihad*, p. 91, where he states (commenting on a tradition in which a fighter returns to the battlefield alone knowing that he will die): "this is proof that it is desirable for the Muslim to fight, even alone, and even if he is certain of death, if this is to the benefit of the Muslims...and it is a proof that it is desirable for the Muslim to carry out suicide

attacks (`amaliyyat al-intihariyya`), knowing that he will die during them, if this is for the benefit of the Muslims."

7. Mohammed Hafez, *Manufacturing Human Bombs*, pp. 40–41.

8. For example, Tariq Abu Hamdan, *Misk al-khatam* (December 31, 1987), in *Hizbullah: al-Muqawama wa-l-tahrir*, ii, 11 (a report on the year's operations in which the author discusses the usefulness of suicide operations).

9. For example, Abu Basir al-Tartusi, living in London, for years was one of the major radical intellectuals in support of suicide attacks, but after the London bombings (July 7, 2005) he issued a statement referring to these attacks as `amaliyyat al-intihariyya`: *Mahadhir al-`amaliyyat al-istishhadiyya aw al-intihariyya* at tawhed.ws (20/7/1426 = August 25, 2005); see D. Hazan, "Expatriate Syrian Salafi Sheikh al-Tartousi Comes Out Against Suicide Attacks," at memri.org, Special Report no. 40 (February 10, 2006).

10. Such as the small Palestinian Islamic Jihad group founded by Fathi Shiqaqi.

11. See Farhad Khosrokhavar, *Les nouveaux martyrs d'Allah*, chapter 2; Khosrokhavar, *L'Islamisme et la Mort, le martyre révolutionaire en Iran*; Ian Brown, *Khomeini's Forgotten Sons: The Story of Iran's Boy Soldiers*, especially chapter 2; and the official Iranian version in *Yadnama-yi shuhada-yi sal-i avval-i difa` muqaddas-i Shahristan va-Qumm*.

12. For example, "Iran's Political and Military Leadership Calls for Martyrdom (*shahada*)," at memri.org, Special Dispatch no. 850 (January 20, 2005); "Iranian Volunteer Suicide Organization of 40,000," at memri.org, Special Dispatch no. 929 (July 6, 2005); "Iranian Martyr Recruitment Website," at memri.org, Special Dispatch no. 1106 (March 3, 2006).

13. This operation and the ones following are detailed in Abu Diya, *Dirasa*, pp. 26–81; and Takruri, `Amaliyyat`, pp. 51–52.

14. These are best documented by the collection *al-`Amaliyyat al-istishhadiyya: watha'iq wa-suwar al-muqawama al-wataniyya al-Lubnaniyya 1982–85*, which, however, emphasizes the nationalistic rather than the religious aspects of these attacks.

15. For the martyrology, see *Sijill al-nur* (1998).

16. Note the two victory speeches by Nasrallah, "al-Muqawama faradat al-khuruj al-mudhill," in *Hizbullah: al-Muqawama wa-l-tahrir*, vii, pp. 11–20 (May 24, 2000), and "Mustamirrun ka-l-muqawama," in Nasrallah, pp. 21–30 (June 27, 2000), neither of which mention the suicide attacks in lists of the other tactics that drove the Israelis out, nor does he mention Hizbullah suicide attackers in his "La Madaniyyin fi Isra'il wa-yajib mutabi`at al-`amaliyyat al-istishhadiyya," in Nasrallah, pp. 63–74 (December 15, 2001) while praising the Palestinian suicide attackers.

17. "Buenos Aires Bomber Identified," at bbc.com (November 10, 2005). This "identification" 11 years after the bombing indicates the slow progress of the investigation.

18. "Sadr Warns of Iraq Suicide Bombs," at bbc.com (April 23, 2004).

19. Saddam Husayn during the immediate prelude to the invasion of Iraq (2003) proclaimed the existence of suicide squads to defend Iraq against the coalition forces, and these groups were responsible for the first suicide attacks immediately after the fall of Iraq in March 2003. See Kevin Woods, James Lacey, and Williamson Murray, "Saddam's Delusions," *Foreign Affairs* (May–June, 2006).

Chapter 3

1. Mishal and Aharoni, *Speaking Stones*, p. 206 (translation of Hamas leaflet #2, January 1988) (I have modified the translation somewhat); the Qur'anic verse is 9:111.

2. Actually the PLO was founded in 1962 as an expression of Egyptian interests, but shortly after 1967 under the leadership of Yasser Arafat it managed to achieve a degree of independence.

3. Michele Esposito, "The al-Aqsa Intifada: Military Operations, Suicide Attacks, Assassinations and Losses in the First Four Years," *Journal of Palestine Studies* 34 (2005), pp. 85–122; Hillel Frisch, "Debating Palestinian Strategy in the al-Aqsa Intifada," *Terrorism and Political Violence* 15 (2003), pp. 61–80.

4. Examples would be the first Intifada of the Palestinians (1987–93), the African National Congress (ANC) against the Afrikaner government of South Africa (far more oppressive than Israel) or the Filipino Moros in the southern Philippines.

5. Little public international protest occurred, but the International Court of Justice filed an Advisory Opinion strongly against the barrier; this opinion has been strongly contested by several states and academics on evidenciary and legal bases. ICJ, Advisory Opinion of 9 July 2004, "Legal Consequences of the Construction of a Wall in the Occupied Palestinian Territory."

6. "A Palestinian Communiqué against Martyrdom Attacks," at memri.org, Special Dispatch series no. 393 (June 25, 2002); see also "Suicide Bomber's Father: Let Hamas and Jihad Leaders Send Their Own Sons," Special Dispatch series no. 426 (October 8, 2002).

7. Confirmed by communication from Reuven Paz, April 12, 2006.

8. For the motivations of failed suicide attackers see Anat Berko, *Ba-derekh le-Gan ha-Eden.*

9. Most are included in Takruri, *al-`Amaliyyat al-istishhadiyya fi al-mizan al-fiqhi* (4 editions since 1997); Muhammad Sa`id Ghayba, *al-`Amaliyyat al-istishhadiyya wa-ara' al-fuqaha' fiha* (2 editions, 1997, 2003); and see also Tu`amat al-Qudat, *al-Mughamara bi-l-nafs fi al-qital* (2001); *Masa'il jihadiyya wa-hukm al-`amaliyyat al-istishhadiyya* (2002); Ibn Jubayr, *al-`Amaliyyat al-istishhadiyya* (2002); Hasan al-Bash, *al-`Amaliyyat al-istishhadiyya* (2003); Ghazi Husayn, *al-Irhab al-Isra'ili wa-shara`iyyat al-muqawama wa-l-`amaliyyat al-istishhadiyya* (2003); Nawaf al-Zarw, *al-`Amaliyyat al-istishhadiyya* (2003); and Ahmad `Abd al-Karim Najib, *al-Dala'il al-jaliyya `ala mashru`iyyat al-`amaliyyat al-istishhadiyya* (2006).

10. In the Palestinian context the process of discussion of the renaming of suicide attacks can be seen within the small tract issued by Hamas in the middle 1990s, *al-`Amaliyyat al-fida'iyya: shahada am intihar?* In which the anonymous writer argues for this change.

11. Takruri, `*Amaliyyat*, pp. 49–51 (summarized using his phraseology).

12. Ibid., p. 51.

13. Justin Sparks, "Freed Terrorist Vows he will complete his Suicide Mission," *The Sunday Times* (February 8, 2004).

14. Note the martyrologies that had developed among Palestinians, both Muslims and Christians, from the first Intifada (1987–93): Lance Daniel Laird, "Martyrs, Heroes and Saints: Shared Symbols of Muslims and Christians in Contemporary Palestinian Society," unpublished Ph.D. dissertation, Harvard University 1998.

15. For how this material is used, see Daphne Burdman, "Education, Indoctrination and Incitement: Palestinian Children on the Way to Martyrdom," *Terrorism and Political Violence* 15 (2003), pp. 96–123.

16. Hamas and other radical Muslim organizations have been asked what the rewards of the female suicide attacker are; so far the emphasis has been moved away from the graphic sexual rewards of the male martyr and to the intercession that the martyr can make for his or her relatives.

17. *Intifadat al-Aqsa*, iv, pp. 89–91 (Mahmud Marmash), pp. 97–99 (Nimr Darwish Abu al-Hayja and `Ala Hilal `Abd al-Sattar Sabah), pp. 167–69 (Nidal Abu Shaduf), pp. 203–04 (`Izz al-Din Misri), pp. 259–62 (Hisham Abu Jamus),

pp. 268–81 (Hasan Husayn al-Hotari), v, pp. 209–10 (Samir 'Umar Shawahina), pp. 266–68 (Ahmad Daraghima), vi, pp. 74–80 (Wafa Idris), pp. 216–17 (Andalib Tiqataqa), vii, pp. 113–15 (Muhammad al-Ghul), viii, pp. 149–51 (Samir al-Nuri and Buraq Khalfa), ix, pp. 59–61 (Ahmad al-Khatib), pp. 102–03 (Hiba Daraghima), pp. 173–76 (Ayhab and Ramiz Abu Salim), x, pp. 84–93 (Hanadi Jaradat).

18. For example, see Muhammad al-Ghul in *Intifadat al-Aqsa*, vii, p. 113 "This operation does not mean that I like to kill or to die, but its goal is to ensure the future safety of the coming generations."

19. See, e.g., Clara Beyler, "Chronology of Suicide Carried Out by Women," at ict.org (February 12, 2003); Joyce Davis, *Martyrs: Innocence, Vengeance and Despair in the Middle East*, chapter 4 (2003); Barbara Victor, *Army of Roses* (2003); Debra Zedalis, *Female Suicide Bombers* (2004); Bloom, *Dying to Kill*, chapter 7 (2005); Claudia Brunner, *Männerwaffe Fraunkörper* (2006); Rosemary Skaine, *Female Suicide Attackers* (2006); and Yoram Schweitzer (ed.), *Female Suicide Bombers: Dying for Equality?* (2006).

20. For example, "Musharikat al-nisa fi al-'amaliyyat al-istishhadiyya," at Palestine-info.com (April 7, 2002); Eric Silver, "Schoolgirl Suicide Bomber Kills Two in Supermarket," *Independent* (March 30, 2002) (Ayat al-Akhras); and on the attitudes of mothers, Aluma Solnick, "The Joy of the Mothers of Palestinian 'Martyrs,'" at memri.org, Special Dispatch no. 61 (June 25, 2001); "Umm Nidal: The Mother of the Shahids," at memri.org, Special Dispatch no. 673 (March 4, 2004); "Mothers of Hizbullah Martyrs," at memri.org, Special Dispatch no. 819 (November 25, 2004).

21. The reaction of the larger Muslim world has also been varied, "Conflicting Arab Press Reactions to the Gaza Suicide Bombing," memri.org, Special Dispatch no. 651 (January 27, 2004).

22. "The Will of Hanadi Jaradat," at memri.org, Special Dispatch no. 766 (August 19, 2004).

23. Whether a sense of liberation or feminism has a part in female suicide attacks has been discussed by Bloom, *Dying to Kill*, chapter 7; and refuted by Schweitzer (ed.), *Female Suicide Bombers: Dying for Equality?*

24. The English translation is widely available on the Internet; it is based upon the Arabic *Hal intaharat Hawa Barayev?*

25. *No Surrender*, available through almaktabah.com (English translation by almaktabah.com).

26. See the full list in Schweitzer, *Female Suicide Bombers*, pp. 64–65. Some dispute the female majority of Chechen suicide attackers, see Anne Speckhard and Khapta Ahkmedova, "The Making of a Martyr: Chechen Suicide Terrorism," *Studies in Conflict and Terrorism* 29 (2006), pp. 429–92.

27. Note the discussions in Sean Yom and Basel Saleh, "Palestinian Suicide Bombers: A Statistical Analysis," *ECAAR News Network* (November 2004); "Terrorists Are Motivated by Cultural and Religious Factors, not Poverty," in memri.org, Special Dispatch no. 853 (January 26, 2005), and the sources cited in chapter 1, note 33 and discussion in chapter 8.

Chapter 4

1. Nasir al-Fahd, "The Ruling on Fighting Americans outside of Iraq" (*Hukm mujahidat al-Amirikan kharij al-'Iraq*), available at tawhed.ws. Nasir al-Fahd is a well-known Saudi radical cleric who has been imprisoned several times since May 2003.

2. See its initial proclamation by 'Abdullah 'Azzam, "al-Qa'ida al-Sulba," *al-Jihad* 24 (April 1988), pp. 4–6.

3. See *Sawt al-jihad*, 18, p. 20 on this operation.

4. For example, al-Bukhari, *Sahih*, iv, p. 39 (no. 3053).

5. These attitudes are brought out clearly by numerous analyses of September 11 from the point of view of al-Qa`ida or other radical Muslim groups: see "al-Qa`ida Activist, Abu `Ubeid al-Qureshi, Compares Munich (Olympics) Attack (1972) to Sept. 11," at memri.org, Special Dispatch no. 353 (March 12, 2002).

6. For example, "al-Tasa'ulat: hal ustudrija al-mujahidin ila ma`araka ghayr mukafa'a?," ascribed to the Saudi al-Qa`ida leader Yusuf al-`Ayyiri at alneda.com (May 1, 2002).

7. For example, see `Adil b. `Ali al-Shiddi, *Min qisas al-shuhada' al-`Arab fi Afghanistan* (2 vols.); *Min qisas al-shuhada' al-`Arab fi al-Bosnia wa-l-Hirsak* at saaid.net; "Killing Infidels in Chechnya: A Foreign Mujahid's Diary," in Adam Parfrey (ed.), *Extreme Islam*, pp. 274–78; and Hamd al-Qatari and Majid Madani, *Min qisas al-shuhada al-`Arab* at tawhed.ws.

8. See Cook, *Martyrdom in Islam*, chapter 3 (forthcoming).

9. The Arabic phrase *al-harb al-salibiyya al-jadida* (the "New Crusader War") was gladly adopted by al-Qa`ida (e.g., used as the title of Yusuf al-`Ayyiri's book justifying September 11, *Haqiqat al-harb al-salibiyya al-jadida*) in their attempt to frame the conflict in terms that arouses the anger of most Muslims. While the English word "crusade" has a number of meanings, some of which are innocuous (so it is possible to understand President Bush's blunder) the Arabic only refers to the historical Crusades.

10. For example, the works of al-`Ayyiri, in his articles "Tasa'ulat" at the al-Qa`ida Web site al-neda.com on Abu Basir and Abu Jandal (Spring 2002).

11. The official figures were 224 killed in Nairobi (of whom 12 were Americans) and approximately 4,000 wounded; 11 killed in Dar es-Salaam (none of whom were American) and approximately 85 wounded.

12. *The 9/11 Commission Report*, pp. 149–50, 153–56.

13. This point has been contested, in our judgment, foolishly; some have suggested that not all of the "muscle" hijackers knew they were going to die. The fact that all of them left suicide videos makes it impossible to support the idea that they did not know September 11 was a martyrdom operation; additionally, it is impossible to believe that after all the careful planning al-Qa`ida would leave the outcome dependent upon deceiving some of the participants who then might have then aborted the mission.

14. From *The Last Night* (my translation) in *Understanding Jihad*, appendix 6, p. 198.

15. Analysis by Quintan Wiktorowicz and John Kaltner, "Killing in the Name of Islam: Al-Qaeda's Justification for Sept. 11," *Middle East Policy* 10 (2003), pp. 76–92.

16. Other justifications were those of Hamud b. `Uqla al-Shu`aybi, "Fatwa on the Events of Sept. 11," at aloqla.com, alsahwah.com; Abu Qatada (spiritual leader of al-Qa`ida in Europe), "Sept. 11: The Legal Vision," at jihadunspun.com (September 2002); `Abd al-`Aziz b. Salih al-Jarbu`a, *al-Ta'sil li-mashru`iyyat ma hasala li-Amrika min tadmir*, at tawhed.ws; Husayn `Umar b. Mahfuz, *al-Ta'sil al-shar`i li-ahdath Amrika*, at tawhed.ws; Sayf al-Din al-Ansari, *Ghazwat New York wa-Washington*; and the unsigned *Kashf al-shubhat `an ahkam al-hujumat*, at tawhed.ws.

17. Arguments along these lines were already developed by Egyptian radical Muslims even during the 1980s and 1990s; see `Abd al-Salam Faraj, *al-Farida al-gha'iba*, pp. 39–41; trans. Johannes Jansen, *The Neglected Duty*, pp. 207–09; Ayman al-Zawahiri, *Shifa' sudur al-mu'minin* (1995), *al-Mas'ala al-thaniya*, pages unnumbered (thanks to Elena Pavlova for providing me with a copy of this text).

18. See the summary translation in my *Understanding Jihad*, appendix 3 "A Communiqué from Qa`idat al-Jihad concerning the Testaments of the Heroes and the Legality of the Washington and New York Operations," pp. 175–81 (April 22, 2002).

19. Bali: al-Ustadz Luqman bin Muhammad Ba`abduh, *Sebuah Tinjauan Syari`at Mereka adalah Teroris: bantahan terhadap buku Aku Melawan Teroris* (of Imam Samudra, the spiritual leader of the Bali bombings); Riyadh: "The Council of Senior Scholars on the Riyadh Suicide Bombings," at fatwa-online.com; London: Abu Basir, *Mahadhir al-`amaliyyat al-istishhadiyya aw al-intihariyya*, at abubaseer.bizland.com (articles 90), also D. Hazan, "Expatriate Syrian Salafi Sheikh al-Tartousi Comes Out Against Suicide Attacks," memri.org, Special Report no. 40 (February 10, 2006); `Amman: Abu Muhammad al-Maqdisi, Y. Yehoshua, "Dispute in Islamist Circles Over the Legitimacy of Attacking Muslims," memri.org, Inquiry and Analysis, no. 239 (September 11, 2005).

20. For example, the attack against tourists in Jerba, Tunisia on April 11, 2002 killing 19 and injuring 26.

21. "Al-Hurub al-Nawawiyya wa-l-Kimawiya wa-l-Bialojiyya fi al-Mizan al-fiqhi," at tawhed.ws (from part 1); see also *Sawt al-jihad* 16, pp. 46–47.

Chapter 5

1. Muhammad Siddique Khan (leader of the July 7, 2005 London suicide bombings), CNN transcript, September 1, 2005.

2. Note the "credits" in the appendices of Pape, *Dying to Win* and Pedahzur, *Suicide Terrorism* are nowhere near as clear as the authors would like to have us believe.

3. On him, see Fu'ad Husayn, *al-Zarqawi: al-Jil al-thani li-l-Qa`ida.*

4. See Abbas Akhtar Avan, *Karvan-i shuhada: Kabul se Kashmir*; Faridulislam Janju'ah, *Jihad, shahadat, jannat*; Sa`id Rashid, *Shahid-i Kashmir.*

5. In general, see Amir Rana, *A to Z of Jehadi Organizations in Pakistan*, chapters 9, 14.

6. See Kanchan Lakshman, "Jammu & Kashmir: Suicide Terror," in *Kashmir Herald* (January 2003), at kashmirherald.com; see also satp.org "Major Incidents of Terrorist Violence in Jammu and Kashmir."

7. `Abd al-Rahman Makki, "Fidayee Activities in [the] Shari`a," at markaz-dawa.org (November 30, 2001); and on the history of these types of groups, Ahmad Sharbasi, *Fida'iyyun fi al-ta'rikh al-Islam.*

8. For example, April 19, 2000 (4 injured) December 25, 2000 (9 soldiers killed), April 30, 2002 (suicide attacker killed), October 9, 2004 (5 soldiers killed, 50 wounded), July 20, 2005 (6 soldiers killed).

9. We do not agree with Pape's classification of the December 13, 2001 attack by Jaysh-i Muhammad on the Indian Parliament in New Delhi was a suicide attack (Pape, p. 259, category #16, num. 3). This was the operation of a suicide squad, but there was no attempt by the attackers to kill themselves. Their mission was to kill as many people as possible and to provoke tensions between India and Pakistan (which they did).

10. "Kashmir Woman Suicide Attacker," at bbc.com (October 13, 2005).

11. Musa Jalalzai, *Dying to Kill Us*, pp. 152–53; and satp.org "Fidayeen [Suicide Squad] Attacks in Pakistan."

12. Rana, *Jehadi Organizations*, pp. 9–18.

13. Ron Moreau, Sami Yousafzai, and Michael Hirsh, "The Rise of Jihadistan," *Newsweek* (October 2, 2006).

14. Omid Marzban, "The Foreign Make-up of Afghan Suicide Bombers," at jamestown.org, Terrorism Focus 3:7 (February 21, 2006).

15. See, e.g., "Suicide Bomber Kills 17 in Afghan Town," Associate Press (August 28, 2006); Terry Pedwell, "Taliban Distance Themselves from Suicide Attacks," Canada Press, www.canada.com (August 25, 2006). Many of the attackers seem to be foreigners, mainly Pakistanis, see Marzban, "The Foreign Make-up of Afghan Suicide Bombers," at jamestown.org (vol. 3:7, February 21, 2006).

16. Kyrgyzstan and Tajikistan have some radical Islamic elements, but these are mostly connected to their Uzbek minorities. Turkmenistan is an outright dictatorship; both the Kazakh and the Kyrgyz populations have been little influenced by radical Islam.

17. Ahmed Rashid, *Jihad: The Rise of Militant Islam in Central Asia*, chapter 8; see also discussion in Vitaly Naumkin, *Radical Islam in Central Asia: Between Pen and Rifle*, chapter 2.

18. Personal communication, Bakhtiyar Babajanov, July 27, 2004.

19. "Uzbekistan's Affluent Suicide Bombers," at iwpr.net (Institute for War and Peace Reporting) (April 20, 2004).

20. Based upon interviews conducted by Olivia Allison in the immediate wake of the bombings in Tashkent, Uzbekistan (May–July 2004).

21. Andrew Tan, "The Indigenous Roots of Conflict in Southeast Asia: The Case of Mindanao," in Ramakrishna and Tan (eds.), *After Bali: The Threat of Terrorism in Southeast Asia*, pp. 97–116.

22. *Philippines Terrorism: The Role of Militant Islamic Converts*, International Crisis Group, Asia report no. 110, December 19, 2005.

23. See *Berjihad di Pattani*, translated in Rohan Gunaratna, Arabinda Acharya, and Sabrina Chua, *Conflict and Terrorism in Southern Thailand*, pp. 118–45.

24. See Ken Conboy, *The Second Front: Inside Asia's Most Dangerous Terrorist Network*, chapter 13; and for the al-Qa'ida analysis, see "Shifa sudur al-mu'minin: bayna yaday al-'amaliyyat fi Molucca, Fulayka wa-Bali," freedomination.org (alneda.com) (October 27, 2002).

25. Imam Samudra, *Aku Melawan Teroris*, pp. 171–73.

26. See *Fatwa Majelis Ulama Indonesia tentang Terorisme* (Jakarta, 2005), especially p. 17 (which, however, does not condemn suicide attacks in all circumstances, only against civilians).

27. The principal link between al-Qa'ida and JI was JI's operational leader Hambali (captured in August 2003) who was also a member of al-Qa'ida's *shura* council (the only non-Arab).

28. "One in 10 Indonesians backs Suicide Bombings," at msnbc.com (March 16, 2006).

29. Bruce Lawrence, *Messages to the World: The Statements of Osama bin Laden*, p. 183.

30. Takruri, *'Amaliyyat al-istishhadiyya*, p. 54 claims that suicide attacks took place in the Sudan against the southern Christians; however, we have been unable to confirm this report. Interviews with the Mujahidin in Juba (capital of southern Sudan) on January 31, February 1, 2005 did not reveal any use of suicide attacks or knowledge of this one.

31. See "Rare Footage of Saudi Comedian and Al-Majd TV Employee turned Suicide Bomber Muhammad Shazzaf al-Shehri" for one of the perpetrators, at memri.org, Special Dispatch no. 1076 (January 24, 2006).

32. See Najih Ibrahim 'Abdallah, *Tafjirat al-Riyad*, passim.

33. Note how well connected they were: "Abiqaiq Suicide Bombers Hail from Leading Saudi Families," at arabianews.org (Saudi Information Agency) (February 25, 2006).

34. Pedahzur, *Suicide Terrorism*, appendix lists 3: January 3, 1995 in Algiers (killing 42), August 7, 1995 in Boufarik (killing 8 and wounding 25); and August 31, 1998 in Algiers (killing 25 and wounding 61). On the methods of the GSPC, see the interview with Nabil Sahrawi, their commander, memri.org, Special Dispatch no. 642 (January 13, 2004).

35. Rashid Khashana, "Moroccans in Quest of Martyrdom," *al-Hayat* (June 22, 2005); also Ahmed Benchemsi, "Mémoires d'un kamikaze," *Tel-quel* 228 (September 14, 2006), at telquel-online.com.

36. See Faraj, *al-Farida al-gha'iba*, p. 45; trans. Jansen, *The Neglected Duty*, pp. 215–16; and the translation of Abu Umama, *The Absent Obligation*, pp. 94–99 (an appendix added on by radical Muslims trans. from *The Islamic Ruling on the Legitimacy of Martyrdom Operations*).

37. See his *Shifa' sudur al-mu'minin*.

38. "Cairo Bombing claims Third Victim," at bbc.com (April 11, 2005); "Cairo Tourists Come under Attack," at bbc.com (April 30, 2005). The Egyptian government claimed to have identified all of the bombers.

39. One of the Sharm attackers, Yusuf Badran, was identified as a radical from al-`Arish, but his connections are still unclear.

40. Raphaeli, "Iraqi-Jordanian Tension over the Most Lethal Suicide Bombing in Iraq," at memri.org, Inquiry and Analysis no. 214 (March 29, 2005).

41. This hotel had also been the target of the intended "Millennium Plot" of 1999, along with other tourist locations, for which the American Raed Hijazi was sentenced to death in 2002.

42. Attacks of all types have been virtually continuous against the U.S. and international forces in the center of the country (the Sunni Triangle) since the summer of 2003, but for the most part have been rocket attacks, roadside bombings, or formal warfare (Falluja, Tell Afar, etc.), and not suicide attacks. These other methods will not be covered in this book.

43. Southern Iraq was converted to Shi`ism for the most part during the nineteenth and early twentieth centuries.

44. Hafez notes 443 suicide attacks between March 22, 2003 to February 20, 2006: Mohammed Hafez, "Suicide Terrorism in Iraq: A Preliminary Assessment of the Quantitative Data and Documentary Evidence," *Studies in Conflict and Terrorism* 29 (2006), pp. 591–619, at p. 591. There have probably been about another fifty until the time of writing in September 2006.

45. Hafez, pp. 593–94.

46. Ibid., pp. 595–99.

47. Another example has been the Noralwizah Lee Abdullah, wife of the Jama`a Islamiyya leader al-Hambali (captured in August 2003), who has expressed public interest in carrying out a suicide attack. Also, note Steven Stalinsky, "Arab and Muslim Jihad fighters in Iraq," memri.org, Special Report no. 19 (July 27, 2003).

48. "Video purports to show Mosul bombing," at msnbc.msn.com (December 27, 2004). CNN's use of this video is discussed in chapter 7.

49. Hafez, pp. 616–19.

50. Further discussion on this operation in chapter 8; see also the case of Pascal Cruypeninck, a Belgian convert to Islam, who tried to persuade his Rwandan fiancée to go to Iraq and carry out a martyrdom operation: "Zarqawi's European Network," at the Counterterrorism Blog (December 30, 2005).

51. "New Internet Footage of Fatima's Fiancé," at memri.org, Special Dispatch no. 1095 (February 16, 2006).

52. Hafez, pp. 601–11.

53. Evan Kohlmann, *Al-Qaida's Jihad in Europe*, pp. 152–53.

54. Ibid., pp. 165–66.

55. Based on research conducted in Turkey (Cook and Allison) in May 2005.

56. On the justifications for this bombing, see Reuven Paz, "Islamic Legitimacy for the London Bombings," at ict.org.il (July 18, 2005).

57. "Somali Leader Escapes Attack," *International Herald Tribune* at iht.com (September 18, 2006).

58. "Hariri Killed by a 'Suicide Bomber'," bbc.com (September 25, 2006).

59. For example, *An Analysis of al-Qaida Tradecraft*, lesson 4, pp. 27, 38; alluded to in *The 9/11 Commission Report*, p. 167.

60. *9/11 Commission Report*, p. 163.

61. H.G. Reza, "Unlikely Candidate for Car Bomber," *Los Angeles Times* at latimes.com (April 16, 2006).

62. There is little research on this subject; see the French police study, *Les Conversions á l'Islam radical*, excerpted "Fundamentalism in French Workplace," at latimes.com (November 26, 2005); also *Philippines Terrorism: The Role of Militant Islamic Converts*, Asia Report #110, crisisgroup.org (December 19, 2005).

63. For example, *Sawt al-jihad*, 9, pp. 25–26.

64. For example, the Madrid bombers: Keith Richburg, "Madrid Attacks May Have Targeted Election," msnbc.msn.com from *Washington Post* (October 17, 2004); and the JI leader Azahari Husin (November 9, 2005).

Chapter 6

1. Abu Musa`b al-Suri (Mustafa Setmariam Nasar), *Da`wat al-muqawama al-Islamiyya al-`alamiyya*, p. 1126; for a discussion of al-Suri's influence, see Craig Whitlock, "Architect of New War on the West," *Washington Post*, May 23, 2006.

2. Debra Zedalis, *Female Suicide Bombers*, p. 20.

3. See, e.g., Jonathan Alter, "The Other Air Battle," *Newsweek* (April 7, 2003); "Rumsfeld Blasts Arab TV Stations," BBC (November 26, 2003); Dorrance Smith, "The Enemy on Our Airwaves," *Wall Street Journal*, (November 4, 2005); "Al-Jazeera Promotes Global Terrorism," *Accuracy in Media Report* (August 1, 2006).

4. Joyce Purnick, "Censorship is Patriotism to Big Board," *The New York Times* (March 27, 2003).

5. Abraham Miller, "Terrorism and the Media: Lessons from the British Experience," The Heritage Foundation, May 1, 1990.

6. Cited in Bethami A. Dobkin, "The Television Terrorist," *Terrorism, Media, Liberation*, p. 129.

7. See Lawrence, *Messages*, pp. 103–29 (Taysir al-Alwani of al-Jazeera, October 7, 2001); and further by Robert Fisk (June 12, 1996); Peter Arnett (March 1997); John Miller (May 28, 1998); Salih Najm and Jamal Ismail (June 19, 1999); *Daily Ummat* (October 19, 2001); and Hamid Mir (November 7, 2001).

8. M.J. Kelly and T.H. Mitchell, "Transnational Terrorism and the Western Elite Press," in *Media Power in Politics*, p. 284.

9. "Most books, articles, essays, and speeches on the topic are comprised of sweeping generalities, conjecture, supposition, anecdotal evidence based on dubious correlations, and endless repetition of equally weak arguments and nonscientific evidence offered by other writers on the subject of terrorism. As one reviews the literature it becomes shockingly clear that not a single study based on accepted social science research methods has established a cause-effect relationship between media coverage and the spread of terrorism." (Picard in *Media Power in Politics*, p. 315.)

10. Iraqi suicide bombings especially have been filmed in real-time, but they usually emphasize the bomber's statements before the bombing, while the camera crew maintains significant distance during the operation, such that all that is visible is an explosion from afar.

11. M.J. Kelly and T.H Mitchell, "Transnational Terrorism and the Western Elite Press," in *Media Power and Politics*, p. 284.

12. Bloom, *Dying to Kill*, p. 77 argues there are two audiences for suicide bombers: international and domestic, with a lesser third audience of potential donors and supporters. Earlier, Ralph E. Dowling ("Terrorism and the Media,"

Journal of Communication 36 [1986], pp. 16–18) had chosen two more general audiences, "insiders" and "outsiders."

13. Kim A. Cragin and Sara Daly, "The Dynamic Terrorist Threat: An Assessment of Group Motivations and Capabilities in a Changing World," RAND (2004), p. 37.

14. See, e.g., Adam Gadahn's ("Azzam the American") recent video, calling all people to Islam, which was an attempt to appeal to more neutral publics that had not yet been radicalized. Cited in personal communication with Elena Pavlova, October 2006.

15. See Zarqawi, *Wasaya li-l-mujahidin*, at tawhed.ws; other wills or statements are translated by Hafez, *Manufacturing Human Bombs*, appendix B. Wills of Kuwaitis killed in Iraq were published in the booklet: *Sarakha fi wajh al-batil, mutadammina Usud al-Kuwayt fi bilad al-rafidayn* (thanks to Elena Pavlova).

16. "An Analysis of Zarqawi's Message—From a Soldier to His Emir (Prince)," SITE Institute (May 31, 2005).

17. From the martyrdom will attributed to Abu Anas al-Tuhami, released by Al-Qaeda's Jihad Committee in Mesopotamia, 2005, cited in "Profiles of Saudi Arabian Islamic Militants Killed in Iraq: 2004–2005," GlobalTerrorAlert.com (2005).

18. Only 11 percent of Jordanians, 31 percent of Egyptians, 54 percent of Lebanese, 40 percent of Syrians and 7 percent of Palestinians polled in 2004 called al-Qa`ida "terrorist." Low percentages of people in Jordan and Palestine labeled the September 11 attacks "terrorist." No more than 60 percent called attacks on Israeli citizens "terrorist," and no more than 25 percent in any of the countries surveyed gave the label to attacks on U.S. forces in Iraq. *Revisiting the Arab Street: Research from Within*, Center for Strategic Studies, University of Jordan, pp. 72–74 (February 2005).

19. Bruce Hoffman, *Al Qaeda Trends*, pp. 4–5; see the analysis in Hoffman, "Underground Voices: Insurgent and Terrorist Communication in the 21st Century," unpublished paper presented to the Insurgency Board, RAND (August 2002).

20. See Hafez, *Manfacturing Human Bombs*, pp. 33–34, and 87–92; also see the extensive testaments cited in the 10 volumes of *Intifadat al-Aqsa*; and further "Will of Hannadi Jaradat," in memri.org, Special Dispatch no. 766 (August 19, 2004).

21. Based upon our field research in the Middle East, North Africa, Central Asia, Indonesia, Pakistan, and Afghanistan (January–August 2005).

22. Based on research conducted in Syria (Cook) May 2002, (Cook) June 2003, and (Cook and Allison) June 2005.

23. *Revisiting the Arab Street*, op. cit.

24. "Farewell Message from Azzam Publications," at azzam.com (November 20, 2001).

25. GIMF, however, is not directly affiliated with Al-Qa`ida, e.g., see Bouchaib Silm, "Al Qaeda Wants Its Own TV," *IDSS Commentaries*, No. 73, October 24, 2005, p. 2; "Al Qaeda calls for Muslim Journalists to Join in," *Al Farouq* (October 15, 2005), at http://www.al-farouq.com/vb/showthread.php?t=3044; "GIMF Introduces a New Animated Video on Hostile Websites," *Global Issues Report*, Center for International Issues Research (January 24, 2006).

26. For example, see "Profiles of Saudi Arabian Islamic Militants Killed in Iraq: 2004–2005," *Global Terror Alert*, at http://www.globalterroralert.com, p. 9; Stephen Ulph, "Global Jihad's Internet Front," *Terrorism Focus*, Jamestown Foundation, 2:23 (December 13, 2005), p. 5.

27. "Twelve of the martyrs were then featured in a concluding segment accompanied by the voiceover: 'Rejoicing in what their Lord has given them of His bounty, and they rejoice for those who stayed behind and did not join them; knowing that they have nothing to fear and that they shall not grieve.' " Quote from a martyrdom video seized by CIA in 2002, containing pictures of 27 martyrs, Bruce Hoffman,

"Al Qaeda, Trends in Terrorism and Future Potentialities: An Assessment," RAND (2003), p. 10. (Qur'anic citation is 3:170; translation has been changed to accord with the other translations in this book).

28. Discussions on such Web sites as http://clearinghouse.infovlad.net, where many people post links to radical Muslim videos and other materials, contain lengthy discussion threads new logos for militant organizations and analysis thereof. Sometimes members post logos they cannot identify or request logos for certain groups, and other members sometimes respond to identify them.

29. Bloom, *Dying to Kill*, p. 31.

30. See chapter 5, section on Iraq.

31. Scott Baldauf, "Militia's Other Weapon: Videos," *Christian Science Monitor* (August 25, 2004), at http://www.csmonitor.com/2004/0825/p01s03-woiq.html.

32. By sectarian here, we primarily mean the Pakistani and Iraqi suicide attacks (interview with Amir Rana of the Pakistan Institute for Peace Studies, Lahore, Pakistan, May 16, 2006, confirmed that there are no such videos in circulation for Pakistani bombings).

33. Note the fact that there are a number of suicide attacks whose authors are unknown, see Pedahzur, *Suicide Terrorism*, appendix for examples.

34. See, e.g., Joel Greenberg, "7 Killed, 17 Hurt in Ambush of Bus by Palestinians," *The New York Times* (July 17, 2002); "7 die in Terror Attack on Immanuel Bus," *Ha'aretz* [English edition] (July 17, 2002).

35. Robert Brym and Bader Araj, "Palestinian Suicide Bombing Revisited: A Critique of the Outbidding Thesis," (Unpublished paper), p. 8.

36. Gabriel Weimann, "www.terror.net: How Modern Terrorism Uses the Internet," *United States Institute of Peace Special Report*, No. 116 (March 2004), p. 5.

37. "Suicide Bomber Kills 17 in Afghan Town," AP, reprinted in CBSNews.com (August 28, 2006).

38. Terry Pedwell, "Taliban Distance Themselves from Suicide Attacks," *Canadian Press* (August 25, 2006).

39. *Revisiting the Arab Street*, op. cit.

40. Bloom, *Dying to Kill*, p. 29.

41. "Al-Qaeda in Iraq Denies Media Reports That It Claimed Responsibility for an Attack in al-Hillah Killing 125" at SITE institute (March 1, 2005) at http://siteinstitute.org/.

42. Globalterroralert.com (July 20, 2005) at http://www.globalterroralert.com/archive0704–02.html. (accessed April 8, 2006).

43. Lawrence, *Messages*, p. 56.

44. See Whitlock, "Architect of New War on the West," *Washington Post* (May 23, 2006).

45. Suri, p. 1126.

46. Ibid., pp. 1127–28.

47. Araj and Brym, in "Suicide Bombing as Strategy and Interaction" (p. 5), write that "Arabic sources...provide more consistent and detailed evidence [than American and Israeli sources] drawn from interviews with organizational leaders and suicide bombers' family members, official organizational statements, and statements made by suicide bombers before their attacks."

48. On the influence of al-Jazeera, see Hugh Miles, *al-Jazeera: How the Arab Media Challenged the World*; and Marc Lynch, *Voices of the New Arab Public*.

49. al-Suri, 571.

50. Al-Qureshi, "The Sept. 11 Raid: The Impossible becomes Possible," trans. Foreign Broadcast Information Service, also "al-Qa'ida Activist, Abu Ubeid al-Qureshi, compares Munich (Olympic) attack (1972) to Sept. 11," at memri.org, Special Dispatch no. 353 (March 12, 2002).

51. Phone interview (Olivia Allison) with Basha Basrahil, Sanaa, Yemen (February 28, 2005).

52. Interview (Olivia Allison), Muhammad Agha, Damascus, Syria (June 22, 2005).

53. Interview (Olivia Allison) with Dr. Fuad Sharbaji, Damascus, Syria (June 23, 2005).

54. "We have to ask, will this increase or decrease public opinion in Europe? The answer has to be it will decrease." Hilali, "The Testament of the Martyr: Between the Telling of al-Jazeera and the Failure of the Brothers," at aloswa.org., also in Muslimeen.co.uk. (April 18, 2002).

55. Ibid.

56. Reuven Paz, "Al-Qaeda's Search for New Fronts: Instructions for Jihadi Activity in Egypt and Sinai," Global Research in International Affairs (GLORIA) Center, PRISM Occasional Papers (October 2005).

57. Ibid., pp. 4–5.

58. Ibid., p. 4.

59. Baldauf, "Militia's Other Weapon," *Christian Science Monitor*, August 25, 2004.

60. Al-Nawawy, *Al-Jazeera* (2003), pp. 171–72. This was the interview with Taysir al-`Alwani, translated in Lawrence, *Messages to the World*, pp. 107–29 and is arguably the most informative interview that has ever taken place with Bin Laden. The more likely reason for its not having been aired is the fact that Bin Laden is quite clear about his responsibility for the September 11 attacks, a fact widely disbelieved in the Arab world then and now.

61. Anthony Shadid, "A Newsman Breaks the Mold in the Arab World," *Washington Post* (May 1, 2006).

62. Nacos, pp. 74–90.

63. Al-Suri, pp. 1127–28.

64. Weimann, *Terror on the Internet*, op. cit.

65. Posted on the al-Hesbah Jihadi forum: http://www.alhesbah.org, cited in Akil Awan, "Transitional Religiosity Experiences," *Islamic Political Radicalism* (forthcoming), p. 225 n. 17.

66. Weimann, p. 5; note the guide *39 wasila li-khidmat al-jihad* (*39 Ways to Help the Jihad*, by Muhammad b. Ahmad Salim) lists several different types of "electronic jihad" including "jihad of hackers" (pp. 44–45).

67. Paz, p. 2.

68. Ibid., p. 4.

69. Weimann, *Terror on the Internet*, op. cit.

70. YouTube's terms of use, which a user must agree to when joining, include a clause prohibiting the submission of "material that is unlawful, obscene, defamatory, libelous, threatening, pornographic, harassing, hateful, racially or ethnically offensive, or encourages conduct that would be considered a criminal offense, give rise to civil liability, violate any law, or is otherwise inappropriate" (http://youtube.com/t/terms). The definitions of these terms are not, however, given anywhere in the terms of use. Google Video did not have the same terms of use, but has recently bought and is merging with YouTube.

71. Edward Wyatt, "Anti-U.S. Attack Videos Spread on Web," *The New York Times*, October 6, 2006.

72. See, e.g., "Hamas Fighters Suicide Car Bombing" (added July 28, 2006, http://youtube.com/watch?v=y9Jy_6HO6Ew); "Iraq Al Qaeda Suicide Car Bomb against US Convoy" (added August 1, 2006, http://youtube.com/watch?v=0e1tguspf9c); "A Martyr's Will" (added March 10, 2006, http://youtube.com/watch?v=zPx1UgFTpc0); "Jihad Hidden Camera" (added January 26, 2006, http://youtube.com/watch?v=LxokJ0rWeZE) (all accessed August 2006). All of

these have videos have been removed since we originally accessed them, due to "terms of use violations," and few new similar videos have been posted. Although there are hundreds of results to a search term, however, it should be noted that many of the videos are duplicates and there are usually several copies of a single video, especially if it is "popular."

73. A cursory glance at some of the comment areas for some of these videos proves there is a very partisan audience. A popular "Majlis Shura Counsel" video, was loaded on the site at the end of August 2006 and, in addition to hundreds of views, had several comments in less than a week. The first comment said, "Masallah!" and the second said, "Why???? It doesn't make sense> [sic] Nothing about this stupid insurgency movement makes sense." The latter is one of the tamer anti-insurgent comments viewable in response to such videos. This video was posted many times; see, e.g., "Mujahideen Shura Council Suicide Carbombing against Shi'ite" (added August 26, 2006, http://www.youtube.com/watch?v=g8RiXC3qlJg).

74. Aimal Khan, "Future Shock," Pakistan: *The Herald Annual* (January 2006).

75. Brigitte Nacos, "Mass-Mediated Terrorism in the New World (Dis)Order," in J. David Slocum, ed., *Terrorism, Media, Liberation*, pp. 185–208 at p. 203.

76. "Remarks by President Bush to the U.S. University Presidents Summit on International Education," State Department, www.state.gov (January 5, 2006).

77. Djerejian, *Changing Minds; Winning Peace*, p. 32.

78. In a poll conducted by Zogby International and Shibley Telhami in October 2005, only 1 percent of Arabs polled said they selected al-Hurra as a first choice, and 5 percent claimed to watch the station as a second-choice. See, e.g., Alvin Snyder, "Alhurra's Struggle for Legitimacy," USC Center on Public Diplomacy (November 22, 2005), "Middle East: Poll Finds U.S.-Funded Al-Hurra TV Has Least Viewers in Region," BBC Monitoring International (December 5, 2005).

79. Lorraine Ali, "This Is Your Street Mid-Bombing," *Newsweek* (June 20, 2006).

Chapter 7

1. Kelly and Mitchell, pp. 287–88.

2. See, e.g., Kirsten Mogensen, Lauran Lindsay, Xigen Li, Jay Perkins, and Mike Beardsley, "How TV News Covered the Crisis: The Content of CNN, CBS, ABC, NBC, and Fox," *Communication and Terrorism*, pp. 101–20; Amy Reynolds and Brooke Barnett, " 'America Under Attack,' " *Media Representations of September 11*, pp. 85–102; Michelle Brown, Leia Fuzesi, Kara Kitch, Crystal Spivey, "Internet News Representations of September 11," *Media Representations of September 11*, pp. 103–16; Maggie Wykes, "Reporting, Remembering, and Reconstructing September 11, 2001," *Media Representations of September 11*, pp. 117–35; and *Media in an American Crisis*, 2005.

3. Carter and Stanley, "On Television, Networks Ask if 'Message' is Really News," *The New York Times* (October 10, 2001). Bin Laden himself has ridiculed this suggestion, saying in a CNN-aired interview with al-Jazeera from 2002, "It's as if we were living in the time of mail by carrier pigeon, when there are no phones, no travelers, no Internet, no regular mail, no express mail, and no electronic mail.... They discount people's intellect." (Al-Jazeera interview with Usama bin Laden, aired by CNN, February 1, 2002. Transcript available on CNN.com: http://transcripts.cnn.com/TRANSCRIPTS/0202/01/ltm.04.html.)

4. Robert G. Picard, "News Coverage as the Contagion of Terrorism: Dangerous Charges Backed by Dubious Science," *Media Power in Politics*, 2nd edition, p. 320.

5. Kelly and Mitchell, p. 283.

6. Ibid., pp. 285–88.

7. See, e.g., Eric Black, "Newspapers Turn Page in New Media Age," Minneapolis: *Star Tribune* (October 11, 2005); "Tribune Co. to Pare its Foreign Bureaus," Reuters (July 8, 2006). There are some exceptions; when the McClatchy Company bought Knight Ridder Newspapers, it vowed to open more foreign bureaus (Chris Serres and Mike Meyers, "The Knight Ridder Deal," Minneapolis: *Star Tribune* (March 14, 2006)). Nonetheless, this is the exception in an environment when downsizing foreign reporting is the rule.

8. To compile our research database, we used the searchable Vanderbilt Television News Archive, which contains one hour of world news coverage per day. According to the Archive's director John Lynch, the Archive has recorded CNN's major "evening news" show, but the timing and name of this show has changed over the years. Therefore, these results cannot be judged wholly conclusive. While it is possible that a suicide bombing was covered very briefly throughout the course of the day but did not get covered during this hour, this scenario is somewhat unlikely. Because the cost of recording and producing such materials are so high, they are usually repeated throughout the day. The network CNN was chosen because of its high reliability ratings and the general perception of objectivity; Fox News frequently gets higher overall ratings, but more Americans claim to get their news from CNN than from Fox. The Vanderbilt archive is an archive of the hour of "evening news" on these channels; for CNN, the shows and times have changed over the years but have always been the show that most closely approximates an evening news magazine.

9. This list is not entirely complete, but because it is organized according to campaign, it is the most helpful such list that exists.

10. CNN's fatality-coverage correlation was 0.39 (r = 0.388), and NBC's was 0.33 (r = 0.334); including September 11, both correlations were above 0.9—that is, highly correlated. Correlations can range from -1 to 1. In a positive correlation, as the values of one of the variables increase, the values of the second variable also increase. In a negative correlation, as the values of one of the variables increase, the values of the second variable decrease. A correlation value of 0 means there is no relationship between the variables. In order to prove two ideas are correlated, the r value should approach 1.

11. CNN's fatality-coverage length correlation was 0.35 (r = 0.351), and NBC's was 0.29 (r = 0.292), excluding September 11.

12. Because there was not yet a comprehensive list of suicide bombings in Iraq at the time of writing, we cannot perform the same type of statistical analysis performed earlier in this section.

13. February 22, 1996; March 4, 1996 (twice, once saying, "A large percentage of Palestinians, along with significant percentages of Jordanians, Syrians and Lebanese don't want peace, don't like Israelis, think that the conflict should continue"); November 6, 1998; May 7, 2002; May 8, 2002; June 5, 2002; May 17, 2003.

14. April 4, 2002; June 24, 2004 (Gen. George Casey stated that the point of an insurgency is making the president seem worse).

15. April 29, 2003.

16. November 8, 2003 (regarding Saudi Arabia); July 14, 2004 (regarding Baath party attempting to take over Iraq).

17. March 4, 1996 (regarding Israel's elections); May 8, 2003 (regarding road map in Israel); February 11, 2004 (regarding handover of power to Iraqis).

18. August 13, 1997.

19. The upcoming-election rationalization of suicide bombings was used extremely frequently in 2004 regarding U.S. presidential elections and over a period of years regarding ongoing debates on Iraqi elections. See, e.g., September 17, 2004, when both types of elections were cited as reasons, and December 2005.

20. August 19 and 20, 2003 (both about bombing of UN headquarters in Baghdad, Iraq); November 11, 2004 (about Iraq); December 26, 2004 (Iraq).

21. See, e.g., September 17, 2004; December 20, 2004.

22. Reference made February 16, 2002; August 19, 2003 (includes only a side reference to Islamic Jihad leader killed by Israelis); December 25, 2003 (the attack "came shortly after" Israelis blew up a terrorist leader); January 29, 2004 (trying to revenge killings of Palestinians in Gaza).

23. Reference made March 2, 2002; August 19, 2003; February 22, 2004 (incursion into Gaza earlier that month, in which a dozen Palestinians, "mostly armed militants," were killed).

24. Stating: "Palestinian children are being taught and raised to believe they have a right to go back to villages that they've never seen."

25. May 8, 2002.

26. August 30, 2003.

27. March 31, 1997.

28. Ibid.

29. March 27, 2004.

30. October 4, 2003.

31. Zedalis, p. 14.

32. CNN (February 28, 2002).

33. See chapter 5 for discussion concerning this attack.

34. CNN, December 13, 2005.

35. Geoffrey Kemp, February 25, 1996.

36. July 30, 1997.

37. June 5, 2002.

38. January 28, 2002.

39. See, e.g., a segment discussing preparing Iraqi troops for the daily reality of suicide attacks, aired December 13, 2005.

40. BBC evening news, August 7, 1998, 9/10 p.m.

41. These two explanations were given in the October 13, 2002 broadcast by experts and anchors.

42. BBC, October 14, 2002 broadcast.

43. BBC, October 13 and October 14, 2002 broadcasts.

44. June 2, 2001.

45. August 19, 2003.

46. Ibid.

47. August 20, 2003.

48. In the U.S. media, the question of whether a government could stop suicide bombing was frequently debated—usually with the answer "no," as discussed above.

49. July 7, 2005.

50. This quote is taken from an interview on BBC's Newsnight in 2004 ("Al-Qaradawi Full Transcript," BBC (July 8, 2004)). Yusuf al-Qaradawi is one of the most prominent Muslim scholars in support of suicide attacks.

51. "War, Terror and Emergencies," *BBC Editorial Guidelines* (June 29, 2005). The Canadian Broadcasting Corporation has similar guidelines.

52. "Bombers Are Terrorists, Says Grade," *NewsWatch*, bbc.co.uk (July 19, 2005).

53. October 13, 2002.

54. Nacos, *Terrorism, Media, Liberation*, p. 205.

55. Ibid., p. 135.

56. J. David Slocum, "Introduction: The Recurrent Return to Algiers," *Terrorism, Media, Liberation* (2005).

Chapter 8

1. Abu Hafs al-Masri Brigades (Kata'ib Abi Hafs al-Masri), *Kharitat al-tariq li-l-mujahidin* (*Road-Map for Mujahidin*), p. 13 (July 1, 2004), at tawhed.ws. This group claims to be al-Qaida's branch in Europe.

2. Pape, pp. 211–16; Krueger and Maleckova, "Education, Poverty, Political Violence and Terrorism," BNER Working Paper 9074.

3. "Terrorism: Blocking the Road to Terrorism," European Union Web site, Geographical Themes (undated).

4. Simon S.C. Tay and Tan Hsien Li, "Southeast Asian Cooperation on Anti-Terrorism: The Dynamics and Limits of Regional Responses," *Global Anti-Terrorism Law and Policy* (2005), p. 408. The United Nations and its leadership has made similar statements and resolutions. We do not dispute the fact that radicalization is occurring in economically disadvantaged areas around the world, but we do not tie poverty to suicide bombing as such.

5. Zedalis, p. 26.

6. While comprehensive data on identities of suicide bombers in Iraq is not available, most of the media releases regarding suicide bombings in Iraq have been about Saudi Arabian citizens. See, e.g., Susan B. Glasser, " 'Martyrs' in Iraq Mostly Saudis: Web Sites Track Suicide Bombings," *Washington Post*, Page A01 (May 15, 2005).

7. "Terrorism: Blocking the Road to Terrorism." European Union.

8. Akil Awan, "Transitional Religiosity Experiences: Contextual Disjuncture and Islamic Political Radicalism," in T. Abbas (ed.) *Islamic Political Radicalism: A European Comparative Perspective* (forthcoming); note "German Mother Planned Bombing," bbc.com (May 31, 2006).

9. See Cook, *Contemporary Muslim Apocalyptic Literature*, chapters 1–3.

10. Awan, op. cit.

11. In the case of Sri Lanka, which has more secular suicide bombings, suicide bombers may not believe in eternal rewards, but they believe they will be revered by their community as a martyr or hero.

12. For further discussion of altruistic suicide, see Pape, *Dying to Win*, chapter 9; Brym and Araj, "Palestinian Suicide Bombing Revisited: A Critique of the Outbidding Thesis" (Unpublished paper, revised July 2006), p. 16.

13. Pape, pp. 207–11 (unfortunately Pape never defines his terms "religious" and "secular" which mean quite different things in the Middle East from what they mean in the west, and does not take into account last-minute conversion that is so frequent among suicide attackers, so that a person who for their entire life might have been perceived as "secular" on the outside could change radically); for counter-numbers see Sean Yom and Basel Saleh, "Palestinian Suicide Bombers: A Statistical Analysis," *ECAAR News Network* (November 2004); Pedahzur, *Suicide Terrorism*, pp. 56–57.

14. Leonard Weinberg, Ami Pedahzur, and Daphna Canetti-Nisim, "The Social and Religious Characteristics of Suicide Bombers and Their Victims," *Terrorism and Political Violence*, Vol. 15, No. 3 (Autumn 2003), p. 143.

15. See Samuel Huntington, "The Clash of Civilizations?" *Foreign Affairs* 72 (1993), pp. 22–49.

16. See al-Bukhari, *Sahih*, iiv, p. 78 (nos. 3167–68); discussion in Yohanan Friedmann, *Tolerance and Coercion in Islam*, pp. 90–93.

17. The Saudi government foiled a suicide attack on an oil facility in February 2006 ("Saudis 'Foil Oil Facility Attack,' " bbc.com (February 24, 2006)).

18. "Weakening Indonesia's Mujahidin Networks," crisisgroup.com, Asia report no. 103 (October 13, 2005), p. 3.

19. Although we cannot be sure these attacks have ceased forever, at the time of writing no further attack had taken place.

20. See, e.g., Zhao Dagong, "Suicide Bombing: An Alarm for the CCP," *The Epoch Times* (April 17, 2006); "Official Killed by Suicide Bombing in Sichuan," Xinhua news service (July 25, 2004); Jun Wang, "Suicide Bomber Shocks China— Was Health Care the Catalyst?" Pacific News Service (August 16, 2006); Richard Spencer, "Suicide Blast Kills 10 at Ex-Wife's Wedding," *Telegraph.co.uk* (June 7, 2006).

21. *Creating Enemies of the State: Religious Persecution in Uzbekistan*. Human Rights Watch report (2004).

22. John M. Broder, "F.B.I. Hunts Terror Clues in California," *The New York Times* (August 18, 2005).

23. The bombing in a market in the Khan al-Khalili area in Cairo prompted loud protests, and the grand imam of Al-Azhar University condemned these attacks. See "Prominent Egyptian figures, protestors condemn Cairo blast," MENA News Agency Web site (April 8, 2005).

24. See, e.g., Bruce Pannier, "Uzbekistan: One Week Later, Many Questions Still Unanswered," *Eurasianet.org* (April 8, 2004).

25. See Cook, *Understanding Jihad*, chapter 5.

26. See, e.g., (thanks to Elena Pavlova).

27. Fred Burton, "Ansar el-Mehdi and Terror Potential in Morocco," Stratfor World Terrorism report, *www.stratfor.com* (September 6, 2006).

28. There are some about whom it is difficult to obtain information, see the story about the British Jewish convert who blew herself up in Afghanistan during 2001 in Cook, "The Recovery of Radical Islam in the wake of the Defeat of the Taliban," *Terrorism and Political Violence* 15 (2003), pp. 41–42; and the German women who were arrested for plotting to go to Iraq to become martyrs, "German Mother 'Planned Bombing,'" bbc.com (May 31, 2006).

29. See, e.g., Craig Smith, "Raised Catholic in Belgium, She Died a Muslim Bomber," *The New York Times* (December 6, 2005); Nicola Smith, "Making of Muriel the Suicide Bomber," *The Sunday Times* (December 4, 2005). See also chapter 5. Note also the case of the unnamed Dutch policewoman who wanted to carry out a suicide attack: "Former Dutch Policewoman convert to Islam arrested for links to terrorists—farewell note indicating planned suicide attack found," at militantislammonitor.org (December 8, 2005).

30. One neighbor reportedly also said, "Once he became Muslim, it was just 'Good morning' and he would nod." (Serge F. Kovaleski, "Plot Suspects Are Remembered As both Harmless and Sinister" *The New York Times* [August 15, 2006].)

31. Lizette Alvarez, "New Muslim at 15, Terror Suspect at 19," *The New York Times* (July 18, 2005).

32. "Who is Richard Reid?" BBC (December 28, 2001); see also Alan Cowell, "The Shadowy Trail and Shift to Islam of a Bomb Suspect," *The New York Times* (December 29, 2001).

33. See, e.g., Awan (2007), pp. 210–11; Vadim Rechkov, "Ya odnazhdy sprosila, kak mozhno stat' shakhidom [I Once Asked How it is Possible to Become a Shahid]," *Izvestiya* (June 18, 2004).

34. For biographical information, see, e.g., Nick Paton Walsh, "Tracing a Tragedy," *Guardian* (September 30, 2004); "In Fact, His Last Name is Not Khodov, but Samoshkin," RIA Novosti news agency, reprinted on http://military-en.rian.ru (November 2004). Rumors, however, abound about his true orientation to the seige, including that he was a Russian spy and that he was not killed in the seige but committed suicide in prison ("Slukhi o tom, chto terrorist Khodov zhiv, neobosnovany" ["Rumors that Terrorist Khodov is Alive are Unfounded"], RIA Novosti, reprinted at http://www.Regions.ru (November 10, 2004)).

35. Yuriy V. Maksimov, " 'Russkiy islam' v. internete—shkola novykh yany-char?" [" 'Russian Islam' on the Internet—School of New Jannisaries?"], http://www.um-islam.nm.ru (undated).

36. Katie Fretland, "3 British Suspects Converted to Islam," Associated Press (August 13, 2006); Adam Fresco, Elsa McLaren, Lewis Smith, Lucy Bannerman, and Nicola Woolcock, "Who Are the 'Bomb Plot' Suspects?" *Times Online* (August 11, 2006).

37. "It is not clear that they all worshiped in a single mosque, though it does appear that some knew each other that way." Ian Fisher, "Shock Reverberates Among Acquaintances of the Young Suspects" *The New York Times* (August 12, 2006).

38. "Shoe-Bomb Suspect Linked With E-Mail across Europe," *The New York Times* (January 20, 2002).

39. Brym and Araj, "Suicide Bombing as Strategy and Interaction," pp. 5–6; interrogation of failed or aborted suicide attackers in Nasra Hassan, "An Arsenal of Believers: Talking to the Human Bombs," *The Atlantic Monthly* (November 19, 2001) at newyorker.com; Barbara Victor, *Army of Roses*, pp. 260–64; Anat Berko, *Ba-derekh li-Gan ha-Eden*.

40. Ibid., pp. 6–7; Pedahzur, *Suicide Terrorism*, chapter 6.

41. Vadim Rechkov, "Ne zhivi na zleme, Zhaga! [Don't Live on the Earth, Zhaga!]," *Izvestiya* (April 1, 2004).

42. For example, Hannadi Jarradat (memri.org, Special Dispatch no. 766 [August 19, 2004]); and further examples in Hafez, *Manufacturing Human Bombs*, appendix B.

Chapter 9

1. Hizbullah leader Hasan Nasrallah, quoted in Avi Jorisch, *Beacon of Hatred*, pp. 81–82.

2. See *The 9/11 Commission Report*, chapters 12–13; *Countering Suicide Terrorism*, pp. 159–60.

3. Jorisch, op. cit.

4. "Terrorism Act 2006," available at U.K. Home Office Web site, www.homeoffice.gov.uk. See, e.g., Section 16(5)(6)(i) of the law.

5. When the law was under consideration, Human Rights Watch issued several criticisms of how the law threatens fundamental rights. See, e.g., "Proposed Anti-Terrorism Measures Threaten Fundamental Rights," HRW (August 10, 2005), which insists that " '[t]here must be a link between words that incite and acts of violence for speech to be criminal. The government risks choking free expression.' "

6. Laws in the U.K. have been criticized for this reason, as were the amendments proposed in Australia in 2005. See, e.g., "Law Council launches Final Assault on Counter-Terror Laws," Law Council of Australia, www.lawcouncil.asn.au (December 4, 2005); "Cameron Criticises Terror Effort," BBC, bbc.co.uk (August 15, 2006).

7. See, e.g., Internet Haganah, www.haganah.org.il.

8. "Secretary Rumsfeld Interview with Al-Jazeera TV," Department of Defense, www.defenselink.mil, (February 25, 2003).

9. "National Security Advisor Interview with Al-Jazeera TV," WhiteHouse.gov (October 16, 2001).

10. Zvika Krieger, "Voice of America," *Newsweek* online, www.msnbc.msn.com (August 29, 2006).

11. Neela Banerjee, "State Dept. Official Apologizes for Criticism of Iraq Policy," *The New York Times*, October 23, 2006.

12. For example, Djerejian, *Changing Minds; Winning Peace*; *9/11 Commission Report*, chapter 12; and Susan Epstein and Lisa Mager, "Public Diplomacy: A

Review of Past Recommendations," Congressional Research Service Report (September 2, 2005).

13. Lorraine Ali, "This is Your Mid-Street Bombing," *Newsweek*, Web edition (June 20, 2006).

14. Shaul Shay, *The Shahids*, p. 85.

15. See, e.g., "U.S. Muslim Religious Council Issues Fatwa against Terrorism," CAIR (July 28, 2005); "Pakistani Fatwa against Suicide Bombing," CobraPost.com (May 19, 2005); and "UK Muslims Issue Bombings Fatwa," bbc.com (July 19, 2005).

16. Y. Yehoshua, "Re-education of Extremists in Saudi Arabia," memri.org, Inquiry and Analysis no. 260 (January 18, 2006).

17. See, e.g., the United States' April 2006 National Intelligence Estimate (Mark Mazzetti, "Spy Agencies Say Iraq War Worsens Terrorism Threat," *The New York Times*, September 24, 2006).

18. See, e.g., Michelangelo Guida, "The Turkish Islamist Media in the Era of the War on Terror between 'Sevres Syndrome' and 'Komplo' Theories," 2006; and chapters 7–8.

19. *Islamist Terrorism in the Sahel*, crisisgroup.com (March 31, 2005); interviews with journalists in Sudan (February 2005) and Suliman Baldo (December 13, 2005) (Allison).

20. "Lapses in Human Rights Screening in North African Countries Indicate Need for Further Oversight," Government Accountability Office (July 2006).

Glossary of Terms

Al-`amaliyyat al-intihariyya. Suicide Attacks.

Al-`amaliyyat al-istishhadiyya. Martyrdom Operations.

Dar al-Harb. The Area Subject to War.

Dar al-Islam. The Area Under the Control of Islam.

Dar al-Sulh. The Area Under a Truce.

fatwa. A Solicited Legal Opinion.

fedayin. Suicide-Seeking Squads.

hadith. The Traditions of the Prophet Muhammad.

hajj. The Pilgrimage to Mecca.

houris. The Eternally Virginal Women of Paradise.

ijma`. Consensus of the Scholars.

Intifada. Literally "To Shrug Something Off", The Name of Two Palestinian Revolts Against Israel (1987–93, 2000–05).

jihad. Struggle, Fighting, Exertion.

madrasa. A Religious School.

mufti. One Who is Qualified to Give a *Fatwa*.

mujahid(in). Fighters.

mushrikin. Those Who Associate Beings or Deities with God, Christians.

pesantren. A Religious School in the Context of Southeast Asian Islam (especially Indonesia).

qadi. A Religious Judge.

shahid. A Martyr or Witness.

shari`a. The Divine Law of Islam.

shirk. Associating Other Beings or Deities with God; The Fundamental Sin in Islam.

sura. A Section of the Qur'an (114 in total).

takfir. The Declaration of a Muslim to be an Infidel.

tawhid. The Belief in the Absolute Unity of God; The Fundamental Concept of Islam.

`ulama'. The Religious Leadership of Islam.

Glossary of Groups

Abu Hafs al-Masri Brigades (*Kata'ib Abi Hafs al-Masri*). This group claims to be al-Qaida's branch in Europe.

Abu Sayyaf. A radical Philippine Muslim group, founded by Abu Bakr Janjalani in 1990. More extreme in its ideology than any of the other Muslim groups operating in the southern Philippines, Abu Sayyaf today exists largely as a bandit group.

African National Congress (ANC). A South African multiethnic organization founded in 1912 to support the rights of the black majority population. Its armed wing, *Umkhonto we Sizwe* (Spear of the Nation), carried out terrorist acts against the apartheid government of South Africa during the period 1961–94, when the ANC became the ruling party of the country.

Amal (*Harakat Amal*). The oldest radical Shi`ite party in southern Lebanon, founded by the charismatic Musa al-Sadr in 1975, and after his disappearance in Libya in 1978, headed by Nabih Berri. Amal does not currently engaged in violent activities.

Amida Tong. A society of assassins in medieval Japan associated with a militant Zen Buddhist order.

Ansar Allah. The group associated with Hizbullah that (probably) carried out the 1994 Buenos Aires suicide attack.

Ansar al-Islam. A radical Sunni group founded by Mullah Krekar (presently in Norway) that was based in the Sulaymaniyyeh district of northern Iraq. For the most part it has not been active in the Iraqi insurgency.

Ansar al-Sunna. One of the major radical Muslim groups in Iraq, and an offshoot of Ansar al-Islam, led apparently by Abu `Abdallah Hasan b. Mahmud (captured August 2006), and based in the northern and western parts of the country. Ansar has support from both Arab and Kurdish Sunnis and has carried out numerous suicide attacks.

Al-Aqsa Martyrs Brigades (*Kata'ib shuhada al-Aqsa*). A militant group associated with the ruling Fatah party of the PNA in the West Bank and the Gaza Strip. It was founded in 2000 at the beginning of the Second Intifada (2000–05) and carried out military operations including suicide attacks against Israel.

Al-Arabiya. Saudi Arabia–based Arab satellite channel, funded by Saudi government and said to be less critical of Western governments than its rival, al-Jazeera.

Ba`ath Party. The ruling party in Syria (1970 to the present day) and Iraq (1970–2003) founded by Michel Aflaq in the 1950s. Ba`athists stand for pan-Arab nationalism and are nonsectarian and generally follow socialist principles.

Dar ul-Islam. A radical Islamic movement and rebellion in Indonesia (specifically West Java) founded in 1949 by Sekarmadji Maridjan Kartosuwirjo designed to create a Muslim state. The rebellion of Dar ul-Islam against the authorities was finally crushed in 1962, but support for it remains strong in parts of Java. Some of its members are connected with Jama`a Islamiyya (JI).

Egyptian Islamic Jihad (EIJ, *al-Jihad al-Islami, Tala'i` al-Jihad*). One of the radical Islamic organizations in Egypt, it was headed by Ayman al-Zawahiri (later partially amalgamated to al-Qa`ida). EIJ viewed itself as an avant-garde group and unlike the Gama`at al-Islamiyya did not attempt to make itself into a mass movement or a countersociety. It was responsible for the suicide attacks in Bosnia and Islamabad (1995), and its operatives in Egypt may be connected to the suicide attacks of 2005–06.

*Gama`at al-Islamiyya.* The larger of the two major Egyptian radical Islamic groups, the Gama`at's spiritual leader was Shaykh `Umar `Abd al-Rahman (convicted in the United States of the failed 1993 attempt on the World Trade Center in New York). The Gama`at and its ideological allies fought the Egyptian regime during the 1990s, but after the Luxor massacre of 1997 it renounced violence and became quietistic. Some of its elements may have amalgamated with al-Qa`ida.

Global Islamic Media Front. The media organ that, while not directly affiliated with al-Qa`ida, claims to have some affiliation with the organization and is best known for its role producing the serial video news program *al-Sawt al-Khilafah* (Voice of the Caliphate).

Groupe Islamique Armeé (GIA, *al-Jama`a al-Islamiyya al-Musallaha*). The most violent and radical of the Algerian militant organizations, the GIA was founded in 1994 by dissident elements from a number of radical groups that agreed to combine forces. The GIA used violence against civilians, under the general accusation of *takfir* and frequently murdered foreigners and prominent intellectuals in Algeria. In 1998 the group collapsed as a result of these controversial tactics and many of its fighters left to form the GSPC.

Groupe Islamique Combatant Marocain (GICM, *al-Jama`a al-Islamiyya al-Maghribiyya al-Muqatila*). Founded perhaps in the late 1980s by Moroccans returning from Afghanistan (and perhaps connected with the Harakat al-Shabiba al-Islamiyya), the GICM existed as an underground organization until approximately 2001. It is thought to be ideologically allied with al-Qa`ida and carried out the 2003 Casablanca suicide attacks.

Groupe Salafiste pour la Prédication et le Combat (GSPC, *al-Jama`a al-Salafiyya li-l-Da`wa wa-l-Qital*). An Algerian radical group founded in 1998 by dissidents from the GIA, its tactics have been to attack government and military targets without killing civilians. In 2006 it announced its amalgamation with al-Qa`ida.

Hamas (*Harakat al-muqawama al-Islamiyya*). The principle Palestinian radical group founded in 1987 by Shaykh Ahmad Yasin (assassinated 2004). Hamas has a national radical Islamic vision that claims all of historical Palestine (Israel, the West Bank, and the Gaza Strip) as the patrimony of Muslims, and it has carried out numerous terrorist and suicide operations against Israel since its foundation. In 2006 Hamas assumed the government of the PNA.

Harakat al-Mujahidin (HM). The major Pakistan-based radical Muslim group fighting in Kashmir founded by Fazlur Rahman in mid-1990s, and responsible for a number of terrorist activities against Indians and foreigners. Most of its fighters abandoned HM in favor of Jaysh-i Muhammad in 2000–01. Fazlur Rahman was one of the signatories to Usama bin Laden's 1998 fatwa.

Hizb al-Mujahidin. A major Pakistan-based radical Muslim group fighting in Kashmir associated with the Jama`ati Islami. Hizb avoids attacking civilians and does not use suicide attacks. It is the only major jihadi group in Pakistan that has remained unbanned after 2001–03.

Hizb al-Tahrir. A shadowy quietist radical Muslim group that is calling for the return of the caliphate founded by the Palestinian Taqi al-Din Nabhani in the 1950s. Its current leader is unknown. Strength is in Pakistan, Central Asia, among British Muslims, and in Europe in general.

Hizbullah. The major Shi`ite grouping of southern Lebanon with both militant and social-support wings, led by Shaykh Hasan Nasrullah. Hizbullah was founded approximately in 1983, perhaps as an amalgamation of a number of militant Shi`ite groups that had existed prior to that time and consistently fought Israel and the SLA during the period 1985–2000 when Israel withdrew from southern Lebanon. During part of this period, Hizbullah used suicide attacks. Since 2000 Hizbullah has translated itself into a major political party in Lebanon, but remained dominant in the southern area of the country, and in July 2006 provoked a war with Israel.

Al-Hurra. American-funded and -run TV station, intended to provide an Arabic-language, pro-American media outlet in the Middle East.

Islamic Jihad (*al-Jihad al-Islami*). The smallest of the Palestinian radical factions, founded by Fathi Shiqaqi in mid-1980s, it was responsible for pioneering suicide attacks among the Palestinians. As a small, revolutionary organization (with connections to Iran), it has never enjoyed popular support among Palestinians.

Islamic Movement of Uzbekistan (IMU). One of the militant factions of Uzbekistan founded in the early 1990s by Tahir Yuldashev and Juma` Namangani, IMU carried out militant operations throughout the country during the period 1999–2003. Currently the IMU seems to have disentigrated.

Jagrata Muslim Janata Bangladesh. A radical Muslim group in Bangladesh founded by Mawlana Abdur Rahman and Siddiqul Islam (Bangla Bhai) in 1998, closely related to the Jama`at ul-Mujahidin that carried out suicide attacks in 2005. Both groups were suppressed shortly thereafter and their leaders condemned to death.

*Jama`a Islamiyya* (JI). An Islamic countersociety in Indonesia founded by `Abdallah Sungkar and Abu Bakr Ba`asyir in the early 1980s, JI was designed to unite all the Muslims of southeast Asia into one state. Sections of some of its radicals carried out suicide attacks starting in 2002.

*Jama`at-i Islami.* A Pakistani and Indian Muslim radical group founded by Abu al-`Ala al-Mawdudi in the 1960s. Its militant expression is Hizb al-Mujahidin.

Jama`at ul-Mujahidin. A violent Bangladeshi group that is an offshoot of the Jagrata Muslim Janata Bangladesh.

Jaysh-i Muhammad. A violent radical Pakistani group associated with the Deobandi school operating in Kashmir with supporters in parts of Pakistan, founded by Mahmud Azhar after his release from prison in India in 2000. It has carried out a number of suicide attacks both in Kashmir and in Pakistan for which it was banned (and has gone through several name changes).

Al-Jazeera (al-Jazira). Theoretically independent, Qatar-based Arab satellite channel, funded by the Qatari government and often critical of Western governments, and enjoying wide popularity.

Lashkar-i Tayba. A violent radical Pakistan group associated with the Ahl-i-Hadis school operating in Kashmir, founded by Hafiz Muhammad Saeed in 1989 and associated with the Markaz al-Da`wa wa-l-Irshad. Lashkar has carried out numerous terrorist attacks and suicide attacks in Kashmir and in India (but not in Pakistan).

Liberation Tigers of Tamil Eelam (LTTE). A violent organization fighting for independence for the Tamil minority of Sri Lanka since mid-1970s, founded by Velupillai Prabhakaran. It has carried out hundreds of suicide attacks in Sri Lanka and India.

Mahdi Army. A radical Iraqi Shi`ite organization headed by Muqtada al-Sadr.

Majlis al-Shura al-Mujahidin (The Mujahidin Shura Council). The coordinating group for the radical Muslim groups of Iraq; works with al-Qa`ida, Ansar al-Sunna, and Ansar al-Islam.

Moro Islamic Liberation Front (MILF). A violent radical Islamic national movement in the southern Philippines, founded by Hashim Salamat as an Islamic alternative to the MNLF. Since 2001 the MILF has moved away from globalist radical Islam.

Moro National Liberation Front (MNLF). A nationalistic movement fighting for self-determination or at least autonomy for the Muslims in the southern Philippines. Since mid-1980s the MNLF has been involved in periodic negotiations with the Philippine government.

Northern Alliance. The name given to the coalition of various Afghan movements fighting against the Taliban from 1996 to 2001 when they defeated the latter and reoccupied Kabul.

Palestine Liberation Organization (PLO). A Palestinian nonsectarian group founded in 1962, but receiving its independence in 1968 when it was taken over by Yasir `Arafat (who dominated it until his death in 2004). The PLO recognized Israel in 1993 under the Oslo Accords and took over the government of the West Bank and the Gaza Strip. However, dissatisfied with terms offered to it in the final status talks in 2000 the PLO initiated the second Intifada (2000–05). The al-Aqsa Martyrs Brigades was the major violent group associated with the PLO during this later period and it carried out dozens of suicide attacks against Israel.

Palestinian National Authority (PNA). The governmental manifestation of the PLO since 1993.

Partiya Karkaren Kurdistan (PKK). A violent Marxist Kurdish organization fighting for self-determination for the Kurdish minority in Turkey, founded by `Abdallah

Ocalan in the early 1980s. It carried out a number of suicide attacks during the 1990s, but enforced (for the most part) a moratorium since 2000.

POLISARIO. A group fighting for independence for the Western Sahara against Morocco since 1975.

Popular Front for the Liberation of Palestine (PFLP). A violent Marxist Palestinian organization founded by George Habash in the early 1970s, it has carried out dozens of terrorist attacks in Israel and other countries. Although the PFLP is small in the West Bank and the Gaza Strip, it has carried out a number of suicide attacks in Israel since the beginning of the second Initfada (2000).

*al-Qa`ida.* The most important globalist radical Muslim organization dedicated to *jihad*, founded by `Abdallah `Azzam in 1988, and taken over by Usama bin Laden during the 1990s, al-Qa`ida has branches and operatives in a wide range of countries and fights to establish a unified Islamic state under a caliph, and to remove all foreigners and foreign influence from the Muslim world.

*al-Qa`ida fi Bilad al-Rafidayn* (al-Qa`ida in the Land of the Two Rivers or Mesopotamia). A violent radical Muslim organization in Iraq, founded by the Jordanian Abu Mus`ab al-Zarqawi (killed in June 2006) in 2003 as al-Tawhid wa-l-Jihad and then amalgamated with al-Qa`ida in 2004; it is currently led by Abu Hamza al-Muhajir (an Egyptian). It was and continues to be responsible for hundreds of attacks and suicide attacks in Iraq.

Radio Sawa. American-funded and -run radio station, intended to provide an Arabic-langauge, pro-American media outlet in the Middle East.

Riyad al-Salihin. The suicide brigade of the Chechen rebels.

Al-Sahab Publications. The primary publishing house for al-Qa`ida media relations, which often releases videos and written/electronic statements from al-Qa`ida leadership.

South Lebanese Army (SLA). An Israeli-supported military force that was supposed to protect the interests of the Christians of southern Lebanon (and indirectly also the security of Israel's northern border), founded by Maj. Haddad in the early 1980s and then succeeded by Gen. Lahhad. The SLA disentigrated in 2000, when Israel withdrew from the region.

Taliban. The radical Muslim Afghan organization headed by Mullah `Umar Mujahid that had its origins in the Deobandi schools of Pakistan. During 1994–96 the Taliban occupied most of Afghanistan and ruled it until 2001, giving sanctuary to al-Qa`ida. Since 2001 the Taliban have found refuge in Pakistan and continue to fight the multinational forces in Afghanistan, using suicide attacks since 2004.

Tanzim Qa`idat al-Jihad. A Southeast Asian violent radical Muslim group that broke off from JI under the leadership of Muhammad Nuruddin Top in 2005. Top and his former associate Azahari Husin (killed Nov. 2005) were responsible for numerous suicide attacks.

Al-Thawra al-Islamiyya al-Hurra. The group that perpetrated the 1983 suicide attacks against the Marines and the French in Beirut. Probably related in some way to Hizbullah.

Bibliography

Newspaper articles and articles taken from Internet sources (unless they are book-length) are not reproduced in this bibliography because the full bibliographical details are given in the notes. Similarly, videos accessed on sites such as YouTube are also not reproduced. A great many of the websites used by radical Muslims, including al-neda.com, tawhed.ws and others, have been suppressed over the years.

`Abdallah, Najih Ibrahim, *Tafjirat al-Riyad: al-ahkam wa-l-athar*. Cairo: Maktabat al-Turath al-Islami, 2003.

Abu Basir, `Abd al-Mun`im Mustafa Halima, *Mahadhir al-`amaliyyat al-istishhadiyya aw al-intihariyya*, at abubaseer.bizland.com (articles 90).

———— *al-Tariq ila isti'naf hayat Islamiyya wa-qiyam khilafa rashida `ala daw' al-Kitab wa-l-Sunna*, at abubaseer.bizland.com/.

Abu Da'ud al-Sijistani (d. 888–9), *Sunan Abi Da'ud*. Beirut: Dar al-Jil, 1988 (4 vols.).

Abu Diya, Sa`d, *Dirasa tahliliyya fi al-`amaliyyat al-istishhadiyya fi janub Lubnan*. Beirut: Jami`at al-`Ummal al-Matabi` al-Ta`awuniyya, 1986.

Abu Nasr, `Umar Mahmud, *Nazra Shara`iyya li-l-Ahdath 11 Ellul*, at aloswa.org (May 9, 2002).

Abu Qatada, "September 11: The Legal Vision," at jihadunspun.com (2002).

Abu Ruqaiyah, "The Islamic Legitimacy of the Martyrdom Operations," *Nida' al-Islam* (January 1996–97), at ict.org.il.

`Adwan, `Abd al-Jabbar, *al-Shuhada*. London: Dar al-Intifada, 1989.

Alagha, Joseph, "Hizbullah and Martyrdom," *Orient* 45:1 (2004), pp. 47–74.

Al-`Alwan, Sulayman b. Nasir, *Hal al-qital ma` al-Afghan jihad? Wa-hal al-maqtul shahid?* at tawhed.ws.

———— *Hukm al-`amaliyyat al-istishhadiyya* (parts 1–2), at tawhed.ws.

———— *Hukm qatl al-atfal fi al-`amaliyyat al-istishhadiyya*, at tawhed.ws. (1422/2000).

*Al-`Amaliyyat al-fida'iyya: shahada am intihar?* Gaza: Markaz al-Quds li-l-Dirasat wa-l-I`lam wa-l-Nashr, 2001.

*Al-`Amaliyyat al-istishhadiyya: Watha'iq wa-suwar al-muqawama al-wataniyya al-Lubnaniyya 1982–85*. Damascus: al-Markaz al-`Arabi, 1985.

Al-`Amili, Abu Sa`id, *al-`Amaliyyat al-istishhadiyya dhurwat sanam al-istishhad*, at aloswa.org.

Al-Ansari, Sayf al-Din, *Ghazwat 11 September: Ru'iya mutakamila li-l-hadath al-ladhi hazza al-`alam*. In *Majallat al-Ansar* (September 2002), at tawhed.ws.

"Annex to the Report from the Commission Based on Article 11 of the Council Framework Decision of 13 June 2002 on Combating Terrorism." Brussels: Commission of the European Communities, June 8, 2004.

Atran, Scott, "Genesis of Suicide Terrorism," *Science* 299 (March 7, 2003), pp. 1534–39.

Avan, Abbas Akhtar, *Karvan-i shuhada: Kabul se Kashmir*. Lahore: Idara-yi Matbu`at-i Tulbah, 1994.

Awan, A.N., "Transitional Religiosity Experiences amongst British Muslims: Contextual Disjuncture & Political Radicalism," in T. Abbas (ed.) *Islamic Political Radicalism: A European Comparative Perspective*. Edinburgh: Edinburgh University Press (forthcoming).

Ayoub, Mahmoud, "Martyrdom in Christianity and Islam," in Richard Antoun and Mary Elaine Hegland (eds.), *Religious Resurgence: Contemporary Cases in Islam, Christianity and Judaism*. Syracuse, NY: Syracuse University Press, 1987, pp. 67–77.

———— *Redemptive Suffering in Islam: A Study of the Devotional Aspects of `Ashura' in Twelver Shi`ism*. The Hague: Mouton Publishers, 1978.

Al-`Ayyiri, Yusuf, "The Islamic Ruling on the Permissibility of Martyrdom Operations," at azzam.com; also religioscope.com (documents); trans. of *Hal intaharat Hawa' am ustushihdat?* at www.alsunnah.info; also tawhed.ws.

———— *Haqiqat al-harb al-salibiyya al-jadida*, at alneda.com.

`Azzam, `Abdallah, *Ayat al-Rahman fi jihad al-Afghan*. Peshawar: Markaz Shahid `Azzam al-I`lami, n.d. (available at azzamjihad.com); trans. "Signs of al-Rahman in the Jihad of Afghanistan," at almansura.com.

———— *Basha'ir al-nasr*. Peshawar: Markaz Shahid `Azzam al-I`lami, n.d. (available at azzamjihad.com).

———— *al-Difa` `an aradi al-Muslimin*. Peshawar: Markaz Shahid `Azzam al-I `lami, 1990.

———— *Fadl al-shahada*. Peshawar: Markaz Shahid `Azzam al-I`lami, n.d.

———— *`Ithaf al-`ibad fi fada'il al-jihad*. Peshawar: Markaz Shahid `Azzam al-I`lami, n.d.

Ba`abduh, al-Ustadz Luqman bin Muhammad, *Sebuah Tinjauan Syari`at mereka adalah Teroris: bantahan terhadap buku Aku Melawan Teroris*. Malang: Pustakah Qawlan Sadidan, 2005.

Bash, Hasan, *al-`Amaliyyat al-ishishhadiyya*. Damascus: Dar Qutayba, 2003.

Berko, Anat, *Ba-derekh li-Gan ha-`Eden (On the Way to Paradise)*. Tel Aviv: Yediot Ahronot, 2004 (Hebrew).

Beyler, Clara, "Female Suicide Bombers," at ict.org.il (March 7, 2004).

Bin Laden, `Usama, *Declaration of War against the Americans Occupying the Land of the Two Holy Places*. Trans. Abu Umama in *Declaration of War*. N.p.: Khurasaan Publications, 2000.

———— *Messages to the World: The Statements of Osama Bin Laden*. Ed. and Trans. Bruce Lawrence and James Howarth, London: Verso, 2005.

Bloom, Mia, *Dying to Kill: The Global Phenomenon of Suicide Terror*. New York: Columbia University Press, 2005.

Brown, Ian, *Khomeini's Forgotten Sons, The Story of Iran's Boy Soldiers*. London: Grey Seal Books, 1990.

Brown, Michelle, and Leia Fuzesi, Kara Kitch, Crystal Spivey, "Internet News Representations of September 11: Archival Impulse in the Age of Information," in Steven Chermak, Frankie Y. Bailey and Michelle Brown (eds.), *Media Representations of September 11*. Westport,CT: Praeger, 2005, pp. 103–16.

Brunner, Claudia, *Männerwaffe Frauenkörper: zum Geschlecht der Sebstmordattentate im israelisch-pälestinensischen Konflikt*. Vienna: Bräumuller, 2005.

Brym, Robert, and Bader Araj, "Palestinian Suicide Bombing Revisited: A Critique of the Outbidding Thesis," *Political Science Quarterly*, forthcoming.

——— "Suicide Bombing as Strategy and Interaction: The Case of the Second Intifada," *Social Forces*, 84:4: (2006), forthcoming.

Bukhari, Muhammad b. Isma`il (d. 870), *Sahih al-Bukhari*. Beirut: Dar al-Fikr, 1991 (4 vols.).

Burdman, Daphne, "Education, Indoctrination and Incitement: Palestinian Children on the Way to Martyrdom," *Terrorism and Political Violence* 15 (2003), pp. 96–123.

Çapan, Ergün (ed.), *An Islamic Perspective: Terror and Suicide Attacks*. New Jersey: The Light, 2004.

The 9/11 Commission Report: Final Report of the National Commission on Terrorist Attacks upon the United States. New York: W.W. Norton, 2004.

Conboy, Ken, *The Second Front: Inside Asia's Most Dangerous Terrorist Network*. Jakarta: Equinox, 2006.

Cook, David, *Contemporary Muslim Apocalyptic Literature*. Syracuse, NY: Syracuse University Press, 2005.

——— "The Implications of Martyrdom Operations for Contemporary Islam," *Journal of Religious Ethics* 32 (2004), 129–51.

——— *Martyrdom in Islam*. Cambridge: Cambridge University Press (forthcoming).

——— "Muslim Apocalyptic and Jihad," *Jerusalem Studies in Arabic and Islam* 20 (1996), 66–102.

——— "The Recovery of Radical Islam in the Wake of the Defeat of the Taliban," *Terrorism and Political Violence* 15 (2003), pp. 31–56.

——— "Suicide Attacks or 'Martyrdom Operations' in Contemporary Jihad Literature," *Nova Religio* 6 (2002), pp. 7–44.

——— *Understanding Jihad*. Berkeley: University of California Press, 2005.

——— "Women Fighting in Jihad?," *Studies in Conflict and Terrorism* 38 (September–October 2005), pp. 375–84.

Council of Senior Scholars on the Riyadh Suicide Bombings. Trans. Abu al-`Abbas and Abu `Iyaaad, at fatwa-online.com (May 18, 2003).

Countering Suicide Terrorism: An International Conference. Herzliya: The International Policy Institute for Counterterrorism, 2001.

Cragin, Kim A., and Sara Daly. *The Dynamic Terrorist Threat: An Assessment of Group Motivations and Capabilities in a Changing World*. Prepared for the Air Force. Santa Monica: RAND Corporation, 2004.

Creating Enemies of the State: Religious Persecution in Uzbekistan. Human Rights Watch, March 2004.

Dale, Stephen, "Religious Suicide in Islamic Asia: Anti-Colonial Terrorism in India, Indonesia and the Philippines," *Journal of Conflict Resolution* 32 (1988), pp. 37–59.

Dankowitz, A., "Fighting Terrorism: Recommendations by Arab Reformists," at memri.org, Inquiry and Analysis, no. 232 (July 28, 2005).

Davis, Joyce, Martyrs: *Innocence, Vengeance and Despair in the Middle East*. New York: Palgrave Macmillan, 2003.

Djerejian, Edward (chair), *Changing Minds; Winning Peace: A New Strategic Direction for U.S. Public Diplomacy in the Arab and Muslim World*. Report of the Advisory Group on Public Diplomacy for the Arab and Muslim World (Washington, DC), (October 1, 2003).

Dobkin, Bethami A., "The Television Terrorist," in J. David Slocum (ed.), *Terrorism, Media, Liberation*. New Brunswick: Rutgers University Press, 2005, pp. 121–36.

Dowling, Ralph E., "Terrorism and the Media," *Journal of Communication*, 36 (1986), pp. 12–24.

*Encyclopedia of Islam*². Ed. Bernard Lewis, C.E. Bosworth, *et alia*. Leiden: E.J. Brill, 1960–2002.

Esposito, Michele, "The al-Aqsa Intifada: Military Operations, Suicide Attacks, Assassinations, and Losses in the First Four Years," *Journal of Palestine Studies* 34 (2005), pp. 85–122.

"European Union Plugging the Gaps in the Fight Against Terrorism." European Union document at http://ec.europe.eu. (accessed November 27, 2004).

Al-Fahd, Nasir b. Hamd, *Ayat al-Rahman fi ghazwat September*, at tawhed.ws.

——— *Hukm qital al-Amrikan kharij al-`Iraq*, at tawhed.ws.

——— *Risala fi hukm istikhdam aslihat al-damar al-shamil didd al-kuffar*. 1424/2003, at tawhed.ws.

——— *al-Tibyan fi kufr man a`ana al-Amrikan*, at tawhed.ws.

Falk, Ophir, Yaron Schwartz, Eran Duvdevany, and Eran Galperin, "The Suicide Terrorism Threat," at ict.org.il (January 10, 2005).

Farag (Faraj), Muhammad `Abd al-Salam, *al-Farida al-gha'iba*. Amman: n.p., n.d.; trans. Johannes Jansen, *The Neglected Duty*. New York: Macmillan, 1986; also trans. Abu Umama, *The Absent Obligation*. Birmingham: Maktabat al-Ansar, 2000.

Fatwa Majeles Ulama Indonesia tentang Terrorisme. Jakarta, 2005.

Fawzan, Salih, *Shaykh Saalih al-Fowzaan on the Riyadh Bombings*, trans. Abu Iyaaad, at fatwa-online.com (May 31, 2003).

Feldner, Yotam, "Debating the Religious, Political and Moral Legitimacy of Suicide Bombings," at memri.org, Inquiry and Analysis nos. 53–54, 65–66 (May 2–3, 2001, July 26–27, 2001).

Firghal, Yahya Hashim Hasan, "Kashf al-tawiyya fi al-`amaliyyat al-istishhadiyya," at e-prism.com (from tawhed.ws).

Friedmann, Yohanan, *Tolerance and Coercion in Islam*. Cambridge: Cambridge University Press, 2003.

Frisch, Hillel, "Debating Palestinian Strategy in the al-Aqsa Intifada," *Terrorism and Political Violence* 15 (2003), pp. 61–80.

Ganor, Boaz, "Suicide Terrorism: An Overview," at ict.org.il (February 15, 2000).

Ghayba, Muhammad Sa`id, *al-`Amaliyyat al-istishhadiyya wa-ara' al-fuqaha' fiha*. Damascus: Dar al-Maktabi, 2001.

Ghazwat al-hadi `ashara min Rabi` al-awwal: `Amaliyyat sharq al-Riyad wa-harbuna ma` Amrika wa-`umala'iha. Markaz al-Dirasat wa-l-Buhuth al-Islamiyya, at tawhed.ws (1424/2003).

Grusin, Elinor Kelley, and Sandra H. Utt (eds.), *Media in an American Crisis: Studies of September 11, 2001*. Lanham: University Press of America, Inc., 2005.

Guida, Michelangelo, "The Turkish Islamist Meida in the Era of the War on Terror between 'Sevres Syndrome' and 'Komplo' Theories," unpublished paper presented at "Muslim Media and the 'War on Terror' "conference, University of Bristol, 2006.

Gunaratna, Rohan, *Inside al-Qaeda: Global Network of Terror*. New York: Berkley, 2003.

———— Arabinda Acharya, and Sabrina Chua, *Conflict and Terrorism in Southern Thailand*. Singapore: Marshall Cavendish, 2005.

Hafez, Kai, "International News Coverage and the Problems of Media Globalization. In Search of a 'New Global-Local Nexus,' " *Innovation*, 12:1 (1999), pp. 47–62.

Hafez, Mohammed, *Manufacturing Human Bombs: The Making of Palestinian Suicide Bombers*. Washington, DC: United States Institute of Peace Press, 2006.

———— "Suicide Terrorism in Iraq: A Preliminary Assessment of the Quantitative Data and Documentary Evidence," *Studies in Conflict and Terrorism* 29 (2006), pp. 591–619.

Hassan, Nasra, "An Arsenal of Believers: Talking to the 'Human Bombs,' " *The Atlantic Monthly* (November 19, 2001), at newyorker.com.

Haykal, Muhammad Khayr, *al-Jihad wa-l-qital fi al-siyasa al-shara`iyya*. Beirut: Dar al-Barayiq, 1993 (3 vols.).

Hazan, D., "Expatriate Syrian Salafi Sheikh al-Tartousi comes out against Suicide Attacks," at memri.org, Special Report, no. 40 (February 10, 2006).

Herd, Graeme P., "The Russo-Chechen Information Warfare and 9/11: Al-Qaeda through the South Caucasus Looking Glass?" *European Security* 11:4 (2002), pp. 110–130.

Al-Hilali, Abu Ayman [= Iman], *al-`Amaliyyat al-istishhadiyya: al-mudadd al-hayawi li-l-jurthuma al-Sihyawniyya*, parts 1–2, at aloswa.org (July 21, 2002).

———— *al-`Amaliyyat al-istishhadiyya: tariquna ila tahrir al-Quds*, at tawhed.ws.

Al-Hindi, al-Muttaqi (d. 1567–8), *Kanz al-`ummal*. Ed. Bakri Hayyani, Beirut: Mu'assasat al-Risala, 1989 (18 vols.).

Hizbullah:al-muqawama wa-l-tahrir. Beirut: al-Safir, 2006 (13 vols.).

Hoffman, Bruce, "Al Qaeda, Trends in Terrorism and Future Potentialities: An Assessment." Santa Monica, CA: RAND, 2003.

Hukm istihdaf a'immat al-kufr wa-hum mukhalitun bi-l-Muslimin, at tawhed.ws.

Huntington, Samuel, "The Clash of Civilizations?" *Foreign Affairs* 72 (1993), pp. 22–49.

Husayn, Fu'ad, *al-Zarqawi: al-Jil al-thani li-l-Qa`ida*. Beirut: Dar al-Khayal, 2005.

Ibn `Abd al-`Aziz, `Abd al-Qadir, *Risalat al-`umda li-l-jihad fi sabil Allah*. Silsilat Da`wat al-Tawhid, n.d.

Ibn al-`Arabi, Muhammad b. `Abdallah (d. 1148–9), *Ahkam al-Qur'an*. Ed. `Ali Muhammad al-Bijawi, Beirut: Dar al-Jil, 1987 (4 vols.).

Ibn Jubayr, Hani b. `Abdallah b. Muhammad, *al-`Amaliyyat al-istishhadiyya*. Riyad: Dar al-Fadila, 2002.

Ibn Mahfuz, Husayn `Umar, *al-Ta'sil al-shar`i li-ahdath Amrika*, at tawhed.ws.

Ibn Mahmud, Husayn, *Khawatir fi zaman al-tafjirat*, at tawhed.ws.

Ibn Mahmud, Husayn, *al-Tibyan fi hukm qatl al-Amerikan*, at tawhed.ws.

Ibn Maja (d. 888–89), *Sunan*. Beirut: Dar al-Fikr, n.d. (2 vols.).

Ibn Mar`i, Mar`i b. `Abdallah, *Ahkam al-mujahid bi-l-nafs fi sabil Allah fi al-fiqh al-Islami*. Medina: Maktabat al-`Ulum wa-l-Hikam, 2003.

Ibn al-Mubarak, `Abdallah (d. 797), *Kitab al-jihad*. Ed. Nazih Hammad, Beirut: `Afif al-Zu`bi, 1971.

Ibn al-Nahhas al-Dumyati, Ahmad b. Ibrahim (d. 1411), *Mashari` al-ashwaq ila masari` al-`ushshaq fi al-jihad wa-fada'ilihi*. Ed. Durish Muhammad `Ali and Muhammad Khalid Istambuli, Beirut: Dar al-Basha'ir al-Islamiyya, 2002.

Ibn `Uthaymin, Muhammad b. Salih, *Concerning Suicide Bombings*. Trans. Abu Talhah Dawud Burbank, at fatwa-online.com.

—— *Fatawa al-`aqida*. Cairo: Maktabat al-Sunna, 1993.

Imam, Ahmad `Ali, *al-Shahada wa-hayat al-shuhada*. Beirut: al-Maktab al-Islami, 2000.

Imam Samudra, *Aku melawan teroris!* Solo: Jazera, 2004.

Intifadat al-Aqsa. `Amman: al-Khalil, 2002–6 (10 vols. to date).

Jalalzai, Musa Khan, *Dying to Kill Us: Suicide Bombers, Terrorism and Violence in Pakistan*. Lahore: al-Abbas International, 2005.

Jamal, Amal, *Media Politics and Democracy in Palestine: Political Culture, Pluralism and the Palestinian Authority*. Brightland: Sussex Academic Press, 2005.

Janju'ah, Faridulislam, *Jihad, shahadat, jannat*. Rawalpindi: Markaz-i Matbu`at Kashmir, 2000.

Al-Jarbu`a, `Abd al-`Aziz b. Salih, *al-Ta'sil li-mashru`iyyat ma hasala li-Amrika min tadmir*, at tawhed.ws.

Jawabirah, Basim, *Tafrij al-karb bi-fada'il shahid al-ma`arik wa-l-harb*. Riyad: Dar al-Raya, 1993.

Al-Jihad wa-khisal al-muhajidin fi al-Islam. Beirut: Markaz Baqiyat Allah al-A`zam, 1999.

Jirar, Husni, *Ma`an ila al-janna: shahid al-fajr wa-saqr Filistin*. `Amman: al-Sabil, 2004.

Jorisch, Avi, *Beacon of Hatred: Inside Hizballah's Al-Manar Television*. Washington, DC: Washington Institute for Near East Policy, 2004.

Kashf al-shubhat `an ahkam al-hujumat, at tawhed.ws.

Kelly, Michael J., and Thomas H. Mitchell, "Transnational Terrorism and the Western Elite Press," in Doris A. Graber (ed.), *Media Power in Politics*. Washington, DC: Congressional Quarterly, Inc., 1984, pp. 282–9.

Kelsay, John, and Johnson, James Turner (eds.), *Just War and Jihad: Historical and Theoretical Perspectives on War and Peace in Western and Islamic Traditions*. Westport, CT: Greenwood Press, 1991.

Kharitat al-tariq li-l-mujahidin: Kata'ib Abi Hafs al-Masri, at tawhed.ws. (July 1, 2004).

Khashan, Hilal, "Collective Palestinian Frustration and Suicide Bombings," *Third World Quarterly* 24:6 (2003), pp. 1049–67.

Khosrokhavar, Farhad, *L'Islamisme et la Mort, le martyre révolutionnaire en Iran*. Paris: L'Harmattan, 1995.

—— "Le martyre révolutionnaire en Iran," *Social Compass* 43 (1996), pp. 83–100.

———— *Les nouveaux martyrs d'Allah*. Paris: Flammarion, 2002.

Kohlberg, Etan, "The Development of the Imami Shi`i Doctrine of jihad," *Zeitschrift der Deutschen Morgenländischen Gesellschaft* 126 (1976), pp. 64–86.

———— "Martyrdom and Self-Sacrifice in Classical Islam." *Pe'amim* 75 (1998), pp. 5–26 (in Hebrew).

———— "Medieval Muslim Views on Martyrdom," *Mededelingen der Koninklijke Nederlandse Akademie van Wetenschappen* 60 (1997), pp. 281–307.

Krueger, Alan B., and Jitka Maleckova, "Education, Poverty, Political Violence, and Terrorism," BNER Working Paper 9074. Cambridge, MA: National Bureau of Economic Research, July 2002.

Laird, Lance Daniel, "Martyrs, Heroes and Saints: Shared Symbols of Muslims and Christians in Contemporary Palestinian Society," unpublished Th.D. Dissertation, Harvard University, 1998.

Lawrence, Bruce, and James Howarth (trans.), *Messages to the World: The Statements of Osama bin Laden*, see Bin Laden, Usama.

Lynch, Mark, *Voices of the New Arab Public*, New York: Columbia University Press, 2006.

Madsen, Julian, "Suicide Terrorism: Rationalizing the Irrational," *Strategic Insights* 3 (2004), at http://knxup2.ad.nps.navy.mil/homesec/docs/dod/nps 17–081804–08.pdf.

Makki, `Abd al-Rahman, "Fidayee Activities in [the] Shariah," at markazdawa.org (November 30, 2001); Voice of Islam (July 2001).

Mansdorf, Irwin, "The Psychological Framework of Suicide Terrorism," *Jerusalem Center for Public Affairs* 496 (April 15, 2003), at jcpa.org/jl/vp496.htm.

Margalit, Avishai, "The Suicide Bombers," *New York Review of Books* 50:1 (January 16, 2003).

Martin, Richard, "Discourses on Postmodern Jihad," in Jonathan Brockopp (ed.), *Islamic Ethics of Life: Abortion, War and Euthanasia*. Columbia, South Carolina: University of South Carolina Press, 2003, pp. 155–72.

Masa'il jihadiyya wa-hukm al-`amaliyyat al-istishhadiyya. Beirut: al-Wahda al-Islamiyya, 2002.

Miles, Hugh, *Al-Jazeera: How Arab TV News Challenged the World*. London: Abacus, 2005.

Mishal, Shaul, and Reuven Aharoni (eds.), *Speaking Stones: Communiqués from the Intifada Underground*. Syracuse, NY: Syracuse University Press, 1994.

Misri, Abu al-Ashbal Ahmad b. Salim, *Fatawa al-`ulama al-kibar fi al-irhab wa-l-tadmir*. Riyad: Dar al-Kiyan, 2006.

Mogadham, Assaf, "Palestinian Suicide Terrorism in the Second Intifada: Motivations and Organizational Aspects," *Studies in Conflict and Terrorism* 26 (2003), pp. 65–92.

———— *Suicide Bombings in the Israeli-Palestinian Conflict: A Conceptual Framework*, at e-prism.com (May 2002).

Mogensen, Kirsten, Lauran Lindsay, Xigen Li, Jay Perkins, and Mike Beardsley, "How TV News Covered the Crisis: The Content of CNN, CBS, ABC, NBC and Fox," in Bradley S. Greenberg (ed.), *Communication and Terrorism: Public and Media Responses to 9/11*. Cresskill, New Jersey: Hampton Press, Inc., 2002, pp. 101–20.

Muslim al-Qushayri (d. 875), *Sahih Muslim*. Beirut: Dar al-Jil, n.d. (4 vols.).

Nacos, Brigitte L., "Mass-Mediated Terrorism in the New World (Dis)Order," in J. David Slocum (ed.), *Terrorism, Media, Liberation*. New Brunswick: Rutgers UP, 2005, pp. 185–208.

——— *Mass-Mediated Terrorism: The Central Role of the Media in Terrorism and Counterterrorism*. New York: Rowman & Littlefield Publishers, Inc., 2002.

——— "Mediated Terror: Teaching Terrorism through Propaganda and Publicity," in James J.F. Forest (ed.), *The Making of a Terrorist: Recruitment, Training and Root Causes. Vol. II: Training*. Westport, Connecticut: Praeger, 2006, pp. 98–118.

——— "The Terrorist Calculation behind 9–11: A Model for Future Terrorism," *Studies in Conflict and Terrorism* 26 (2003), pp. 1–16.

Nafisi, `Abdallah, *Ghazwat Manhattan*, at alneda.com.

Al-Najdi, Abu Qudama, *Kashf al-litham `an dhurwat sanam al-Islam*. At tawhed.ws (1424/2003).

Naumkin, Vitaly V., "Militant Islam in Central Asia: The Case of the Islamic Movement of Uzbekistan." Berkeley: Berkeley Program in Soviet and Post-Soviet Studies Working Paper Series, 2003.

——— *Radical Islam in Central Asia: Between Pen and Rifle*. Lanham: Rowan and Littlefield, 2005.

El-Nawaway, Mohammed, and Adel Iskandar, *Al-Jazeera: The Story of the Network That is Rattling Governments and Redefining Modern Journalism*. Cambridge, MA: Westview, 2003.

OAU Convention on the Prevention and Combating of Terrorism: Treaty on Cooperation among the States Members of the Commonwealth of Independent States in Combating Terrorism, 1999. United Nations Treaty Collection (July 19, 1999, Algiers), at http://untreaty.un.org/English/Terrorism/oau_e.pdf.

Pape, Robert, *Dying to Win: The Strategic Logic of Suicide Terrorism*. Chicago: University of Chicago Press, 2005.

——— "The Strategic Logic of Suicide Terrorism," *American Political Science Review* 97 (2003), pp. 1–19.

Parachini, John V., "Combating Terrorism: The 9/11 Commission and the National Strategies." Testimony: House Committee of Government Reform, Subcommittee on National Security, Emerging Threats, and International Relations. September 22, 2004. Washington, DC: RAND Corporation, 2004.

Parfrey, Adam (ed.), "Killing Infidels in Chechnya: A Foreign Mujahid's Diary," in *Extreme Islam: Anti-American Propaganda of Muslim Fundamentalism*. Los Angeles: Feral House, 2002.

Paz, Reuven, "Islamic Legitimacy for the London Bombings," at ict.org.il (July 18, 2005).

——— "Reading Their Lips: The Credibility of Jihadi Web Sites in Arabic as a Source for Information," at e-prism.org.

——— "Al-Qaeda's Search for New Fronts: Instructions for Jihadi Activity in Egypt and Sinai," at Global Research in International Affairs (GLORIA) Center; *PRISM Occasional Papers* 3:7 (October 2005).

Pedahzur, Ami, *Suicide Terrorism*. Cambridge, MA: Polity Press, 2005.

Piazza, James, "Rooted in Poverty: Terrorism, Poor Economic Development and Social Cleavages," *Terrorism and Political Violence* 18 (2006), pp. 159–75.

Picard, Robert G., "News Coverage as the Contagion of Terrorism: Dangerous Charges Backed by Dubious Science," in Doris Graber (ed.), *Media Power in Politics*. 2nd edition. Washington, DC: Congressional Quarterly, 1990, pp. 313–23.

Proposal for Council Framework Decision on Terrorism, Brussels: Commission of European Communities, September 19, 2001.

Protocol to the OAU Convention on the Prevention and Combating of Terrorism, Addis Ababa: African Union Publications, July 8, 2004.

Al-Qatari, Hamd, and al-Madani, Majid, *Min qisas al-shuhada' al-Arab*, at tawhed.ws.

Quillen, Chris, "A Historical Analysis of Mass-Casualty Bombings," *Studies in Conflict and Terrorism* 25 (2002), pp. 279–92.

Al-Qureshi, Abu Ubayd. "The 11 September Raid: The Impossible Becomes Possible." Essay published by *Majallat al-Ansar*, September 1, 2002. Translated by Foreign Broadcast Information Service; see also "al-Qa`ida Activist, Abu Ubeid al-Qureshi, compares Munich (Olympics) attack (1972) to Sept. 11," memri.org, Special Dispatch no. 353 (March 12, 2002).

Al-Qurtubi, Muhammad b. Ahmad (d. 1272), *al-Jami` li-ahkam al-Qur'an*. Ed. `Abd al-Razzaq al-Mahdi, Beirut: Dar al-Kitab al-`Arabi, 2003 (20 vols.).

Raja`i, Ghulam `Ali, *Lahzahha-yi asmani: karimat-i shahidan*. Tehran: Shahid, 2001.

Ramakrishna, Kumar, and See Seng Tan (eds.), *After Bali: The Threat of Terrorism in Southeast Asia*. Singapore: Institute of Defense and Strategic Studies, 2003.

Rana, Muhammad Amir, *A to Z of Jehadi Organizations in Pakistan*. Lahore: Mashal Books, 2004.

Raphaeli, Nimrod, "Iraqi-Jordanian Tension around the most Lethal Suicide Bombing in Iraq," at memri.org, Inquiry and Analysis, no. 214 (March 29, 2005).

Rashid, Ahmed, *Jihad: The Rise of Militant Islam in Central Asia*. New Haven: Yale University Press, 2002.

Rashid, Sa`id, *Shahid-i Kashmir*. Lahore: Book Corner, n.d.

Report to the European Council on the Implementation of the Declaration on Combating Terrorism. Brussels: Committee of Permanent Representatives (Coreper), June 11, 2004.

Revisiting the Arab Street: Research from Within. Amman: Center for Strategic Studies, University of Jordan, 2005.

Reynolds, Amy, and Brooke Barnett, "'America Under Attack': CNN's Verbal and Visual Framing of September 11," in Steven Chermak, Frankie Y. Bailey, and Michelle Brown (eds.), *Media Representations of September 11*. Westport, CT: Praeger, 2005, pp. 85–102.

Richards, Alan, "Socio-Economic roots of Radicalism," at globalsecurity.org.

Rinnawi, Khalil, "Intifada Live: Arab Satellite TV Coverage of the Al-Aqsa Intifada," *Palestine-Israel Journal of Politics, Economics and Culture*, 10:2 (2003), pp. 57–63.

Rocca, Christine, "U.S. Counterterrorism Policy Toward South Asia." Testimony before House Committee on International Relations Subcommittees on Asia and the Pacific, and on International Terrorism, Nonproliferation, and Human Rights. October 29, 2003.

Rosenthal, Franz, "On Suicide in Islam," *Journal of the American Oriental Society* 66 (1946), pp. 239–59.

Al-Rushayd, `Abdallah b. Nasir, *Intiqad al-i`tirad `ala tafjirat al-Riyad*, at tawhed.ws (1424/2003).

Sageman, Marc, *Understanding Terror Networks*. Philadelphia: University of Pennsylvania Press, 2004.

Saleh, Basel, *Socioeconomic Profile of Palestinian Suicide Militants from Hamas, Palestinian Islamic Jihad and the al-Aqsa Martyrs Brigade*. Typescript.

Salih, Amal, *Abtal fawqa al-khayal: qisas shuhada al-intifada*. Beirut: Dar Ibn Hazm, 2003.

Salim, Muhammad b. Ahmad, *39 wasila li-khidmat al-jihad wa-l-musharaka fihi*, at tawhed.ws (1424/2003).

Sawt al-Jihad (online journal of the Saudi Arabian branch of al-Qa`ida), at e-prism.com.

Sayim, Muhammad, *Shuhada al-da`wa al-Islamiyya fi al-qarn al-`ishrin*. Cairo: Dar al-Fadila, 1992.

Schweitzer, Yoram (ed.), *Female Suicide Bombers: Dying for Equality?* Tel Aviv: Jaffee Center for Strategic Studies, 2006, at e-prism.com.

——— "Female Suicide Bombers for God," *Tel Aviv Notes* 88 (October 9, 2003).

Al-Shami, Jabir b. `Abd al-Qayyum al-Sa`idi (Abu Qutayba), *al-Isaba fi talab al-sha-hada*, at forsan.net (August 20, 2002).

Sharbasi, Ahmad, *Fida'iyyun fi al-ta'rikh al-Islam*. Beirut: Dar al-Ra'id al-`Arabi, 1982.

Sharp, Jeremy M., "The Al-Jazeera News Network: Opportunity or Challenge for U.S. Foreign Policy in the Middle East?" Congressional Research Service, Report for Congress, July 23, 2003.

Shay, Shaul, *The Shahids: Islam and Suicide Attacks*. New Brunswick, NJ: Transaction Publishers, 2004.

Al-Shiddi, `Adil b. `Ali, *Min qisas al-shuhada' al-`Arab fi Afghanistan*. Sana`a: Maktabat al-Irshad, 1411/1990.

Shinn, David, "Fighting Terrorism in East Africa and the Horn," *Foreign Service Journal*, 81:9 (September 2004), pp. 36–42.

Shu`aybi, Hamud b. `Uqla', "Fatwa on the Events of Sept. 11," at alsahwah.com.

——— "Mashru`iyyat al-`amaliyyat al-istishhadiyya," at aloqla.com (April 18, 2002).

Sifr, Mahmud b. Muhammad, *al-Islam wa-Amrika wa-ahdath September*. Beirut: Dar al-Nafa'is, 2004.

Sijill al-nur. Beirut: al-Wahda al-I`lamiyya al-Markaziyya, 1998.

Silsilat al-i`dad li-l-jihad, at faroq.org.

Slocum, J. David, "Introduction: The Recurrent Return to Algiers," *Terrorism, Media, Liberation*. Ed. J. David Slocum, New Brunswick: Rutgers University Press (2005), pp. 1–37.

Slone, Michelle, "Responses to Media Coverage of Terrorism," *The Journal of Conflict Resolution*, 44 (2000), pp. 508–22.

Solnick, Alma, "The Joy of the Mothers of the Palestinian Martyrs," at memri.org, Inquiry and Analysis no. 61 (June 25, 2001).

——— "The Shuhada cult of Martyrdom in Islamic Jihad," at memri.org, Inquiry and Analysis, no. 25 (February 24, 2000).

Speckhard, Anne, and Ahkmedova, Khapta, "The Making of a Martyr: Chechen Suicide Terrorism," *Studies in Conflict and Terrorism* 29 (2006), pp. 429–92.

Sprinzak, Ehud, "Rational Fanatics," *Foreign Policy* (September–October 2000), pp. 66–74.

Stalinsky, Steven, "Arab and Muslim Jihad Fighters in Iraq," at memri.org, Special Report, no. 19 (July 27, 2003).

Strenski, Ivan, "Sacrifice, Gift and the Social Logic of Muslim Human Bombers," *Terrorism and Political Violence* 15 (2003), pp. 1–34.

Sturman, Kathryn, "The AU Plan on Terrorism: Joining the Global War or Leading an African Battle?" *African Security Review* 11:4 (2002), pp. 103–08.

Suhaybani, `Abd al-Hamid b. `Abd al-Rahman, *Siyar al-shuhada*. Riyad: Dar al-Watan, 1999.

Al-Suri, Abu Mus`ab, Mustafa Setmarian Nasar, *Da`wa al-muqawama al-Islamiyya al-`alamiyya*, available at http://www.ctc.usma.edu/alsuri.asp.

Al-Suyuti, Jalal al-Din, *Abwab al-sa`ada fi asbab al-shahada*. Cairo: al-Maktaba al-Qiyyama, 1987.

Taarnby, M., "Profiling Islamic Suicide Terrorists," *Center for Cultural Research, University of Aarhus* (November 7, 2003).

Taha, Rifa`i Ahmad, *Imatat al-litham `an ba`d ahkam dhurwat sinam al-Islam*, at tawhed.ws.

Al-Takruri, al-Nawwaf, *al-`Amaliyyat al-istishhadiyya fi al-mizan al-fiqhi*. Damascus: N. al-Takruri, 2003 (4th edition).

Tay, Simon S.C., and Tan Hsien Li, "Southeast Asian Cooperation on Anti-Terrorism: the Dynamics and Limits of Regional Responses," in Victor Ramraj, Michael Hor and Kent Roach (eds.), *Global Anti-Terrorism Law and Policy*. Cambridge: Cambridge University Press, 2005. pp. 399–424.

Al-Tirmidhi, Muhammad b. `Isa (d. 902), *al-Jami` al-sahih*. Beirut: Dar al-Fikr, n.d. (5 vols.).

Tu`mat al-Qudat, Muhammad, *al-Mughamara bi-l-nafs fi al-qital wa-hukmuha fi al-Islam*. Amman: Dar al-Furqan, 2001.

`Ubaydi, `Ali `Aziz, *Shuhada' bi-la akfan*. Baghdad: Dar al-Hurriyya li-l-Tiba`a, 2000.

Victor, Barbara, *Army of Roses: Inside the World of Palestinian Women Suicide Bombers*. New York: St. Martin's Press, 2003.

Vilawi, `Ali Muhammad, *Shahidan-i shahadat*. Tehran: Nashr-i Shahid, 2000.

Waller, J. Michael, "Wartime Public Diplomacy: A Strategy to Deliver the Messages," in Public Diplomacy White Paper No. 2, The Institute of World Politics. March 29, 2006. Weiberg, Leonard, Ami Pedahzur and Daphna Canetti-Nisim, "The Social and Religious Characteristics of Suicide Bombers and their Victims," *Terrorism and Political Violence* 15 (2003), pp. 139–53.

Weimann, Gabriel, *Terror on the Internet: The New Arena, the New Challenges*. Washington, DC: United States Institute of Peace Press, 2006.

——— "www.terror.net: How Modern Terrorism Uses the Internet." United States Institute of Peace Special Report, No. 116, March 2004.

Weinberg, Leonard, Ami Pedahzur, and Daphna Canetti-Nisim, "The Social and Religious Characteristics of Suicide Bombers and Their Victims," *Terrorism and Political Violence*, Vol. 15, No. 3 (Autumn 2003), pp. 139–53.

Wensinck, A.J. (ed.), *Concordance et indices de la Tradition Musulmane*. Leiden: E.J. Brill, 1936–64.

Wiktorowicz, Quintan, and John Kaltner, "Killing in the Name of Islam: al-Qaeda's Justification for Sept. 11," *Middle East Policy* 10 (2003), pp. 76–92.

Wolf, Charles, Jr., and Brian Rosen, "Public Diplomacy: How to Think about and Improve It," Washington, DC: RAND Corporation, Occasional Paper, 2004.

Woods, Kevin, James Lacey, and Williamson Murray, "Saddam's Delusions," *Foreign Affairs* (May–June 2006).

Wykes, Maggie, "Reporting, Remembering, and Reconstructing September 11, 2001," in Steven Chermak, Frankie Y. Bailey, and Michelle Brown (eds.), *Media Representations of September 11*. Westport, CT: Praeger, 2005, pp. 117–34.

Yadnamah-i shuhada-yi sal-i avval-i difa`-i muqaddas-i shahrastan va-Qumm. Tehran: Markaz-i Asnad-i Inqilab-i Islami, 2000.

Yehoshua, Y., "Dispute in Islamist Circles over the Legitimacy of Attacking Muslims, Shiites, Non-Combatant Non-Muslims in Iraq: al-Maqdisi vs. His Disciple al-Zarqawi," at memri.org, Inquiry and Analysis, no. 239 (September 11, 2005).

——— "Re-education of Extremists in Saudi Arabia," at memri.org, Inquiry and Analysis, no. 260 (January 18, 2006).

Yom, Sean, and Basel Salih, "Palestinian Suicide Bombers: A Statistical Analysis," *ECAAR News Network* (November 2004).

Al-Yusuf, Muslim Muhammad Jawdat, *Ishkaliyyat al-`amaliyyat al-istishhadiyya*, at said.net.

Zarqawi, Abu Musa`b, *Mawqifuna al-shari`i min hukumat Karzai al-`Iraq*, at tawhed.ws.

——— "Text from Abu Mus`ab al-Zarqawi Letter," at cpa.gov/transcripts/2004.

——— *Wasaya li-l-mujahidin*, at tawhed.ws.

Zarw, Nawwaf, *al-`Amaliyyat al-ishishhadiyya: `awamil, dawafi`, khalfiyyat, hasad, tada`iyyat, ta'thirat*. `Amman: al-Mu'tamar al-Sha`bi li-l-Difa` `an al-Quds, 2003.

Zawahiri, Ayman, *Shifa' sudur al-mu'minin*. Silsilat nashrat al-Mujahidin bi-Misr, 1995.

Zedalis, Debra, *Female Suicide Bombers*. Honolulu: University Press of the Pacific, 2004.

Zuhdi, Karam Muhammad, *Istratijiyyat wa-tafjirat al-Qa`ida*. Riyad: Maktabat al-Ubaykan, 2005.

Memri articles: Memri.org (ascribed memri articles are listed under their author):

Special Dispatch Series:

"On Suicide Bombings," no. 51 (October 20, 1999);

"Egyptian Opposition Weekly calls for Martyrdom Operations," no. 224 (June 4, 2001);

"Highest Ranking Palestinian Authority Cleric in Praise of Martyrdom Operations," no. 226 (June 8, 2001);

"Friday Sermon on PA TV calling for Suicide Bombings," no. 228 (June 12, 2001);

"Egyptian Government Daily on the Muslims' Love of Death and their Enemies'
    Love of Life," no. 289 (October 19, 2001);

"The Role of the Arab Media: An Historical Perspective," excerpted from *Al Hayat*
    (London), no. 320 (December 21, 2001);

"The Role of Fatwas in Incitement to Terrorism," no. 333 (January 18, 2002);

"Egyptian Government Daily praises the Martyrdom Attack at Jerusalem Café," no.
    356 (March 15, 2002);

"Leading Egyptian Government Cleric calls for 'Martyrdom Attacks that Strike
    Horror into the Hearts of the Enemies of Allah,' " no. 363 (April 7, 2002);

"Suicide, Martyrdom, Terrorist Attacks or Homicide: A Debate in the Arab Media,"
    no. 378 (May 12, 2002);

"Interview with the Mother of a Suicide Bomber," no. 391 (June 19, 2002);

"A Palestinian Communiqué against Martyrdom Attacks," no. 393 (June 25, 2002);

"Suicide Bomber's Father: Let Hamas and Jihad Leaders send their own Sons,"
    no. 426 (October 8, 2002);

"Editors of Egyptian Government Papers hail the Recent Suicide Bombing in a
    Jerusalem Neighborhood," no. 442 (November 25, 2002);

"Hamas Spokesman: Iraq must Establish a Suicide Army," no. 457 (January 9,
    2003);

"Egyptian Opposition Daily Condemns Suicide Martyrdom Operations," no. 474
    (February 25, 2003);

"Saudi Press: Initial Reactions to the Riyadh Bombings," no. 505 (May 15, 2003);

"al-Qaradawi speaks in Favor of Suicide Operations at an Islamic Conference in
    Sweden," no. 542 (July 24, 2003);

"Interview with Algerian Terror Leader Nabil Sahrawi," no. 642 (January 13, 2004);

"Conflicting Arab Press Reactions to the Gaza Suicide Bombing," no. 651 (January 27,
    2004);

"Egyptian Governmental Daily: Suicide Bombings are Legitimate, even if Children
    are killed... " no. 658 (February 6, 2004);

"Umm Nidal: The Mother of the Shahids," no. 673 (March 4, 2004);

"A Testimony on Suicide Bombers recruitment to Ansar al-Islam," no. 686 (March 25,
    2004);

"Hamas Spokesman on UAE TV: On the Recruitment and Training of Palestinian
    Suicide Bombers," no. 741 (July 8, 2004);

"Will of Hannadi Jaradat," no. 766 (August 19, 2004);

"Mothers of Hizbullah Martyrs," no. 819 (November 25, 2004);

"Iran's Political and Military Leadership Calls for Martyrdom (*shahada*), no. 850
    (January 20, 2005);

"Terrorists are motivated by Cultural and Religious Factors, not Poverty," no. 853
    (January 26, 2005);

"Collateral Killing of Muslims is Legitimate," no. 917 (June 7, 2005);

"Iranian Volunteer Suicide Organization of 40,000," no. 929 (July 6, 2005);

"Director of London's al-Maqreze Center for Historical Studies Hani Sibai: There
    are no 'civilians' in Islamic Law," no. 932 (July 12, 2005);

"Iran's New President glorifies Martyrdom," no. 945 (July 29, 2005);

"Turkish Press reactions to the London Bombings," no. 947 (August 3, 2005);

"TV Program on the Culture of Martyrdom," no. 961 (August 19, 2005);

"Leading Progressive Qatari cleric: By permitting suicide operations al-Qaradawi and his ilk have caused a crisis in Islam," no. 969 (August 25, 2005);

"Sheikh al-Qaradawi and other Islamic Scholars debate Suicide Attacks," no. 971 (August 26, 2005);

"New al-Jazeera Video: London Suicide Bomber before entering the Gardens of Paradise," no. 979 (September 2, 2005);

"Commander of Hamas Military Wing Women's Units: Our Members Yearn for Martyrdom," no. 983 (September 9, 2005);

"Religious Cassettes advocate jihad emphasizing the Martyr's Sexual Rewards," no. 1032 (November 23, 2005);

"al-Qaida presents Footage of Preparations for Triple Baghdad Suicide Bombing," no. 1034 (November 24, 2005);

"Iraqi and Arab Mujahideen tell al-'Arabiyya of the Wait List for Martyrdom Operations," no. 1040 (December 6, 2005);

"Rare Footage of Saudi Comedian and al-Majd Employee turned Suicide Bomber Muhammad Shazzaf al-Shehri," no. 1076 (January 24, 2006);

"New Internet Footage of Fatima's Fiance," no. 1095 (February 16, 2006);

"Iranian Martyr Recruitment Website," no. 1106 (March 3, 2006).

Inquiry and Analysis:

"72 Black-Eyed Virgins," no. 74 (October 30, 2001);

"Wafa Idris: The Celebration of the First Female Palestinian Suicide Bomber," nos. 83–85 (February 12–14, 2002);

"Palestinian Debate over Martyrdom Operations," nos. 100–1 (July 4–5, 2002).

Special Report:

"Arab and Irsanian TV Clips in Support of Suicide Bombing," no. 32 (September 1, 2004); "Arab Media Reactions to the London Bombings," no. 36 (July 8, 2005).

Index

About the Author

DAVID COOK is Assistant Professor of Religious Studies at Rice University specializing in Islam. He is the author of *Studies in Muslim Apocalyptic*, *Understanding Jihad*, and *Contemporary Muslim Apocalyptic Literature*.

OLIVA ALLISON is a graduate student at King's College, London, England. A former research assistant on media and terrorism at Rice University, she has published several articles on various topics.